CyberAsia

Social Sciences in Asia

Edited by

Vineeta Sinha
Syed Farid Alatas
Chan Kwok Bun

VOLUME 5

CyberAsia

The Internet and Society in Asia

edited by

Zaheer Baber

BRILL

LEIDEN • BOSTON

2005

This book is printed on acid-free paper.

Library of Congress Cataloging-in-Publication data

CyberAsia : the Internet and society in Asia / [edited] by Zaheer Baber.
     p. cm. (Social sciences in Asia, ISSN 1567-2794 ; v. 5)
     Includes bibliographical references and index.
     9004146253 (pbk. : alk. paper)
     1. Internet—Social aspects—Asia. 2. Civil society—Asia. 3. Social change—Asia.

HN655.2.I56 C92 2005
303.48/33/095 22

                                                                    2005050083

ISSN 1567-2794
ISBN 90 04 14625 3

PRINTED IN THE NETHERLANDS

CONTENTS

LIST OF CONTRIBUTORS

Irina Aristarkhova teaches the pioneering studio-based course, Cyberarts, in the University Scholars Programme at the National University of Singapore. She has published and lectured widely on cyberculture and cyberarts. Irina has a range of research interests including issues of aesthetics and technologies of virtual reality, immersive and interactive virtual environments, critical issues in image processing, ethnicity and gender in cyberspace, technological embodiments, contemporary psychoanalytic theory, postcolonial new media theory, and cyberethics. She is Contributing Editor on the editorial board of the journal, *Radek: Art, Theory, Politics*. Address: University Scholars Programme, National University of Singapore, 10 Kent Ridge Crescent, Singapore 119260. [E-mail: uspia@nus.edu.sg]

Stef Aupers is affiliated with the Faculty of Social Science at Erasmus University. He is the author of a number of articles and a book on the New Age movement and spirituality (co-authored with A. Van Otterloo). His current research interests include classical social theory, new media and society, and new religious movements. Address: Faculty of Social Sciences, Erasmus University, P.O. Box 1738, 3000 DR Rotterdam, The Netherlands. [E-mail: aupers@fsw.eur.nl]

Zaheer Baber holds the Canada Research Chair in Science, Technology and Social Change in the Department of Sociology, University of Saskatchewan. He is the author of *The Science of Empire: Scientific Knowledge, Civilization and Colonial Power in India* (Albany: State University of New York Press, 1996; Delhi: Oxford University Press, 1998) and has published articles and essays in a number of journals including *British Journal of Sociology, Theory and Society, Current Sociology, Sociology, Sociological Inquiry* and *The Times Literary Supplement*. He is Contributing Editor of the *Bulletin of Science, Technology and Society*, Consulting Editor of the *Canadian Review of Sociology and Anthropology* and Associate Editor of the *Asian Journal of Social Science*. Address: Department of Sociology, University of Saskatchewan, Saskatoon, SK, Canada S7N 5A5. [E-mail: zaheer.baber@usask.ca]

James Gomez founded Think Centre (Singapore) [www.thinkcentre.org] on 16 July 1999 and published *Self-Censorship: Singapore's Shame* in September of that year. He also co-founded Think Centre (Asia) [www.thinkcentreasia.org] in Bangkok in August 2001. For his use of the Internet for political communication and mobilizing people, he was identified separately on various occasions in 2001 as one of "Asia's 50 Most Powerful Communicators" by *Asiaweek*, as "An Asian Trailblazer" by *Newsweek*, and as an "Asian Making a Difference" by FEER. Address: Friedrich Naumann Foundation, 26th Floor, SSP Tower, 555 Soi 63 Sukhumvit Road, Bangkok 10110, Thailand. [E-mail: jamegomez@hotmail.com]

Toby E. Huff is Chancellor Professor at the Center for Policy Analysis at the University of Massachusetts Dartmouth. He is the author of a number of books and articles, including *Max Weber and the Methodology of the Social Sciences* (Transaction Books, 1984). The second edition of his book, *The Rise of Early Modern Science: Islam, China and the West* (Cambridge University Press) includes a new epilogue and was published in July 2003. His research interests include the Internet and globalization as well as attitudes towards science in the Muslim world. Address: Center for Policy Analysis, University of Massachusetts Dartmouth, North Dartmouth, Ma 02747. [E-mail: thuff@umassd.edu]

Stella Koh is a graduate student at the Department of Sociology, National University of Singapore. Her research interests include boredom and social meaning, cyberculture, leisure studies, and youth culture. She enjoys continental philosophy, psychoanalysis, cultural studies, abnormal psychology, Sandman comics and shoegazer music. She writes best when fuelled with vanilla lattes. Address: Department of Sociology, National University of Singapore, Singapore 117570. [E-mail: thesweetestache@hotmail.com]

Alwyn Lim is a graduate student in Sociology at the State University of New York, Stonybrook. His research interests include science and technology studies, cultural studies and social theory. He has recently published a paper on information technology in Singapore in the *Bulletin of Science, Technology and Society*. Address: Department of Sociology, State University of New York at Stonybrook, Stonybrook, NY, USA 11794 [E-mail: aylim@ic.sunysb.edu]

Noortje Marres is a lecturer in the philosophy of science and technology at the University of Amsterdam, and is currently working on her Ph.D. dissertation, a rehabilitation of the American journalist Walter Lippmann. Address: Department of Philosophy, University of Amsterdam, Nieuwe Doelenstraat 15,1012 CP Amsterdam, Netherlands. [E-mail: marres@dds.nl]

Michael D. Mehta is Associate Professor of Sociology at the University of Saskatchewan, Saskatoon, Canada. His interests include risk perception and communication on blood safety, nuclear power plant safety, electromagnetic field risks, global climate change, and biotechnology. His work in the sociology of cyberspace involves examining pornography on the Internet, and surveillance and privacy issues. Address: Department of Sociology, University of Saskatchewan, Saskatoon, SK, Canada S7N 5A5. [E-mail: michael.mehta@usask.ca]

Shigeru Nakayama is Professor Emeritus of Science and Technology Studies at Kanagawa University. He taught at the University of Tokyo from 1960 until 1989. One of the leading historians of science in Asia, he was a student of Thomas Kuhn and Joseph Needham. He has been a Visiting Professor at Harvard, UC-Berkeley, Latrobe and Monash universities. He is the author and editor of many books including *A History of Japanese Astronomy* (Harvard University Press, 1969); *Chinese Science* (MIT Press, 1973); *Science and Society in Modern Japan* (MIT Press, 1974); *Science, Technology and Society in Contemporary Japan* (Cambridge University Press, 1999). Address: 3–7–11 Chuo Nakano, Tokyo, 164–0011 Japan. [E-mail: shigeru@info.kanagawa-u.ac.jp]

Richard Rogers is Assistant Professor in New Media at the University of Amsterdam, and Visiting Professor in The Philosophy and Social Study of Science at the University of Vienna. His most recent book is the edited volume, *Preferred Placement: Knowledge Politics on the Web* (Maastricht: Jan van Eyck Editions, 2000). Address: New Media, University of Amsterdam, Nieuwe Doelenstraat 16, 1012 CP Amsterdam, The Netherlands. [E-mail: rogers@hum.uva.nl]

Naubahar Sharif is completing his Ph.D. in the Department of Science and Technology Studies at Cornell University. His research interests include national systems of innovation, business history and technology policy issues. Address: Department of Science and Technology Studies, Cornell University, 306 Rockefeller Hall, Ithaca, N.Y. 14853 [E-mail: ns89@cornell.edu]

INTRODUCTION:
THE INTERNET AND SOCIETY IN ASIA

Zaheer Baber
Department of Sociology
University of Saskatchewan

In the prevailing atmosphere of cynicism generated by the relentless cyberbole, one can be forgiven for underestimating the revolutionary nature of the Internet. There is no doubting the intensity of the sense of betrayal especially by investors and businessmen who, until recently, were unabashedly afflicted with dotcom fever. As most commentators—with the benefit of the proverbial hindsight—repeatedly point out, highly successful and innovative though it may be, the virtual bookshop, amazon.com, is still waiting for its promised profits. The anticipated social consequences of the Internet are, of course, not at all limited to the business world even though it is this aspect that has received publicity. In sectors of the globe that are wired, there is hardly any social sphere that is not affected by this new technology. Areas that are not yet wired are also affected, precisely because the gulf between them and the wired sectors threatens to grow larger than ever. Most technocrats and planners expect the "digital divide" to disappear in the near future. To focus on the social consequences of the Internet is, of course, not to buy into a form of technological determinism that has been questioned—if not completely discredited—by sociologists and historians of science and technology (Smith and Marx, 1994; Bijker, Hughes and Pinch, 1989).

No narrative of the development of the Internet can ignore the social and political factors that were constitutive elements of what appear to be purely technical factors in the construction of the open architecture of this technology (Abbatte, 1999). It is clear that Vinton Cerf, Robert Kahn and their associates specifically chose a particular architecture from a range of possibilities, and that this choice was not driven by purely technical concerns. Fundamental though the social constructivist perspective has been in generating new research agendas for the sociologists of science and technology, problems arising from a fundamentalist constructivist perspective have

begun to surface. Coming from quite a different academic agenda
than the vicious axe-grinding soldiers of the "science wars", such as
Gross and Levitt (1994), a number of "science and technology studiers"
have raised doubts about a social constructivist fundamentalism that
threatens to reduce all technologies to effects of social and political
forces. An exemplar of this strain of critique is Langdon Winner
(1993), whose important paper, "Social Constructivism: On Opening
the Black-Box and Finding it Empty", questions the value of the
work of scholars who are not sufficiently dialectical in their analyses
of society and technology. Winner is critical, perhaps a bit too stri-
dently, of scholars who are content with pursuing only one loop of
the chain—the influence of the social on the technical—while neglect-
ing the reflexive influence of socially constructed technologies on
society itself, even as these technologies themselves are reconstituted
as a consequence of these multifaceted interactions. Thus, the idea that
both social relations and technologies simultaneously affect each other
with an unpredictable mix of intended and unintended consequences,
while certainly not absent, was not a dominant focus of the count-
less reiteration of studies in the constructivist mode. This perspective,
while certainly useful for making sense of any technology, is particularly germane to the Internet as it generates a tremendous amount
of social change even as it is simultaneously transformed by the
socially and culturally specific demands placed on it by diverse global
constituencies of users.

All the contributors to this volume explore the various dimensions
of the dialectical interplay between the Internet and society—a process
that is contributing to the restructuring of existing social formations,
ranging from the intimate sphere of personal relationships to the
larger macrostructures of globalization and the social movements that
connect the two at various levels. Stef Aupers' essay focuses on the
Weberian theme of technology and disenchantment. Through a detailed
empirical analysis, Aupers argues that computer technology is contributing to the possibility of a re-enchanted world, replete with "technoanimism" and other forms of being in the world that were expected
to disappear as a consequence of the growth of instrumental rationality. Focusing specifically on Internet Relay Chat (IRC), Stella Koh
examines the variety of ways in which individuals and groups in
Singapore deploy the Internet for creating virtual communities and
experimenting with virtual identities. Koh explores the flexible possibilities for the reconstitution of social relations that may not be fea-

sible in the real world with skill and imagination. Irina Aristarkhova's essay continues the exploration of the sociological characteristics of virtual communities. Deploying the ideas of a wide range of classical and contemporary social theorists, she takes issue with some of the more utopian aspects of Rheingold's expectations vis-à-vis virtual communities. Her main argument is that virtual communities reproduce and mimic rather than replace existing real communities. Her contention is that insofar as real communities form the structural and discursive basis for the development of Net communications, virtual communities are unlikely to become the borderless, heterogeneous and free entities anticipated by cyberutopians such as Rheingold. Michael Mehta's paper extends the investigation of the nature of virtual communities by pursuing issues such as: How is the wired world affecting our society? What are the impacts on individuals, organizations, and governments? Is it possible to develop virtual community standards in cyberspace, and on what level? Can the Internet really promote a more democratic, egalitarian world? What consequences do the infrastructural needs and costs associated with building and maintaining the Internet have on content-based regulation like the Communications Decency Act?

Nakayama's paper examines the significance of social and cultural factors in shaping the specificity of the Japanese response to personal computers and the Internet, and the transformation of technologies in the process. In an incisive socio-historical account of the introduction of the Internet in Japan, Nakayama elaborates on the factors behind the popularity of the *pokeberu* and *ketai*, and the relative lack of interest in personal computers, especially among younger Japanese. The selective modification of the existing technologies of communication and the emergence of a "digital trivide" are further explored in Nakayama's paper. Toby Huff's contribution explores the issue of the Internet and social change, by examining Malaysia's attempt to connect with the emerging global "information society" by means of the Multimedia Super Corridor. The issue is discussed within the larger framework of globalization and modernity, and the paper also offers an important comparative discussion of Malaysia vis-à-vis other societies that are also trying to connect with the emergent global knowledge economy.

Alwyn Lim's essay maps out the contours of Singapore's narrative of itself as an "intelligent island" by teasing out the connections between historical and contemporary cultures of technology that have played a major role in the formation of the city-state. His paper represents an attempt to explore the social, political and economic ingredients in the making of a technological nation-state as it constantly seeks to align its position with the changing flows of global techno-capitalism. My paper continues the focus on Singapore by examining some of the unintended consequences of the state's policy on the Internet in opening up spaces for meaningful engagement between social groups and the state via civil society organizations and the public sphere. James Gomez's contribution is a personal narrative of his experiences in Singapore and beyond from taking advantage of the new possibilities for a vibrant civil society opened up by the Internet. Michael Mehta's paper shifts the focus away from Asia to the United States of America and Canada. He explores the variety of ways in which in these two nations, the state attempts to censor material on the Net. At issue here are competing definitions of contentious material and, given the nature of Internet technology, the limits to the power of nation-states when it comes to censorship. Finally, Richard Rogers and Noortje Marres focus on a particular anti-globalization protest by farmers in France to unravel the role of the Internet and web sites in providing resources for organization, and for offering richer alternative accounts of reportage in the mass media. These two essays are useful in enriching our understanding of the Asian context, within which many nation-states attempt to mould the consciousness of their citizens by regulating the content of the mass media and the Internet. The last essay by Sharif moves beyond discussions of culture and politics to e-commerce. As mentioned earlier, the spectacular dotcom crashes in the past few years will continue to influence popular perceptions of the Internet. Sharif provides a sober assessment of the state of play by examining the dynamics of e-commerce in Hong Kong. The paper includes a comparative discussion of Singapore and the USA, and offers a number of sound policy recommendations.

Books and articles on the Internet continue to proliferate, possibly at a faster pace than the Internet itself. So much for promises of a paperless office in the wake of the personal computer! What distinguishes this collection of essays from the existing tomes on cyberspace is the fact that its focus is largely, although not exclusively, on Asia—the site of fastest growth of the Internet. One hopes that this volume will accomplish more than the just the destruction of yet more trees in Asia and beyond.

FROM PC TO MOBILE INTERNET:
OVERCOMING THE DIGITAL DIVIDE IN JAPAN

SHIGERU NAKAYAMA
Science and Technology Studies Programme
Kanagawa University

Introduction

In the year 2000, the Mori-led government in Japan adopted a "Basic Strategy for IT" policy and instituted an advisory committee. Even a cursory examination of the committee's recommendations will indicate that nothing particularly innovative has been proposed. Rather, the recommendations are highly imitative of American and European policies of the past few decades. As for infrastructure building, the most praiseworthy aspects are the proposed subsidies for IT-based training courses. For the Japanese, who tend to have little experience of having even used a keyboard, these courses will be highly useful. It must be pointed out at the outset, however, that the actual practice and development of information technology was much less influenced by public sector policy than by the desire of the people themselves. The culture of the people as end-users was a more decisive factor in determining the trajectory of development of this technology. In what follows, I will discuss particular aspects of Japanese IT in the context of minimizing the domestic digital divide.

The Digital Divide and Keyboard Allergy

In this section, I wish to discuss some aspects of Japanese IT in relation to overcoming the digital divide between the Roman alphabet-based West and the ideogram-based East Asia. This has been a very serious, almost insurmountable disadvantage and handicap for East Asians in catching up with the Internet. The alphabet-based keyboard is a bottleneck for Japanese seeking to access the Internet. Indeed, it is a problem for all East Asians who use ideograms, as they become familiar with the alphabet much later than their counterparts in other countries. According to a UNESCO survey of computer literacy in the late 1990s, the Japanese people are far behind Europeans and Americans, simply because the average Japanese person is untrained in the use of the alphabet-based keyboard until the high school level.

Although the Japanese government has recently started teaching English in primary schools, the digital divide between alphabet-friendly Western countries and ideogram-using East Asian countries still cannot be reduced to zero. The average Japanese, until recently, had little to do with the alphabet-based typewriter due to the lack of opportunities to use English in his or her daily life. Unless students possess their own typewriters or personal computers, official school training in English or on PCs does not mean much in terms of the overall promotion of computer usage in Japan. Rather, the Japanese have been strong in developing the non-keyboard area of the IT revolution; namely, audio-visual media, cartoons, videocassette recorders, fax machines, console games, etc. They have been weak in the development of software that relies on the use of keyboards.

The Double Revolution of the Word Processor

Up until the 1970s, I doubted that a word processor capable of generating Chinese characters was a possibility. The introduction of a two-byte system by East Asians made it possible for Chinese characters to be typed into a word processor, and for other developments to be contemplated. The Japanese word processor was invented in 1979 and has been in general use from around 1984, thanks to the installation of a phonetics-ideogram conversion system. While those in the West experienced a step-by-step transformation from handwritten to mechanical means (via the typewriter) and then a second move to electronic means, East Asians experienced a double revolution, jumping from handwritten to electronic communication without taking the intermediate step of typewriting, once the transformation of ideograms on word processors became possible.

Such a double revolution is really significant in East Asian history but people have had to overcome an extraordinarily high barrier. Most people had no need to use typewriters or personal computers in their daily life. Only small numbers of specially trained typists, usually women, used the cumbersome Japanese typewriters for producing official documents. Unlike her Western counterpart, the average

Japanese woman used neither a typewriter nor a word processor in the office. Few could overcome the double revolution involved in learning to use a PC.

Late Introduction of the Internet

The Nippon Telephone and Telegraph establishment was slow to realize the importance of Internet communication. For them, it was only a vehicle for private communication amongst academic researchers. Jun Murai and his academic associates experimentally connected with the Internet in 1984, and usage of the medium soon spread throughout the Japanese scientific community. In 1985, Nifty Serve and other companies started provider services for the personal computer network. Japanese computer hobbyists communicated amongst themselves in the Japanese language without being connected to the Internet, while scientists opted to use it and communicate in English. It was only in early 1992 that Japanese PC networks were connected to the Internet.

The commercial use of the Internet began around 1995. The catchphrase for PC manufacturers was "Let us play with and enjoy the Internet!" Scientists and professionals who used the Internet as part of their day-to-day work frowned at such slogans. I personally tried to promote the use of the Internet among Japanese citizens in order to share with them a wonderful vehicle for free and open communication. Most Japanese, however, do not to find much use for it, with many using the Internet purely for recreation. The so-called "PC boom" referred to in business literature is arguably more wishful thinking than reflective of reality. Many people who were able to afford a PC acquired one but ultimately found little use for it. Business people were late to join the bandwagon and when they did, they mostly used the Intranet within a corporate firewall.

The Success of Mobile Phones

NTT actually started a car mobile phone service in 1979 for elite customers, but mobile or cellular phones were less popular in Japan as compared to Hong Kong and Taiwan, due to the non-competitive aspects of NTT's monopoly of the Japanese market. Following the development of cellular phones were portable, hand-held phones known in Japanese as *keitai*. They started to appeal to a much wider market from 1992.

As early as 1968, NTT had started a paging service that enabled company headquarters to maintain contact with travelling salesmen, and worried parents to stay in touch with their children. The numerical pager then appeared with only a small display screen that could be used to convey the telephone numbers of senders or any numbers that needed to be transmitted. A "pager culture" subsequently emerged in the early 1990s, with schoolchildren using telephones to send messages in the form of numbers, just for fun. For example, "39" is pronounced in Japanese as *san kyuu*, which approximates the English words "thank you". It then became fashionable for young Japanese to have numerical pagers ("pocket bell" or what they call *pokeberu*). These devices were not welcomed in the world of education as they facilitated cheating in examinations and caused disruptions in classrooms. Nevertheless, these devices were developed further and two numbers could be used to denote 50 Japanese syllables.

In 1994, hardware manufacturing and marketing were privatized. What is more significant is that in 1995, the PHS or Personal Handyphone System was launched. This competed with the *keitai*. In the period that followed, there was harsh competition between the *keitai* and the PHS. Mobile phones were sold cheap or even given away. Young Japanese embraced the PHS phones as fashion accessories. Thus, we see a trend away from *pokeberu* in 1995 to PHS phones, and then to the *keitai*. Although the hardware was almost free, the cost of wireless telephone calls was more expensive than ordinary calls. At one time, children paid so much for PHS and *keitai* calls that parents complained in such large numbers, so young Japanese turned to using them for the transmission of messages in the tradition of the *pokeberu* culture.

The DDI Pocket phone service began in December 1996, primarily as a closed mail service among PHS terminals. NTT DoCoMo met this challenge by providing a "short message" service for *keitai* cellular phones from June 1997. Furthermore, with the PHS, NTT Personal started an open e-mail service in March 1998, and the company NTT DoCoMo followed in February 1999 with a *keitai* I-mode service. This mobile Internet service has now become the centre of Japanese youth culture. Ideographic characters are, thanks to two-byte culture, displayed much more concisely than alphabetical representations of European languages. Now, 80 or 90 percent of mobile phone use by young Japanese is confined to e-mail exchange, while adults use mobile phones just as they did previously—mainly for telephone communication. The problem of cost aside, shy youths often prefer communicating with visual images rather than actual speech.

A few years ago, I organized a freshmen seminar to discuss mobile phones; while the students all carried a PHS or a *keitai*, I, the teacher, was the only person who did not. My lectures were often interrupted by the ringing of *keitai*. On the other hand, they were useful for professors who wished to contact students. What is significant is the way in which young Japanese e-mail one another. Teenagers have still not gotten used to the alphabet-based keyboard. Instead, they have been quick to adjust themselves to new systems of communication through the ten-key keypads of mobile phone. The Japanese language involves the use of a system of phonetics or *kana*, which has five vowels and nine major consonants. These phonetics are, perhaps, better suited to the decimal keypads of mobile phones, as consonants are allocated to the decimal ten-key keypad. The vowels can be represented by pushing numbers one to five times. This is, perhaps, more natural than the alphabet-turned-to-decimal keypad of the Western telephone dialling system. In this way, the decimal mobile phone has become an indispensable tool or toy for fashion conscious Japanese youth. They are sometimes called the "thumb-tribe" due to their ability to type on a keypad with one thumb at a rate much faster than adults using PC keyboards and typing with 10 fingers.

In 1999, NTT DoCoMo commenced the I-mode service, which connects to the Internet. This service not only includes an e-mail function but also enables the transmission of various data. Its use for telephone calls has become a less important aspect of the service, so much so that it can be rightly called a mobile Internet service rather than a mobile phone service. This has contributed to the strengthening of a youth subculture. NTT DoCoMo designed I-mode to fit into the already developed digital youth subculture, while the dominant Western culture of the PC-Internet system has spread much more slowly. Although there are few adults who subscribe to I-mode, the subculture of mobile phone use will arguably come to constitute the major culture of the Japanese in a decade or two, when these teenagers make up most of the workforce. The I-mode service is full of information that teenagers like to access, such as horoscope predictions and announcements of various events and entertainment. I, an adult, need only the weather forecast.

The PC versus Mobile Internet

When Bill Gates visited Japan in 2000, a Tokyo University student asked him to assess the future of mobile phones. He responded that the screen was too small and the future of the Internet rested with the PC. Despite his negative assessment, mobile phone sales continued to boom in Japan.

Considering the popularity of I-mode mobile phones not only in Japan but also in Hong Kong, there appears to be a cultural divide between East and West in terms of how the Internet is accessed. While Bill Gates and the alphabet-based peoples of the West (the USA, in particular, and myself included) prefer to use PCs to access the Internet, the average East Asian would prefer to approach it via the mobile phone. Since mobile phones are getting cheaper everywhere, they will eventually bring about the dissolution of the digital divide, especially in non-alphabet-based countries.

Still, there seem to be certain disadvantages associated with mobile Internet, in terms of the input of letters and the display of output. For input, many of my students claim that one-thumb operation is more convenient, easier and faster than typing on a PC keyboard. Students say that they do not require a particularly large display. Those Japanese who are already familiar with the keyboard, like myself, can never cope with one-thumb operation. Teenagers and most adults use the e-mail service to exchange short messages, such as where to meet and at what time. In time, they will use it to find a place to eat or shop. Today, the *keitai* can handle most functions of a PC, despite having only a small display. Most people will never write a long article or a book, but for those who need to produce a large document, a PC is a must-have.

In Japan, where there is no tradition of a keyboard-typing culture, the Internet is penetrating the lives of the common people through mobile terminals rather than PCs. While Japanese academics and professionals prefer to stay with the PC, most people prefer mobile phones. What is more important for younger Japanese is the design of mobile phones, for they are also fashion accessories, not unlike a necklace or a watch. The young mobile Internet generation sees the *keitai* as constitutive of their body and mind, a lifeline to be worn at all times and throughout their lives.

Conclusion

We can sum up this paper by looking at the following table, which represents a digital "trivide" rather than a digital divide.

Figure 1. The Japanese Digital Trivide

Generation	Pre-Revolutionary	Double Revolutionary	Post-Revolutionary
Communication	Hand	PC	Mobile phone
Age (years)	More than 50	25–50	Less than 25
Of the cohort	100%	Less than 30%	80%
Kind of people	All	Professionals, technophiles	Girls more than boys
At school	Encouraged	Non-existent	Discouraged
Cost	None	High	Low
Writing with	Pen, brush	Alphabet keyboard	Ten-key keypad
Writing by	One hand	Both hands	One thumb

The contrast between PCs and mobile phones can be extended in the following way:

Figure 2

PC	Mobile Internet
Instrumental	Consummatory
Official	Private
Daytime	Night-time
Yang	Yin
Confucian	Taoist

It is hard to predict whether it will be the PC keyboard or the mobile keypad that will dominate the market in the future. In the alphabet-based West, keyboard culture remains standard while ten-key keypads are confined to phone dialling. For the Japanese, both will co-exist for the time being. There will be some devices that will serve to bridge the keyboard and keypad, but for most Japanese and East Asians, the mobile ten-key keypad will eventually dominate communication, unless their own languages give way to English.

Even in a high-tech society like Japan, there exists a digital divide within across the social strata. Handicapped people may not be able to afford a new personal computer, which costs around 200,000 yen. Major computer manufacturers have actively discouraged the used-computer market in order to prevent price-cutting. This is despite the fact that most users do not need particularly advanced computers. For most people, the word processing function is the most needed. A friend of mine, Dr. Akiba, the mayor of Hiroshima City, encouraged a small business to manufacture no-frills computers for handicapped people at the price of 50,000 yen. The influential big manufacturers were not in a position to influence the pricing of this computer for "handicapped people", lest they be criticized for being socially insensitive.

The history of technology tells us that while new technology is often resisted by the older generation, it will survive the next generation only if it holds the attention of the younger generation. On a Japanese commuter train, most people read something—a newspaper, a book or a magazine—but you will find teenagers gazing at mobile phones, either to write e-mails or gather information. Neither the Japanese government nor corporations anticipated the emergence of such a subculture, but they are now adjusting themselves to this new digital environment. NEC and Matsushita are co-operating on research and development for the next generation of *keitai*, and even the Japanese government is committed to providing funding support in the hope of setting the world standard, and helping Japan become the world leader in this technology.

For contemporary Japanese, the double revolution from handwriting to the electronic keyboard has hardly been overcome, but with the advent of the mobile Internet, the next generation of Japanese can jump from handwriting to the keypad. The second revolution from keypad to keyboard has yet to be seen. It is not certain whether the second revolution will happen or not, but it is clear that mobile phones with 10 keys will dominate multimedia culture because of their convenience, low cost and digital divide-free nature.

Appendices

Appendix 1. Generation Chart

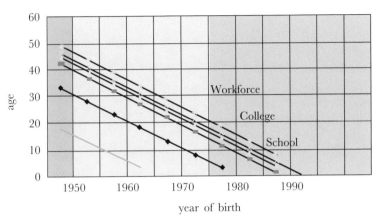

year of birth

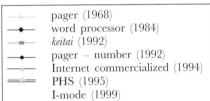

	pager (1968)
	word processor (1984)
	keitai (1992)
	pager – number (1992)
	Internet commercialized (1994)
	PHS (1995)
	I-mode (1999)

Appendix 2. Chronological Table

1966	NTT pager service
1979	Car telephone service
1983	Ichitaro Japanese software
1985	NTT privatized
1987	NCC starts
1987	Pagers with number display
1990s	Youth pager communication
1992–94	Youth pager boom (number)
1995	Commercial use of the Internet
1995	PHS
1995–96	Youth pager boom (letter)
1997	PHS and pager (letter)
1997	NTT DoCoMo *keitai* short message service
March 1998	NTT Personal: PHS e-mail service
February 1999	NTT DoCoMo I-mode service
2000	Mori IT policy

MALAYSIA'S MULTIMEDIA SUPER CORRIDOR AND ITS FIRST CRISIS OF CONFIDENCE

Toby E. Huff

Center for Policy Analysis
University of Massachusetts, Dartmouth

Introduction

Malaysia's Multimedia Super Corridor is that country's unique way of joining the "information society" and assisting the transition to the "knowledge economy". Since the Internet is a *global* construction, it is obviously at the heart of the "second" *great transformation* that is now going on under the heading of "globalization". Moreover, globalization and modernity today are clearly linked. Efforts to modernize forms of education, commerce and government are all linked to the new modes of globalized communication and a mastery of them. At the same time, globalization implies adopting *international* standards, especially international standards of openness with regard to communication, commerce and government, as well as engineering and science.[1]

From a business and commercial point of view, it is important to recognize that globalization is powered by three inexorable trends: globalization of communication, globalization of labour and commodity markets, and the networking of computers (within firms, among firms, nationally, and internationally). With the networking of computers around the world via the World Wide Web, virtually all commercial transactions can be done electronically. Even apart from the Web, it should be noted that retailers and wholesalers alike can send and receive orders automatically and electronically virtually around the world with the use of either fax machines or computers. Transactions that in the past would have taken several days to execute—the time needed to write up an order physically, post it in the mail, and send it to an offsite location—can now be completed

---

[1] This and the following paragraphs are taken from Huff (2001).

within minutes or seconds. All of this is taken for granted now in the
USA and the Western world, but it is not yet a reality in most Muslim countries or underdeveloped countries. The leaders of Malaysia,
however, recognized some of the early signs of this great transformation in early 1990s and proceeded quickly to create an Internet
infrastructure that would adequately connect Malaysia to the Internet,
and lay the foundation for the transition to a knowledge-based economy. They hoped that their "Multimedia Super Corridor" (MSC)
would become a new *engine of economic growth*. The project was launched
in 1996 and by 1999, it was up and running, clearly far ahead of
all other Muslim-majority countries. The many current references to
"failed modernity" in the Muslim world do not apply to Malaysia.[2]
By the summer of 2001, however, a malaise had set in and considerable scepticism was widely expressed.

The MSC Story

The MSC story begins with the "Vision 2020" statement and its
commitment to making Malaysia a fully developed country by the
year 2020. The Vision 2020 statement (Mahathir, 1998: Chapter 1)
was created in 1991 by consultants at the Institute for Strategic and
International Studies (ISIS) and was later fully embraced by Prime
Minister Mahathir. It was realized soon thereafter, however, that
bringing the average Malaysian income up to that of a "fully developed" state—which was estimated to be about $US10,500 (in 1994
dollars) (McKinsey and Associates, as reported in K.J. John, 2001:16)—
by 2020 could not be achieved by focusing mainly on significant
increases in manufacturing (projected to grow by approximately seven
percent per year and topping out at 38 percent of GDP in the mid-
1990s; see Figure 1). To make the grade and to bring Malaysian wages
up to the level of a fully developed country would require another
strategy and another "engine" of economic growth. Consultants and
advisers to the Prime Minister proposed that the incipient ICT revolu-

---

[2] For a compelling analysis of the struggles that Middle Eastern and North African
countries have been having in adjusting to globalization, see Henry and Springborg
(2001).

tion, then becoming apparent, was giving birth to a "new economy"—the "information age" of the global economy. In short, the advisers argued that the ICT revolution had within it the seeds of a new engine of growth that would give rise to the "knowledge economy", and this would be the new engine of economic growth. If Malaysia could position itself as a part of this new global, knowledge-based economy, then it would be able to harness the new technology and propel itself into the status of a fully developed country by 2020.

It is interesting to note that a team of Australian experts had proposed a similar project in the late 1980s. It was called "multifunctional polis" but was turned down by the government because it was thought that creating a platform "to fast-track next generation industries" was a task for private enterprises (*The Edge/**Netv@lue2.0**, 24 September 2001, p. 2). Consequently, one of the original team members, Dr Terry Cutler, later became a member of the International Advisory Panel (IAP) of the MSC, and continues to serve on it.

Figure 1. Leapfrogging Imperative of the MSC Vision

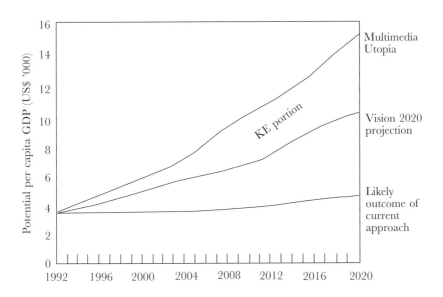

Source: Malaysia's Economic Growth Projection Scenarios by McKinsey and Associates, 1994 (as reported in K.J. John, 2001).

In any event, the Malaysian plan centred on creating a new "platform" of information technology—a local, Malaysian-based version of the Internet-Web platform. It was finally conceived as a "multimedia super corridor", an ICT "utopia" that would be a test bed for all sorts of new multimedia/ICT applications. This new infrastructure and its products would create new jobs, produce new kinds of "value-added" products and services, and transform government, communications and commerce in Malaysia. In the process it would (potentially) attract big multinational ICT corporations; ICT leaders such as Intel, Microsoft, Oracle, Compact, HWP, etc. If the venture were to be successful, it would get Malaysia to its goal of being fully developed *and* it would position Malaysia as a major ICT "hub" in Southeast Asian, and even in the world.

In the end, the concept of a "multimedia super corridor" was adopted, and its construction begun in 1996. By the summer of 1999, the fibre optics core had been laid and was up and running at 2.5 gigabytes/second (expandable to 10 gigabytes/second) in the 50-kilometre-long "corridor" stretching from the Petronas Towers in Kuala Lumpur west to the newly opened Kuala Lumpur International Airport (KLIA). In addition to that, the Malaysian Institute of Microelectronic Systems (MIMOS) had leased a high-speed telecommunications line from Penang in the north (the location of Malaysia's microchip facilities) south through the MSC/Kuala Lumpurcorridor all the way to the southernmost city of Johor Bahru, just a stone's throw away across the straits to Singapore. Not only that, several private telecommunications companies had installed other high-speed lines connecting the north and south of the Malaysian peninsula to the MSC. Furthermore, MIMOS maintains four international lines running from the MSC to Japan and Canada, and two to the west coast of the USA (to San Francisco and Los Angeles). In the summer of 1999, the Japan–Malaysia connection was providing a heavily-trafficked connection to users in China. Locally, Internet cafés were everywhere, and the charge for Internet services ranged between USD0.60 and USD1 per hour (RM2, in September 1999 outside Kuala Lumpur). By the end of 1999, nearly 63,000 kilometres of fibre optic cables had been laid (Malaysia, 2001:375).

During this first phase of the MSC, there were grand hopes for it, which were stated in various brochures and web pages. The MSC was to make Malaysia:

- a vehicle for attracting world-class technology-led companies to Malaysia, and developing local industries;
- a multimedia Utopia offering a productive, intelligent environment within which a multimedia value chain of goods and services will be produced and delivered across the globe;
- an island of excellence with multimedia-specific capabilities, technologies, infrastructure, legislation, policies and systems for competitive advantage;
- a test bed for invention, research and other ground-breaking multimedia developments, spearheaded by seven multimedia applications;
- a global community living on the leading edge of the Information Society;
- a world of smart homes, smart cities, smart schools, smart cards and smart partnerships www.mdc.my/index.html.

Despite the hype, the original conception of the MSC and its initial execution deserves high marks. If we make a comparison between the Malaysian MSC project and those in other parts of the Muslim world, then Malaysia looks very good indeed as it is the most Internet-developed Muslim country (see Figures 2 and 3). I will return to the question of the MSC's status in the Southeast Asian region.

Figure 2. Internet Hosts per 10,000 People (January 2000)

Region	Internet Hosts per 10,000 Pop.
	Jan-00
Middle East and North Africa	0.55
Sub-Saharan Africa	2.73
South Asia	0.22
East Asia & the Pacific	2.69
Low income	0.37
Middle income	9.96
High income	777.22
Low and middle income	5.4
The world	120.02
Malaysia	**25.43**

Source: World Bank Development Report 2000/2001, Table 19, pp. 310–11.

Figure 3. Internet Hosts in Arab/Middle Eastern Countries

Country	Hosts per 10,000 pop. (January 2000)
Algeria	0.01
Egypt	0.73
Iran	0.09
Jordan	1.27
Kuwait	20.5
Lebanon	10.93
Morocco	0.33
Saudi Arabia	1.28
Syria	0
Tunisia	0.1
Turkey	13.92
Yemen	0.02
Malaysia	25.43

First Signs of Crisis: The McKinsey Report

In the spring of 2001, however, a major study was commissioned by the Malaysian government to evaluate the progress of the MSC. The study was carried out by McKinsey and Associates, the international consulting firm that did most of the preliminary work for the original launching of the MSC. Its report was delivered to the Malaysian government in March 2001 but in the meantime, the report was leaked to the press and caused a considerable stir. Since the report remains confidential, the following characterization of the report's findings represents a composite sketch gleaned from various news accounts and editorial comments.[3] One should, however, add the following details. Since the MSC was proposed as a corridor, it became a geographical space, complete with land holdings. A former palm plantation was bought as a location for the new "cybercity" and multimedia corridor. The Malaysian government and the telcos each financed about half the cost of the initial investment. To execute

---

[3] Many of the Malaysian newspapers carried special reports on the MSC in September 2001, as this was when the International Advisory Panel held its annual meeting in Kuala Lumpur. For one of the better and more comprehensive accounts, see Netv@lue2.0, the supplement to *The Edge* ("Malaysia's Business and Investment Weekly"), 3 September 2001 and subsequent issues.

the whole project, a Multimedia Development Corporation (MDC) was set up. The latter was expected to use its position as facilitator of Internet development and—one supposes, as a land- and office-leasing agent—to be fiscally independent.

Within the 15 by 50 kilometre corridor there was a "Bill of Guarantees", especially the guarantee of no censorship and the provision of certain "state of the art" facilities, including fibre optics connections. In addition, special exemptions regarding ownership rights, access to international financial markets and unrestricted use of foreign "knowledge workers" were part of the package. Companies that chose to settle in that zone had to meet certain standards of technical capability and entrepreneurial promise, as well as financial solvency if they were to be given "MSC status". The latter designation would presumably lead to greater visibility and other advantages for the designated companies. It seems likely also that Malaysian leaders had in mind the creation of a Malaysian "Silicon Valley".

With that background in view, the report of McKinsey and Associates offered the following criticisms:

- Too much red tape getting MSC status approval.
- Conflict of interest between the Multimedia Development Corporation's economic interests and those of the companies it is supposed to assist.
- Need to allow MSC companies to locate anywhere they desire.
- Make more areas/cities part of the MSC (for example, Penang).
- MDC needs better, more ICT-qualified leaders.
- MSC/Cyberjaya needs more "world-class" companies.
- MSC project needs more ICT/knowledge workers than the new Multimedia University (MMU) can produce; or MMU is not good enough to draw top-flight regional "intellectual capital".
- MSC has not had a big enough impact on economic development; it needs better venture capital managers, etc.
- Malaysia Telecom (and other Internet Service Providers [ISPs]) have failed to deliver the infrastructure needed to support the MSC's development.
- Not enough attention was given to supporting and promoting Malaysian "small- and medium-sized" enterprises (SMEs).

Much of this criticism is understandable and justified, though it is far too early to make a final judgement on the success or failure of the MSC. It is probably correct to suggest that the top leadership at the MDC needs to be replaced with more professional and sea-soned ICT professionals. This appeared to be taking place in the Fall of 2001 (*Computimes*, 4 October 2001, p. 1).

The issue of insufficient "intellectual capital" is bound up with a variety of indigenous problems, including the government policy of promoting Bumiputeras (that is, people of Malay extraction), which has often been practiced to the neglect of Chinese and Indian citizens. Prime Minister Mahathir has spoken out on many occasions, criticizing Malays for not being hardworking enough, for not achieving top honours in schools, and for not being entrepreneurial enough. Recently, the government has decided to make admission to universities based on merit, starting with the next class of applicants in 2002. Nevertheless, the MSC web page lists 20 universities with "MSC status", which presumably means that they are heavy users of ICT and that they also teach various aspects of ICT (www.mdc.com.my).

In the meantime, the anticipated yield of "knowledge workers" from existing universities by the MDC appears to be adequate, above all given the downturn in the US and global economies. According to the MDC, "the net supply of IT/engineering students expected to be produced between 1999–2001 is about 137,000 while the anticipated demand between 1998–2005 is 104,000" (personal communication with Sumitra, 5 July 2001). Furthermore, plans have been laid for the opening of a joint Malaysian–American graduate school focusing on high technology.[4]

When the Malaysian governmental elite launched their Web project, nobody knew what direction the Web would take. When I heard the original presentation of the MSC project at a conference in Malaysia in 1996, it was clear that this was an *experimental* adventure, that *nobody* could say what the direction(s) would be taken— neither computer visionaries, policy planners or religious officials. For example, we can now see (as we could not in 1996) that the Internet entails the following functional dimensions. It is:

- a new, digitised, global communication system;
- a massive data storage and retrieval system for economic, governmental, historical, medical and scientific information;
- an electronic "bulletin board" ("Usenet");

---

[4] Interview with Tan Sri Datuk Dr Omar Abdul Rahman, former Science Adviser to Prime Minister Mahathir, in Putrajaya, 11 October 2001.

- an automated post office;
- a translocal, transnational shopping mall;
- a potential medium for political mobilization and action;
- an experimental location for new "communities";
- a new medium spawning new types of crime;
- an international meeting place in which new international laws must be worked out;
- a new medium of entertainment and "self expression".

Even this list has to be expanded to include Malaysia's hopeful idea, that the Internet/ICT, can be a new *engine of economic growth*. Consequently, it made perfectly good sense to say that the project was taken on as an experiment. Indeed, the Malaysian leadership was so cautious at the outset that it did not dare to give the job of providing the basic Internet infrastructure to private enterprise out of fear that it would exclude too many Malaysians although shortly thereafter, it did indeed privatize most of the project.

Similarly, in that context it made sense to talk about a corridor of high-tech, multimedia development, since it would have been far too costly to wire the whole country. In addition, it would have been very difficult politically to offer the "Bill of Guarantees" to any and all foreign companies that might wish to locate anywhere in Malaysia with their special exemptions for ownership rights, capital market access, and unlimited knowledge worker importation. At the time, the idea of a corridor was "in the air" and this seemed to be the solution to the problem.[5]

This geographic limitation, however, was soon to become a liability. For among the critics of the MSC, the view that the MSC is a "big land deal" frequently surfaces. At the same time, the island of Penang, off the northwest coast, is the site of many high-tech industries, especially computer chip design and manufacture, which were very successful before the launch of the MSC. Consequently, a strong case could be made for its inclusion in the MSC, and for giving companies located there MSC status, but this has been rejected by the Prime Minister for reasons mentioned above.[6] Nevertheless, there are plans to create a series of "cyber-cities" in the country that would provide the benefits of the Bill of Guarantees and would grant MSC status to companies locating in them.

---

[5] Interview with Dr Tengku Azzman Shariffadeen at MIMOS, 23 July 2001.
[6] Interview with Dr K.J. John, 22 October 2001.

As for the criticism that not enough companies, international or otherwise, have located in Cyberjaya, a spokesman for the MSC quickly shot back that, in fact, the target number of MSC-status companies located in Cyberjaya has surpassed expectations and schedules (*The Edge*/Netv@lue2.0, 6 September 2001). Indeed, at the end of October 2001, there were 585 MSC-status companies (www.msc.com.my/mdc/statistic/default.asp), and 50 of these were World Class companies. At the same time, the MDC could say that about 65 percent of the companies were Malaysian companies and that, therefore, this project was benefiting the Malaysian business community and, above all, its fledgling ICT community. Subsequently, the MDC revised upwards the targeted number of MSC-status companies from 500 to 650 by the end of 2002.

With regards to the economic impact of MSC-related activities, it is clearly too soon to make any judgment about that. On the one hand, MSC-status companies located in Cyberjaya have spent hundreds of millions of dollars in the course of their work, both on infrastructure development and R&D. Estimates of how much e-commerce has been generated by the MSC have not yet been produced. The research firm, IDC, has estimated that by 2005, e-commerce in Southeast Asia will reach US$9 billion (www.idc.com.my). As the number of MSC-status companies grows, it is clear that the growth of e-commerce and ICT-related businesses will also grow in tandem.

Lastly, the claim that the telcos have not fully delivered the Internet service expected seems to be right. On the issue of cost, clearly, access costs are too high for residential and business users. This is widely attested to. DSL service is not widely available because it requires fixed lines in relatively dense settlements, thus, frequently requiring the installation of new fixed lines. The charges are reported to be well over RM1000 (about US$260) per month—clearly an exorbitant rate. To be sure, the MSC does provide state-of-the-art high-speed broadband access to businesses and universities in the country. Nevertheless, some users (despite all the fibre optic cables that have been laid), even in newly-opened Putrajaya (the new high-tech government centre outside Kuala Lumpur), have the sense that service is not as fast and reliable as it should be. Most users have only dial-up service (at about 45kbps), and even in the Kuala Lumpur Civic Center (KLCC) at the foot of the Petronas Twin Towers (one of the anchor points of the MSC), there is only dial-up and not broadband service available in the main concourse demonstration area. Of course, there are technical problems of going "the last mile" from fibre optic cables at the curb to the user, but here again it should be the job of the telcos to overcome those obstacles. The Prime Minister has recently suggested putting more resources into wireless communication, and that seems like a modest short-term solution. In response to the criticism that the MDC did not place enough emphasis on SMEs, the MDC leadership has now announced a new programme that will target the SMEs.

In brief, there are a number of criticisms of the MSC after two years of operation, some of which merit more credence than others. The criticism of the failure of the telcos to fully deliver their part of the infrastructure is perhaps one of the more serious ones. Most of the criticisms, in this writer's view, are signs of intelligent vigilance and the obvious need to fine-tune the parts of a very large and ambitious national project. Given the rapid pace of technological innovation and the constantly evolving international standards of ICT management, it makes sense for the MDC to look for new management options. Singapore has often done this in its various national endeavours, and this has kept its leadership well positioned to deal with the high level of competition in Southeast Asia.

There is, however, another source of serious criticism that concerns e-government but first, I turn to the "Flagship Applications", which were to be developed and rolled out in Phase 2 of the MSC project.

Flagship Applications

The original concept of the MSC included the idea of "flagship applications", which were intended to provide some kind of "content" that would offer inducement to use Malaysia's new Internet infrastructure. The original design of the MSC called for the creation of six flagship applications, though the list eventually got expanded to eight—the eighth just now appearing and designed to enhance "technopreneurship". There seems to be, however, some re-evaluation going on. In September of this year, the MDC web page listed seven flagships, and the eighth, for technopreneurship, had just been announced. In November, however, the web page reverted to six applications, divided into two groups: "multimedia development" and "multimedia environment" applications. The first group includes:

- electronic government;
- a multi-purpose card;
- smart schools;
- telemedicine.

The second cluster of "multimedia environment" applications include:

- an R&D cluster;
- borderless marketing (www.msc.com.my/mdc/flagships).

The "Worldwide Manufacturing Web" had been dropped from the list.

The first of these flagship applications, the e-government application, is actually a combination of several specialized pieces of software:

- a Project Monitoring System (PMS);
- a Human Resource Management Information System (HRIMS);
- a Generic Office Environment (GOE) groupware;
- an Electronic Procurement (EP) system that would automate the process of procuring goods and services between buyers and government offices;
- an Electronic Delivery Services application (this is an alternate method for transactions and interactions between the public and government via electronic delivery channels of Wireless Application Protocol [WAP]).

There is also a sixth part here, a generic Electronic Labour Exchange (ELX) for tracking workers. A Knowledge Workers' Exchange (KWX), however, has already been up and running for several years.

Each of these applications is in a different stage of development and readiness for rolling out. Some parts of the e-government application have been at least pilot-tested, but none have been fully rolled out. The so-called "Smart Card" ("MYKAD") was just being released in August of 2001 in the Klang valley (the area stretching from Kuala Lumpur to port Klang) and two million people are expected to have it by the end of the year. In principle, it will be a national identity card, a driver's licence, a healthcare information card and a bank transfer card, all secured by the owner's thumbprint. When the Smart Card was conceived, it was probably a "world's first" idea.

The Smart Schools project intends to make Internet training and facilities more available to the general population. Another part of that project utilizes a bus, fully equipped with computer equipment, that can accommodate about a dozen students. It is driven around the country to provide local schools with temporary access to computers.

The Telemedicine application is being designed to help manage and deliver healthcare on site and over the Web, and is being developed in conjunction with a new and very high-tech medical centre.

The R&D Cluster application strives to ensure that the MSC is an attractive location for companies to develop next-generation multimedia technologies and innovations. In addition, the R&D Cluster is intended to assist the improvement of Malaysia's human resource development, provide a test-bed for experimenting with innovations, promote indigenous technology and encourage technology transfer to Malaysia.

The e-Business (or Borderless Economy) application seems to be only in the very early stages of development. Its developers hope to create and shape an electronic business environment that can compete with the major economic powers. The MDC thinks that this cluster will have an enormous potential market that could be one of the driving forces for future economic growth in Malaysia.

Lastly, there is the Technopreneurship application. Whether this ought to be run and managed by the MDC when the MTDC (the Malaysian Technology Development Corporation) already has nearly ten years of experience with high-tech start-ups is another question. All would agree, however, that there is need for such a support and training centre for MSC-related firms. Finally, the "Worldwide Web manufacturing application", which appears to have been shelved, aspires to make Internet-based technologies located in Malaysia accessible anywhere in the world for the purpose of carrying out manufacturing processes.

E-Government?

I turn now to the question of implementing e-government. Here, the idea was that Web-based government would revolutionize the nature of government, making services more available to citizens and, hopefully, make the government more democratic.

In recent years, governments around the world have moved towards using the Web to provide various governmental services. In the early part of 2001, a study was done by the international ICT consulting firm, Accenture (formerly Anderson Consulting). It carried out a study of 22 countries and compared them in terms of the actual delivery of government services via the Web. Accenture investigated both the range of services provided by the governments and the degree to which various governments had improved their delivery of Web-based services over time. This comparison served as a basis for estimating the "Web maturity" of governments as they improved their Web-based delivery of services. The researchers also noted that no governments around the world had reached the maturity of Web-based service delivery found in private enterprise (www.accenture.com/xd/xd.asp?it=enWeb&xd=industries/government/gove_method.xml).

The results of the Accenture study yielded a typology of four groups of countries: Innovative Leaders, Visionary Followers, Steady Achievers and Platform Builders (see Figure 4). It is in the latter category that the Accenture team placed Malaysia and, I think, correctly. For Malaysia's approach to the Flagship Applications was indeed to start "from scratch". Instead of taking some available programmes "off the shelf" and modifying them to fit Malaysia's needs, it started from ground zero and worked its way up. It is too soon tell whether or not this approach will pay off, although it seems unlikely on the face of it. As a sort of "work-fare"—giving Malaysian ICT workers a real job to do and paying them while they were training to create something entirely new—it might be a feasible state policy, but it is unclear whether or not that was the best way to proceed. Several parts of the new software design, however, were contracted out to established software companies.

The researchers attempted to determine whether or not citizens could do such things as pay their taxes, get a driver's licence or apply for a passport online. As noted, they compared each country's situation in 2001 with what it was in 2000 to determine how much progress had been made with regard to e-government delivery.

Before turning to those results, I should point out that Malaysia was the only Muslim country that made it into the sample, and one presumes that is because Malaysia has indeed embarked upon a real project of creating electronic government.

This was the central task of Phase 2 of the MSC project, that is, to develop various flagship applications that would give people a reason to use the MSC and, thus, serve as a drawing card for others outside Malaysia to locate their businesses there and to use the facilities of the MSC.

At the time of the study, the MSC's flagship applications designed to provide e-government were only in their developmental stages;

Figure 4. Estimates and Rankings of e-Government Maturity by Country

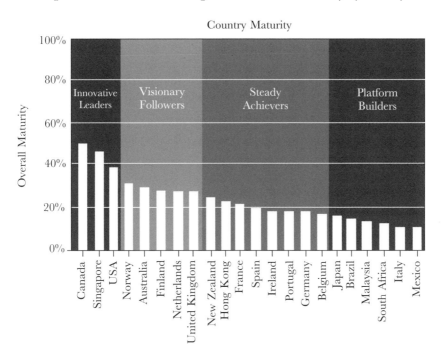

most of them were far from ready to be rolled out or pilot-tested. Consequently, Malaysia's ranking on the scale places its delivery of e-government towards the bottom among the "platform builders", yet it is in the same group as Japan. Given Japan's image as a successful high-tech developer, this might be seen as a considerable achievement for Malaysia, though it needs to be recognized that Japan is a laggard with regard to Internet development (see Nakayama's article in this volume).[7]

This raises the question of how well Malaysia's MSC will compete in the Southeast Asian region. Looking at Figure 5, one can see that Malaysia's Internet preparedness places it somewhere in the middle, below Singapore, South Korea and Hong Kong, but above Thailand, Indonesia and the Philippines. These simple measures of computer ownership and Internet connectedness tell us very little about the

---

[7] A reporter for *The Edge* reported that Malaysia ranked in the top 10 percent "of similar initiatives in the world" (Jayasaeelan, 2001).

underlying infrastructure and the complicated set of resources that
have to be marshalled to be successful in this ICT world of the
information age. If there is truly an incipient economic transformation going on that entails a major shift from a "production economy" to a "knowledge economy", then a far broader range of assets
and human resources have to be considered. Remarkably, the Malaysian leadership has thought deeply about these issues and their resulting strategies merit additional attention. This is the subject of the
"K-economy."

Figure 5. Internet Hosts and Computers in Southeast Asia by Country

	Hosts/10,000— (January 2000)	Computers/1000 pop. (1998)
Singapore	452	458
Hong Kong	162.82	254.2
Korea	60	156.8
Malaysia	25.43	58.8
Thailand	6.46	21.6
Philippines	1.58	15.1
Indonesia	1	8.2
China	0.57	8.9

Source: World Bank, *World Development Report 2001.*

The K-Economy

This is actually at the heart of the whole project. It is the belief that
the modern global economy is shifting towards a *knowledge-based* economy. This vision incorporates the leading themes of sociologists (Bell,
1976; Castells, 1996) and other social scientists who have pointed to
the rise of the "network society", the increasingly rapid flow of information around the world, the revolutionary changes in ICT and the
rapidly expanding commodification of ideas as economic products.
Towards that end, the architects of the MSC created a "National
Information Technology Agenda" (NITA) to promote the knowledge
economy. The latter idea was a mainstream endeavour from the
beginning of the MSC vision. It appears, for example, in all of Dr.
Tengku Azzman's early papers promoting the MSC and, subsequently,
it became institutional. This was accomplished first by the establishment of a National Information Technology Council (NITC) in

1993 and then, the NITA. The NITC, especially the staff at MIMOS, went on to spell out the practical and policy-focused implications of this new IT agenda. It was called the "Integrated Platform for Transformation into the E-World" (www.nitc/org.myresources/inte-gratedplatform.html). The people at MIMOS took the idea of the emerging knowledge economy seriously and spelled out five domains of social, economic and political life that would become dominated by electronic technology and, hence, could be called "e-worlds". These include the e-economy, e-public service, e-community, e-learning and e-sovereignty" (www.nitc.org.my/resources/integratedplatform.html).

The Malaysian leadership has devoted a considerable effort to understanding the ubiquitous "K-economy". The staff at the National Information Technology Council (NITC) held seminars and com-missioned a variety of papers to spell out the practical economic significance of the new economy. They also explored visionary science and technology writers such as Michio Kaku (1997). He identifies ICT, biotechnology and quantum physics as the three rev-olutionary sciences that will both transform our understanding of biological and natural processes, and give us the ability to control and manipulate them.

In a series of related papers, MIMOS/NITC staff attempted to work out in detail the presumed transition from a "P-economy" (pro-duction economy) to a "K-economy" (knowledge economy) (NITC/ MIMOS 1999a,b,c; 2000). The assumption is that ICT, quantum physics and biotechnology are now going through major transfor-mations, and will transform both the nature of work and the types of products that will be produced. According to this line of thinking, a major transformation of modern economies is to be expected as these scientific and technological revolutions mature and make their way through the production cycle.

The NITC agenda calls for a "migration" of Malaysian workers from the current state of development into five new e-worlds. It is recognized that in each sphere, there is a new set of skills needed, which Malaysian workers must acquire (the "knowledge imperative"). Towards that end, the NITC and other key actors have set up a committee, the Strategic Thrusts Implementation Committee (STIC), which is charged with implementing the NITC Strategic Agenda, the integrated platform for transformation into e-worlds (www.nitc. org.my/resources/integratedplatform.html).

Specific individuals and agencies have been appointed to support and monitor progress in each area.

Whatever the criticisms of the MSC—and they are mostly about the lack of speedy execution—it should be said that each step in the process has been carefully thought out by the Malaysian technocratic elite who advise the government. The Malaysian public is generally unaware of any of the background details that have led up to the development of the MSC. In Malaysia, the MSC is seen as Prime Minister Mahathir's brainchild when, of course, it is the product of months and years of committee meetings and intellectual debates involving experts from all over the world, as well as key movers within Malaysia's own technical elite. Nevertheless, Malaysia's leadership here in connection with its efforts to think through the steps necessary for transition to the K-economy have been recognized internationally. It has served as consultant to the technical elite of a variety of Middle Eastern countries and most recently, MIMOS has been named the Secretariat of the Global Knowledge Partnership.[8] The efforts of the National Information Technology Council, however, are only the tip of the iceberg in terms of Malaysia's national drive for transition to the K-economy and the creation of an "ecology" of creativity and innovation in the country.

National Innovation System

Malaysia's efforts to harness the economic and social benefits of advancing science and technology (S&T) go back to the mid 1980s and to the 5th Malaysia Plan, 1986–1990. This planning was underway even before the Vision 2020 statement was embraced by Prime Minister Mahathir in 1991. Starting with the budget of the 5th Malaysia Plan (1986), policy planners realized that "the development of science and technology (S&T) is essential for Malaysia's overall socio-economic advancement" (Malaysia, 1991:187). They proceeded to put in place the rudiments of a national innovation system, more than RM400 million was dedicated to S&T research and development, an amount

---

[8] This is an international partnership designed to aid developing countries by creating a data bank, and a network of people that is engaged in all the issues associated with developing knowledge-based societies throughout the world (gkaims. global-knowledge.org/index.cfm).

that was over and above institutional operating costs. That funding has been significantly increased in each subsequent budget, reaching RM1.6 billion for the period 2001–2005, with an additional RM2.8 billion (about US$737 million) for S&T infrastructure development (Malaysia, 2001:360). In addition, in 1987, a programme of "intensified research in priority areas" (IRPA) was put in place in order to direct research and development into commercialization and other priority areas. Malaysian policy makers are aware, however, that this amount is still below OECD levels of investment in S&T.

The concept of a national innovation system has been defined as the complex set of national agents, actors and institutions that enable and promote economic innovation.[9] Widespread and serious attention to national innovation systems only began to be evident among academics in the late 1980s, so it is impressive that Malaysia's political elite has focused attention on this aspect of economic development, even as early as 1986.

In the summer of 2001, the Malaysian Academy of Sciences produced an advisory report on the state of national science and technology policy, which included a chapter entitled "The National Innovation System: The Driver for Change",[10] and listed such components as financial infrastructure, R&D facilities, technology acquisition systems, human resource development, and a public awareness of science programme. Even prior to that, however, the former Science Adviser to the Prime Minister, Dr Omar (who was also the President of the Malaysian Academy of Sciences in 2001) produced two policy reports outlining the accomplishments of the government in developing a national innovation system, and laying out future steps to be taken to flesh out the system. As can be seen in Figure 6, the policy envisions both "buying" and "making" various strategic technologies that can be turned into commercialized products. The chart also indicates that there is a necessity to develop a sequence of intermediate components

---

[9] For the general literature on national innovation systems (NIS), see among others, Freeman (1995), Nelson (1993), Lundvall (1988, 1999), and Archibugi (1999). For references to Malaysia's NIS, see Felker and Jomo (199). For the official view of Malaysia's national innovation system, I relied on Omar (1, 2).

[10] This document is intended only for internal use and is only advisory; Akademi Sains Malaysia, *Consultancy Report from Academy of Sciences Malaysia to the Ministry of Science, Technology and the Environment, Review of National Science and Technology Policy Final Report* (2001).

that lead from knowledge creation through institutional incubation, financial support, enabling laws and legislation, commercial process- ing and management to the packaging and production of the final product. When the initial funding to potential R&D scientists and engineers was granted in the 1980s, none of the intermediate struc- tures and institutions were in place, except perhaps, university research facilities.

There are a number of additional components of this fledgling system that need to be carefully examined but for present purposes, this sketchy overview should suffice. These policies and their imple- mentation are at the centre of the Malaysian national innovation system that includes not only this essential governmental planning and institution-building, but universities (both public and private), private industry, technology parks, "incubators", various components of infrastructure and, above all at this juncture, the MSC. The broader point is that the Malaysian leaders are not stuck in failed modernization, and that Malaysia stands out as a successfully moderniz- ing Muslim country that generally has embraced modern science and technology, with all their ambiguous offshoots. It stands in marked contrast to many Middle Eastern and North African countries that are having considerable difficulty, not only with Internet develop- ment but with coping with and adjusting to globalization (see Henry and Springborg, 2001).

Discussion and Conclusion

Malaysia embarked upon a bold national project of Internet devel- opment in the early 1990s. The blueprint for the development of the MSC has been laid out with considerable care. The basic infra- structure has been put in place, two new "cyber" cities (Cyberjaya and Putrajaya) have been established, and government functionaries have relocated to the new headquarters in Putrajaya. Five hundred and eighty-five MSC-status companies have located in Cyberjaya, and Malaysians have been making the transition to the Web with reasonable alacrity. The path to the knowledge economy has been surveyed and the necessary steps have been identified. Enabling gov- ernmental structures have also been put in place and major steps have been taken to establish a viable national innovation system.

It is entirely appropriate that a national innovation system be the

Figure 6. Outline of the Components of Malaysia's National Innovation System

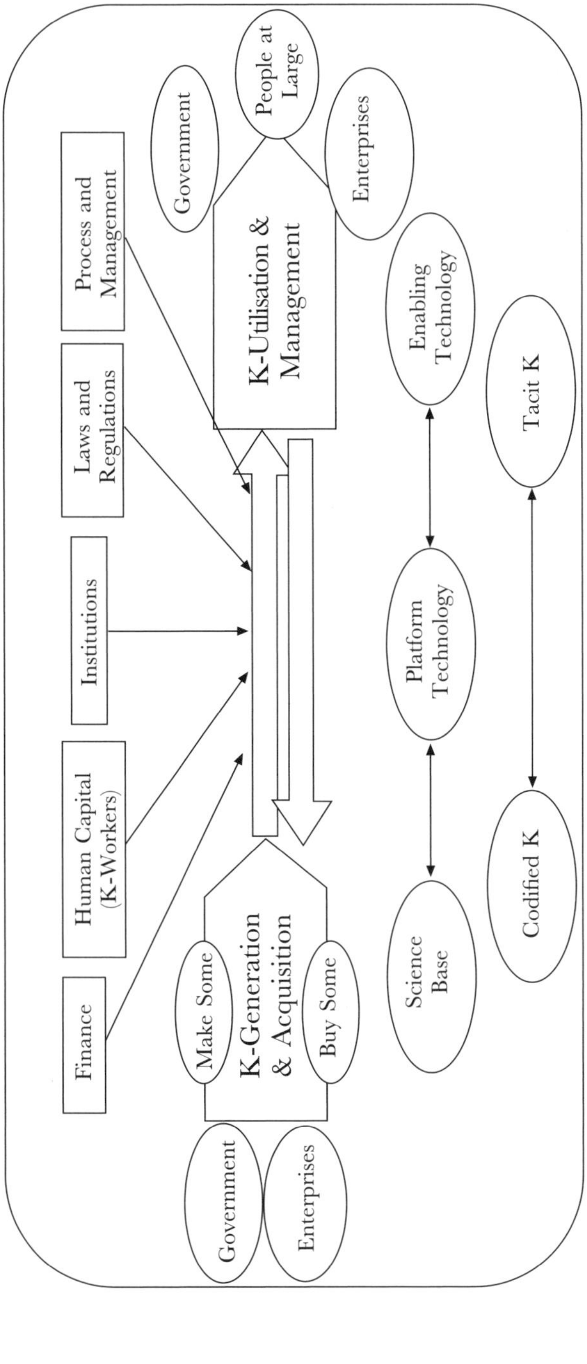

Source: Dr Omar (1)

object of governmental design and policy-making, above all, in a developing country. It is also true that in developing countries, such large enterprises as Internet development (for example, the MSC) have to be undertaken by the government rather than the private sector.

On the legal front, new "cyber laws" have been enacted while others have been adjusted to allow and encourage the emergence of the new "e-worlds", although this is an endless process. Part of it entails allowing the admittance of foreign workers and foreign capital; part of it requires the fashioning of new laws to govern Internet activities, "property" rights, and appropriate Web conduct; and still another task is grappling with the nature and consequences of encryption in a variety of Web contexts.

A new "multimedia university" has been built and is fully functional (on two campuses with up to 8,000 students); and a variety of venture capital funds (both private and governmental) have been created to aid aspiring entrepreneurs, along with other grant schemes designed to encourage ICT entrepreneurs. In addition, multiple locations have been chosen for "incubators", which have been established to house and support ICT developers and technopreneurs—not just in Cyberjaya, but in other locations as well. Plans are now underway to create a whole network of such incubator clusters (*Computimes* 27 August 2001, p. 4).

Likewise, several technology parks have been constructed; some have real research capacity while others are hopeful business ventures.[11] All of these efforts suggest that the Malaysian leadership is on the right track. At least in principle, it seems reasonable to assume that the MSC—the Malaysian Internet—in its enabling function, could serve as a new "engine of economic growth". Wisely used, it also has the potential to serve as the integrating linchpin of a national innovation system that would co-ordinate the salient elements of such a system.

Internally, however, there has been a debate about how large the K-economy will be, and whether or not the MSC and ICT are the vehicles for growing the K-economy or whether ICT *is* itself the K-economy. This is a natural question, and no doubt others around the world are trying to work out this theoretical and conceptual

---

[11] For those related to the *Malaysian Technology Development Corporation* see <www.mtdc.com.my/tc/ssp.html> For the "relaunch" of the Selangor1 Science Park, see Netv@lue2.0, September 24, 2001, p. 2f.

puzzle. It is essential to recognize, however, that the MSC is only *one piece* in the national innovation system, and that high-level research ("world class" scientific research) is necessary in certain fields in order for Malaysia to grow into a technologically self-sufficient economy and country.

On this question, the Prime Minister has seemingly given the official view. While he affirms that it is necessary to have a "paradigm shift" from the production-driven economy to the knowledge-driven economy, "the basic structure of the Malaysian economy will not be fundamentally altered in the short to medium term", and the shift to the K-economy "does not mean the abandonment of our industrial backbone, which today contributes more than 37 percent of our GDP, which provides 30 percent of all jobs" (speech made on 8 March 2000, as reported in Dr Omar 1:[10]).

When it comes down to the actual configuration of government, private industry, universities, research parks, incubators and the MSC, there will be ample room for debate. Some commentators may doubt that the MSC will itself be the location for "world-class" high-tech research. Recently, the Intel Corporation has said that it intends to establish a research facility in Cyberjaya, the geographic heart of the MSC ("New Straits Times", 3 August 2001). At the same time, it is to be recognized that the fledgling Cyberjaya is only in its infancy, and only slowly will it produce both indigenous and international ICT firms with world-class research capabilities; yet, it appears to have made a very good start, given the 585 firms now located there. Already, Lucent Technology, in collaboration with the MMU faculty, has filed multiple patent applications.[12]

Expecting the MSC to be responsible for generating *all* high-level scientific research in Malaysia, however, is misguided. The country, after all, has more than 20 colleges and universities and it should be their responsibility, though not exclusively, to undertake such research. It is difficult to imagine a fully developed modern economy without a robust Internet infrastructure, but it is a mistake to think that the K-economy is totally absorbed by the Internet, or that all major research should be conducted via the Web, or even mostly in a single "cyber" city (or "Silicon Valley") such as Cyberjaya. In the USA, Silicon Valley is only one of many other (at least four) ICT centres,

---

[12] Interview with Sumitra at MDC in Cyberjaya, 15 August 2001.

and still more ICT research is conducted in the nation's universities. Likewise, in Malaysia, the island of Penang is an independent source of first-rate ICT research and development.

When the MSC is viewed as a large-scale national project designed to give Malaysia a new and efficient access point to the *global* Internet work, as well as a "platform" for economic growth in the context of the highly competitive region of Southeast Asia, it deserves fairly high marks. As pointed out earlier, if we make the comparison between Malaysia and the larger Muslim world, then Malaysia has indeed done well and is ahead of the pack. On the other hand, if the comparison is with other Southeast Asian countries (Figure 5), then it falls in the middle of the pact, below Singapore and Hong Kong, but above Thailand, the Philippines, Indonesia, and probably Vietnam. At the same time, it has been noted that Malaysia's Internet project has been presented in excessively boastful terms, spoken about as its "gift to the world" and with ambitions to be a major regional hub. Such hubris attracts undue criticism. Malaysia should devote all its efforts to making *Malaysia* as efficient as possible. Visitors to Malaysia get the impression that there is a great deal of inefficiency, that it seems to take three people, especially in government bureaucracies, to do anything. Malaysian banks are well known for their inefficiency, with plans underway to eliminate thousand of redundant workers (estimates go as high as 30,000) via outsourcing ("New Straits Times", 24 August 2001). It is on these issues that Malaysia should focus its attention. It is to be hoped that the MSC and its new flagship applications will have a real impact on this aspect of Malaysian daily life. At the same time, Malaysian ambitions to do at least some world-class scientific research and to be a leader, "not just a follower" in some fields, is commendable.

Malaysia deserves considerable praise for its steady and impressive economic growth over the last two and half decades, and for the general civility of its public life—notwithstanding the Anwar affair. Whatever one's feelings about the justice of that case, it is a feather in Malaysia's cap that it did not abandon the openness of the Internet during the crisis, and that *precedent* will surely be an asset in future political contests. Likewise, during the aftermath of the attacks on the World Trade Center in New York, Malaysians were both very sympathetic to Americans (though in disagreement regarding the Afghan war), and very civil in the minor demonstrations that some carried out in opposition to the International Coalition's bombings in Afghanistan. Notwithstanding the present national scepticism regarding the MSC, the MSC has been reasonably well designed and launched. In the final analysis, however, it is only a part of the larger structure of national innovation systems that function equally as "engines of economic growth". Whether Malaysia's NIS is more or less adequate or developed than that of the other Asian countries is an important research question.

THE CULTURE OF TECHNOLOGY OF SINGAPORE

ALWYN LIM
Department of Sociology
State University of New York at Stonybrook

Introduction

The impact of information technology on society has been the focus of current academic inquiries into science, technology, and society. Certainly, as Manuel Castells points out in his three-volume *The Information Age* (1997; 2000a; 2000b), this change has been both intensive as well extensive. That is to say, this radical transformation of society necessarily takes place at both global as well as local levels. Together with Castells' *Rise of the Network Society* (2000a), such studies as David Lyon's *The Information Society* (1988) and Andrew Webster's *Science, Technology, and Society* (1991) have brought the question of the relationship between technology, society, economy and culture to the forefront of sociological inquiry.

The Information Society?

The validity of the notion of "the information society" has been put forward by several different conceptions of what such a society might constitute. I intend to argue that given the processes of increasing globalization and the rapid increase in the convergences of computer technologies and mobile communications, we are seeing the development of specific technological hubs that are linked across space in complex political, social and economic networks. These networks constitute technological activity that spans anything from production and dissemination, to research and development. This much is the object of inquiry of studies such as Castells' *The Informational City* (1989) and Castells and Peter Hall's *Technopoles of the World* (1994).

While authors like Castells and Hall concentrate on the development of technoscience parks, and research and development institutions, I argue that it is also important to study the entire cultural complex of societies that promote themselves as such technological hubs. That is to say, the study of the constitution and construction of "informational societies" cannot be undertaken using empty tropes such as "knowledge" or "technology" without considering the unique developmental trajectories of each specific technological society. As the development processes of the construction of these various "technopoles" depend on different historical circumstances and contingencies, a socio-historical approach is necessary to determine the very social and cultural conditions of existence of such "technopoles". Although reflecting different conceptual concerns, prime examples of such an approach include studies by Merton (1970) and Baber (1996).

Castells admits as much when he considers the East Asian experience of industrialization and how developmental states appropriate technology in attempting to assimilate themselves into the network enterprise (2000a:197–199). He argues that the "historical expression of this societal project [of transforming social order] took the form of the affirmation of national identity, and national culture, building or rebuilding the nation as a force in the world, in this case by means of economic competitiveness and socio-economic improvement" (2000a:198). In his study on space and technology, part of his cornerstone theory on the constitution and reproduction of modern social reality, he argues that "the Information Age is ushering in a new urban form, the informational city" and "in spite of the extraordinary diversity of cultural and physical contexts there are some fundamental common features in the trans-cultural development of the informational city" (2000a:429). Nevertheless, despite Castells' acknowledgement, I intend to allow this paper to demonstrate the importance of a sociological inquiry into the particular development of such an informational society, that is, Singapore; and to explore the unique and specific socio-historical condition on which such a development has been possible.

The "Intelligent Island" Today

To write a history of the development of Singapore is also to write a history of technology in Singapore. Several simple statistics allude to the ubiquity of (new) technologies in Singapore society. Over a short period of five years, for example, dial-up Internet subscriptions have risen phenomenally from 2,000 in 1994 to 583,000 in 1999 (Department of Statistics, 2000:157). Likewise, the Singapore government's operating expenditure on communications and information technology has increased from S$4.10 million in 1989 to a massive S$458.0 million in 1999, a more than tenfold increase (ibid.: 194). Another expression of this fact is the increase in enrolment of polytechnic students in information technology courses, from 2,410 students in 1994 to 6,397 students in 1999 (ibid.: 231).

A recent survey of electronic commerce in Singapore revealed that of the top 1,000 enterprises in Singapore, 91 percent have access to the Internet, and that 45 percent of the top enterprises have their own corporate web sites. Revenues derived from electronic commerce supporting services increased from S$144 million in 1997 to a massive S$256 million in 1998. Total business-to-business (B2B) electronic commerce sales had increased significantly from S$197 million in 1997 to a staggering S$1.2 billion in 1998.

June 1998 saw the commercial launch of Singapore ONE, a national initiative to deliver a new level of interactive, multimedia applications and services to homes, businesses and schools throughout Singapore. It is one of the first few implementations of multimedia broadband networks and applications in the world that promises to encompass such scope and depth, followed by a complete liberalization of the telecommunications market in January 2000. A recent household survey (1999) conducted by the National Computer Board showed that there was high information technology deployment in Singaporean households, with home computer ownership and home Internet penetration rising to 59 percent and 42 percent, respectively—these figures look set to rise further. The survey also indicated a general trend towards having more than one computer at home, which is currently at 16 percent (representing an increase of more than 10 percent since 1990).

These various figures should be seen in the light of developments in new technology policies which have been elaborated on throughout the years of Singapore's independence—*Science and Technology for 2 Million* (Ministry of Science and Technology, 1975), the *National IT Plan* (National IT Working Committee, 1985), *A Vision of an Intelligent Island* (National Computer Board, 1992), the *National Science and Technology Plan: Securing Our Future* (National Science and Technology Board, 1997), and *IDA2000: Bringing Singapore to the World* (Infocomm Development Authority, 2001).

"Information technology", "intelligent island", and "knowledge-based economy" are just some of the common tropes (among a constant barrage of others) through which the image of Singapore/

Singaporeans is expressed and represented. Huge financial investments, the significance of which is alluded to above, further points
to a significant material dimension that far transcends the tropes and
rhetoric employed in the official government literature. It would
appear that the cultural economy of technology in Singapore has
had deep effects, from the nation-level visions of a future Singapore
down to the organization of the everyday lives of Singaporeans. To
sociologically study this cultural economy of technology is, therefore,
to attend to the historical sites of discourse where statements on the
status and development of technology in Singapore have been author-
itatively produced, disseminated, and debated over.

Colonial Science and Technology

Historically, it is almost a truism that Singapore under British colonial rule was founded, developed, and maintained in the nineteenth
and twentieth centuries strictly as a port-city (Turnbull, 1989; Wright
and Cartwright, 1989; Pearson, 1956; Makepeace et al., 1991).
Founded by Stamford Raffles in 1819 under the auspices of the
British East India Company and being the foundation for modern
global networks, it is in fact inconceivable to examine colonial
Singapore without situating her within the context of Western impe-
rialist interests. There are very few sources that explicitly detail the
development of science and technology during Singapore's colonial
period. Any historical information must, therefore, be reconstructed
from the various historical texts, documents and journals that commented on British rule in Singapore. With limited urban development to facilitate the colonial administration, Singapore as a Far
Eastern colony was to play a significant economic role in Britain's
colonial network, serving as both a port-of-call for trade as well as
a communications outpost supporting Britain's colonial economic system (Goh, 1995:24; Headrick, 1981; 1988). The potential for financial
gain had attracted regional traders and labourers, whose sole aim
was economic profit.

Technological *transfer* from the British colonial administrators and
industrial/manufacturing know-how was scarce except perhaps for
the construction and maintenance of physical infrastructure, for example, port facilities and warehouses to facilitate efficient trading and
goods storage, and bridges and roads to facilitate easy transporta-

tion and linkages to other built-up sectors of the island. Significant events during this period include the developments in shipping technologies (for example, shipbuilding, and engineering facilities) and the laying of submarine cables that linked Singapore to a larger colonial network via the telegraph.

Advancements in marine technology in the form of improved shipbuilding were the most explicit forms of technology that directly concerned the port status of colonial Singapore (Headrick, 1988:259). The consequence of these developments was a change in the physical landscape of Singapore as wharf and dock facilities were constructed to facilitate trade as well as to serve as a coaling station for British traders (Goh, 1995:30–1; Cameron, 1965:35; Bogaars, 1956; Gibson-Hill, 1956). By the end of the nineteenth century, the port of Singapore had already undergone significant structural changes to accommodate the increase in shipping and trade. Further, the advent of telegraph communications technology was to have implications on Singapore's role in the British Empire. The British Colonial Defence Committee certainly believed that:

> The maintenance of submarine cable communications throughout the world in time of war is of the highest importance to the strategic and commercial interests of every portion of the British Empire (in Kennedy, 1971:729).

As early as 1859, Singapore was linked via submarine cables to Batavia, even though the technology was at an experimental stage and failed on several occasions (Goh, 1995:39). Improvements in cable technology, however, meant that Singapore was connected to the world via telegraph by 1882 (ibid.: 40). This was instrumental in Singapore playing a strategic role in the defence telegraph networks of the British Empire—in the relaying of messages while serving the needs of traders and the business community (Kennedy, 1971:730–1). Of course, the impact of rapid commercial growth as a result of these technological advancements meant an improvement in colonial Singapore's urban infrastructure. Urban planning was initiated as an attempt to systematize the colony, while modern modes of transportation and electricity were introduced but only to the benefit of the business and colonial communities (Goh, 1995:65).

Education in colonial Singapore was a haphazard affair largely due to the colonial government's view of Singapore as a trading port-city within the imperial trading network. This would seem to have an adverse effect on the upgrading of English and technical education in Singapore from 1900 to 1940. Industrial and technical education was administered with reluctance, with higher technical education rejected by an education committee convened in 1925 (Wong and Gwee, 1980:93). Surveys conducted by this very same committee revealed that science-related education, and technical skills upgrading were not popular. In fact, pioneering night science classes at the Raffles Institution in 1922–23 each boasted a maximum of only 15 students (ibid.: 95). Established education institutions concentrated on providing administrative skills to staff a civil service in supporting the trading economy. Educational progress seemed to depend on the needs of British colonial administrators instead of the need to develop any long-term educational system for the local population (Goh, 1995:111), with science-related and technical education being unpopular and deemed unpractical.

The lack of technology transfer from Great Britain to colonial Singapore, either in terms of hardware, skills or knowledge, basically affirms that Singapore's position within Britain's colonial empire was merely as a trading city and an outpost in the Far East. While providing the physical infrastructure as well as overseeing the development of a modern city, education policies were haphazardly implemented, leaving the vernacular schools to the respective ethnic communities. Science and technical education were limited and considered unnecessary by the colonial administration. Basically, the British colonial government had only concentrated on the development of Singapore as a trading outpost—a site of commerce—rather than with the possibility of industrialization.

Establishing an Industrial Economy

In the aftermath of World War II and the Japanese Occupation, Singapore's independence from Malaysia in 1965 had signalled doubt of her viability as an independent economic entity. With Singapore's independence, the ruling People's Action Party (PAP) attempted in the 1960s and 1970s to rapidly push for policies to establish an industrial base, which the British colonial government had failed to clearly develop. In terms of economic strategy, this meant a focus on manufacturing industries and an export-oriented industrialization plan (United Nations, 1963).

Faced with the simultaneous problems of ensuring social and political stability in a rapidly decolonizing Southeast Asian region, the Singapore government planned to integrate the country into an already global capitalist economy while launching attempts to foster a national identity for a largely immigrant population. Couched in the political rhetoric of "crisis and survival", technology was seen as the key for leapfrogging the initial stages of industrialization already experienced by the advanced capitalist nations. These various strategies relied on mobilizing the Singaporean population through several methods, including disciplining the labour force as well as through education in a highly centralized school system (Chua, 1995:59–60; Castells, 1992:35–37, 53; Wilson, 1978:235). In many ways, the foundation and economic survival of this new nation was explicitly connected to the personal responsibilities of each citizen to fulfil his or her role in these systems of correct training. Contrary to popular opinion at the time, the Report stated that Singapore could, in fact, be viable as an independent economic entity, and it seemed that the key to political and economic survival lay in industrialization and labour discipline, rather than Asian values: "The gist of the Singapore solution was plain and straightforward—Industrialise or Bust (Devan-Nair, 1973:65)!"

The immediate concerns for stability "survival" had inadvertently established the ruling party's reactive orientation for the next 35 years (Chua, 1995:48–50; Chan, 1971:32). Occupied with problems of providing employment and improving the living standards of the Singaporean population, little attention was naturally paid to establishing or developing indigenous scientific/technological capabilities despite the considerations made by instituting an ad hoc advisory committee to the government on science and technology in 1966, the Singapore Science Council in 1967, and a Ministry of Science and Technology in 1968 (cf. Ministry of Culture, 1969). This saw the development of a governmental directive to attract foreign multinational corporations as a catalyst for technological leapfrogging (United Nations, 1963:74). A similar attempt was made to engage foreign management personnel, engineers and technicians (Goh, 1972:279). Little attention was given to research and development as the local government aimed at solving the more "pressing" issues of securing a stable and disciplined labour force and establishing Singapore as an international production base so that she could then take advantage of her competitive labour costs.

Following a somewhat conventional developmental model, sophistication and broadening of the industrial base followed (1974–78), showing that the ruling government took no chances in securing its rising position in the global economy despite rising local labour costs (Murray and Perera, 1995:25). This advance is congruent with what has been advanced as the "developmental state" thesis (Johnson, 1995; Manuel Castells, 1992:56). The societal project of modernization, as undertaken by the Singapore government in this case, is also at once the construction and assertion of national identity—a Singaporean modernity—through economic success and socio-economic progress.

This, however, was to anticipate certain core problems that affected the dissemination of technological skills and knowledge. One main problem was that the education system had a difficult time of enhancing the status of technical education since it was associated with blue-collar work, a condition also previously noted in France and Japan (Bourdieu, 1998:29). There was a concern that this was to affect the supply of a pool of skilled workers required to facilitate the industrialization process. Until recent years, the transfer and diffusion of technology and skills from multinational corporations to local workers had been scarce (Goh, 1995:162), with local workers acting merely as facilitators of foreign technologies. Although the industrialization programme and the manufacturing industry were successful in alleviating the problem of mass unemployment, industrial firms in Singapore were largely "labour-intensive, low wage and low-productivity enterprises, requiring the mere repetition of simple operations along the assembly and production lines" (Goh, 1995:166). The initial stages of industrialization lacked a clear science and technology policy. The Ministry of Science and Technology, established in 1968, was to have an ambiguous role in promoting science and technology, and folded little more than 10 years after its inception.

With independence in 1965, the Singapore government's urgency to leapfrog technologically resulted in many contradictory policies and outcomes. Being dependent on foreign multinational corporations, her objective of developing an indigenous technological base was very much in conflict with the fact that technological development was tied to foreign technology, hardware and skills. With policies aimed specifically at making technological research and development economically profitable, there is still controversy over whether scientific/technological research should be adopted for its own sake.

This tension between fundamental and applied research in the context of the government–university–industry linkage would be a growing global concern and is suitably expressed by Etzkowitz (1996; 1997). This has led some authors to believe that the explicit economic motive is what is inhibiting the development of an indigenous and autonomous technological base in Singapore (see, for example, Goh, 1995:297–324). The irony here is that in a drive to promote a technological rationality for Singapore society, the result has been an economic "rationality" that restrains technological innovation.

En Route to the "Intelligent Island"

Restructuring of the Singapore economy took place between 1979 and 1984 with an explicit emphasis on higher value-added industries and services. This move had, in fact, succeeded in achieving some of the government's goals, including rapid growth between 1980 and 1984—much higher than in other Asian New Industrializing Economies. The severe recession of 1985–6, however, led to a convening of a special high-level economic committee, and new directions for the economy were charted. It is significant that two of the new growth areas identified were the high-tech industry and information technology. This urgency was captured with the publication of the *National IT Plan* (National IT Plan Working Committee, 1985), which unreservedly stated that:

1. Companies in both manufacturing and services must fully exploit the advances in IT [information technology] to gain a competitive edge.
2. It is not enough just to computerise. To be able to compete better, our industries need strategic and creative exploitation of IT.
3. Singapore should exploit the opportunities of IT as a new growth industry.
4. A consolidated national IT strategy should be implemented, to be spearheaded by NCB [National Computer Board], subsuming the present national computerisation effort.
(National IT Plan Working Committee, 1985:i)

Despite the fact that manufacturing and other industries are still a large part of economic development in Singapore, the specific focus and the rhetoric employed suggests that embracing new technologies would be the key to Singapore's economic survival and social stability.

The development of a technological trajectory in the 1980s would see a "second industrial revolution" with foreign technology and corporations playing a central role in economic development (Mirza, 1986). In the early half of the 1980s, the Singapore government required foreign and local investors to upgrade speedily from labour-intensive operations to capital-intensive and high-technology operations. The government's explicit endorsement and reliance on foreign multinational corporations to spearhead Singapore's drive towards a high-technology future is an affirmation of a *new* economy—one that is *informational, networked,* and potentially *global* (cf. Castells' definition, 2000a:77), and Singapore's position within that economy. In 1986, backed by ministerial promotion missions to major foreign investor countries as well as advertisements in international publications, the Economic Development Board embarked on an aggressive campaign to attract new investments with high technical content.

Singapore's high reliance on foreign technology and capital investment at this stage of development, however, has led some scholars to dispute Singapore's status as "newly-industrialized" or as having had any "industrial revolution" at all (Yoshihara, 1988). Yoshihara's controversial thesis was that Singapore, one of the so-called "newly-industrialized" Southeast Asian states, did not have any indigenous techno-scientific base and was instead relying heavily on her service industry and foreign technology and skills. Doubts had also been cast over whether this influx of foreign technology and highly skilled management had resulted in any significant transfer of skills or knowledge (Lim, 1978; Chng et al., 1986:40, 78) or even in any beneficial research and development linkages.

Nevertheless, in developing a science and technology framework in the 1980s, the determined economic objective was to create employment for "national survival" and sustainable development, essentially through the attraction of foreign investments. Three interrelated issues were given priority: (i) that research and development in Singapore should be "market-pulled" instead of "science-pushed"; (ii) that the country should hope to achieve technological self-reliance through, amongst other measures, the appropriate alterations in the education system; and (iii) that high-technology foreign investors were seen as indispensable channels to transfer and diffuse technology and skill

(Goh, 1995:222). The Strategic Economic Plan had even stressed the need for "innovation", and that "major progress needs to be made here in the next phase of economic development" (Ministry of Trade and Industry, 1991:28).

The *National Technology Plan* of 1991 followed by 1992's *A Vision of an Intelligent Island* were then to spell out the next technological trajectory, not only for the economy but for general Singapore society as well, in transforming Singapore into an "intelligent island". The "intelligent island" would be the central figure and objective in Singapore's development, portrayed in the popular media by various new technological innovations (EduNet, TradeNet, Electronic Road Pricing, smart cards, electronic funds transfer, etc.). In fact,

> To the extent that Singapore has become one of the most highly computerised nations in the world, with a burgeoning IT industry and a track record of sophisticated, sometimes world-beating, IT applications in business and government, Singapore's computer policy management maybe judge a success (Choo, 1997:58).

The construction of Singapore as intelligent island would also be akin to a nationalist project, since the exhortations of the official government literature demand that embracing new technologies be both a personal as well as a national responsibility. A typical way of representing the situation would be:

> Despite the anticipated social problems, Singapore cannot avoid becoming an information society. The strategic position of Singapore as an international telecommunication node, the openness of the economy to international influences, the desire for a higher standard of living and the push to be a brain centre blends well with the requirements of becoming an information society, the society of the future (National IT Committee, 1985:30).

It is in instances like these that the technological project is offered up as a historical necessity, not only that (i) the transition to an intelligent island is inevitable and essential but also that (ii) this fundamental shift is a trans-national one and potentially global in nature, and (iii) that this shift relies on a mode of economy that is large determined by international flows of knowledge, skills and technology.

In a decisive move, the Infocomm Development Authority (IDA) would be instituted in 1999 to punctuate the government's dedication at establishing Singapore as a knowledge-based economy as well as a life sciences/biotechnology hub. Facing the 2001 recession, it might be suggested that the Singapore government is using its current technological focus as yet another instrument to legitimize and strengthen its political leadership.

With Singapore in the twenty-first century, "information technology", "life sciences" and "innovation" have become catchphrases that have gained cultural milieu in official speeches and statements, even though very few of these speeches are able to articulate exactly what it means to be "innovative" or "creative", or how exactly new technologies are supposed to be appropriated and utilized. Given the current ongoing economic recession, the Singapore government's rarefied ideology of practical survival becomes more entrenched in an ad hoc contextual rationality where technology policies are concerned. Such reactive and contextual interventions by the government have been expressed by a smattering of policies trying to push for science and technology innovation in a confused array of new areas such as technopreneurship, information technology, communications technology, life sciences, stem cell research, etc.; all of which still rely on a great degree of "foreign talent" as little attempt has been made to encourage research and development without an economic motive.

The Logic of Singapore's Culture of Technology

This socio-historical survey of Singapore's culture of technology indicates that the construction of a technological nation-state/intelligent island is much more complex than is normally portrayed in the popular media. The progression of Singapore from a colonial port-city to an intelligent island is certainly not of a linear development and involves a constant negotiation among social, education, economic, industrial and technological policies that are constantly being revised in light of the ephemeral nature of the global capitalist economy. In the attempt to map the history of Singapore's culture of technology, I have found it important to emphasize the historical continuities and discontinuities, for example in the convergence of the discourses of technological progress and the attempt at making technological development a nationalist project.

From some of the tentative conclusions I have drawn, I attempt to identify the working logic by which we might identify the conditions of existence of Singapore as an intelligent island today. This basically consists of a matrix of four interrelated discourses that underpin the development of Singapore's culture of technology.

i. The relationship between postcoloniality and globalization.
ii. Nation-building and the problem of national identity.
iii. The rhetoric of "survival" within the narratives of crisis and utopia.
iv. Technocapitalism and the notion of modernity.

When the obsession with technology is seen in light of these discourses, it is these four concerns that identify why and how technology is to be discoursed in Singapore today. Coupled with the developmental state thesis, it identifies how Singapore attempts to integrate herself into the global, networked informational economy (Castells, 2000a:77–147).

Tentatively, we might identify the conditions of existence of Singapore's culture of technology not as a response to modernization and societal rationalization, but an *expression* of that very condition of modernity. Achieving independence in an already globalizing world economy and in a rapid decolonizing region, the problem of nation building and forging a national identity and the integration of these economies into the global capitalist formation was, and still is, a significant project for the Singapore government and Singaporeans as well. Independence in 1965 had, after all, meant that Singapore would at once have to be politically and economically viable in an already globalized economic network led by the advanced industrialized nation-states.

While it might seem that new technologies have by now been readily embraced by the better part of the Singaporean populace, it would be erroneous to view this process as a result of unilateral state decisions to impose the use of new technologies on Singaporeans. Instead, it might be suggested that this culture of technology is built up on everyday practices that are already taking place, despite them being disparate and uncoordinated. The need for integrated government IT strategies, then, attempts to bring these practices in line with state aims and objectives. Therefore, what is needed is:

> (a) very positive attitude towards IT, fully appreciative of its potentials and the adjustments that will have to be brought about with its extensive use. Our IT vision will not be achievable if we do not bring about the necessary attitudinal change among our citizens (National IT Working Committee, 1985:48).

Consequently, this mode of inducing "attitudinal change" has, as its objective, the institution of self-regulating practices of the Singaporean individual with regard to embracing new technologies, upgrading skills, making technology a personal responsibility, etc. When the "globalizing world" is depicted as one in which intensified connectivities and instantaneous transborder transactions constitute massive uncertainty (Du Gay, 1996), the embracing of new technologies in this global context is offered as a solution to the challenges shored up by global forces. As Lee Kuan-Yew himself reiterated:

> The environment is different, our neighbours are different, the world is different, the technology, the challenge is different. And it's easier in some ways because there are more resources, but in some way it is more difficult because you need more high-calibre manpower to run this economy (*The Straits Times*, 13 December 1999).

There has been much commentary on the "crisis and survival" narratives used by the state in interpreting the history of Singapore (Chan, 1971; Lau, 1992; Chua, 1995). What is not explicit, however, is the flipside of that narrative—utopia. Utopia for Mannheim is that set of ideas which "transcends the present and is oriented toward the future" (1936:97). The promise of technological development is certainly one of the most significant tools used to construct a representation of a future technological utopia in line with Singapore's "core beliefs and values". The narratives of crisis and survival cannot be delinked from the accompanying narratives of utopia.

The official government literature and media reports on technological development in Singapore establish that the use and exploitation of information-communications technology is necessary for her survival, future, the processes of nation building, and the defining of a national identity. Given her precarious economic situation with independence, "technology" is often used as a signifier in a historical tension between crisis and utopia. That is to say, technological development is seen as both a method to transcend Singapore's physical smallness and lack of exploitable natural resources as well as an offering of a vision of a future technological utopia. For example, the *National IT Plan* exhorts:

> The impact of IT will be all pervasive with significant social and cultural changes taking place in Singapore's society . . . in the office environment . . . in factories . . . in the service industry . . . in personal services . . . in the home of the future (National IT Committee, 1985:v).

Contra strategies to root national identity in terms of a common "past", discourses on technological progress, and development appropriate such far-reaching and comprehensive utopian visions to invest national identity in a future Singapore.

Indeed, with meritocracy as one "founding myth", Singapore's leaders "have to look towards the future and the importance of economic achievements to articulate their conception of the nation" (Hill and Lian, 1995:31). With the task of abandoning colonial identities and establishing viable alternatives in Singapore's formative years, the PAP government had to resort to a careful politics of identity given the geopolitical contingencies of the time. By the late 1990s and early twenty-first century, the expressions of these visions of utopia will be commonplace in the Singaporean popular media. These include community songs, government advertisements and glossy brochures, etc., all of which promote the idea of a utopia through embracing technological progress (Lim, 2000).

The notion of progress is a deeply rooted and problematic social condition, especially for the so-called developmental states of Southeast Asia. This incessant drive for newness and innovation, and a forward-looking and destructive impulse had once been described by Berman (1988) as the "experience of modernity". This notion of progress is certainly associated with the belief that technological progress can help define a Singaporean modernity and a unique national identity by helping to carve a niche in the global economy.

Conclusion

"Technology" and "technological development" play an important role in the justification and legitimation of political, economic and social practices in Singapore. This works through the rhetoric of "survival", especially through the deployment of narratives of crisis and utopia that stress the notion of the smallness and vulnerability of Singapore. As "technology" is seen to be the key to economic survival and social stability, a form of techno-capitalism is embraced as the means to constructing a Singaporean modernity. Conflicting ideals and goals as a result of this very modernity, however, mean that government policies and social practices involving technology can only revolve around reactionary responses to the fleeting and ever-shifting global economy.

Consequently, technology is a pertinent sociological issue in Singapore today. This paper has sought to demonstrate the social context in which technology is appropriated by mapping the social history of technology from Singapore's position as a colonial port-city to its current status of "intelligent island" by arguing that the development and employment of technology in Singapore is neither an uncontested nor problem-free project. In so doing, I hope to have demonstrated why current studies on the information/network societies must account for the development of each specific culture of technology. These societal nodes in the global knowledge network should, of course, not be studied in isolation but in relation to the ongoing linkages among societies, that are a consequence of more intensive globalization processes.

THE UNINTENDED CONSEQUENCES OF TECHNOLOGICAL POLICY: THE INTERNET AND CIVIL SOCIETY IN SINGAPORE

ZAHEER BABER
Department of Sociology
University of Saskatchewan

Regardless of whether one is wired or not, it is impossible to avoid the hype or cyberbole surrounding the Internet. Given the dramatic escalation of uncertainties generated by the processes of uneven "globalization" (Robertson, 1992), "reflexive modernization" (Beck, Giddens and Lash, 1994) and the "risk society" (Adam, Beck and van Loon, 2000), it is not surprising that that the emergence of a unique technology of communication should simultaneously generate radically utopian and dystopian expectations. In the context of generalized anxieties about the trajectory and consequences of globalization, the Internet continues to contribute to a modern cargo cult (Worseley, 1968) that some expect will resolve existing contradictions ranging from personal relationships to global inequalities, to eventually create the kinder and gentler society that has so far eluded us. Prior to the events of September 11, after which he changed his mind on this issue, John Perry Barlow, the ex-lyricist for rock band The Grateful Dead and co-founder of the Electronic Frontier Foundation, expected the Net to flatten hierarchies, encourage cross-cultural communication and, eventually, usher in participatory democracy. Such millenarian longings can be contrasted with dystopian visions of the Internet consolidating an ever-expanding network of surveillance and social control. Both viewpoints dramatically exaggerate scenarios that are not in a complete state of disconnectedness from the actual processes at work. Somewhere in between these views is the philosopher of science Hubert Dreyfuss (2001), who is sceptical of the desirability of the Net's capacity to expand the public sphere. Setting up Kierkegaard against Habermas, he endorses the former's view to the effect that a dramatically expanded public sphere leads to alienation rather than robust civic engagement (Drefuss, 2001:78). Much of Dreyfuss' philosophical commentary on the Internet is driven by his exaggerated concern about its consequences of accelerating the production of disembodied selves, disconnected from any specific locale.

Those who have examined the consequences of the dramatic augmentation of surveillance capacity made possible by the Internet have prudently avoided crude technological determinism (Lyon, 1993; Lyon and Zureik, 1996; Gandy, 1993). They have correctly pointed out that the Internet facilitates existing social trends, even while opening up new and dramatically more efficient modes of social control. Indeed, as Ian Hacking (1990) argues, the social imperatives of surveying, measuring, classifying and controlling were implicated in the development of social statistics as a technology of control, long before material artefacts entered the picture. This is also the objective of Manuel Castells' (1996; 1997; 1998) magisterial trilogy that further develops and reconstitutes a line of argument proposed in his *The Informational City* (1989). He seeks to map out the broad contours of the information age such that the novelty of the network society is highlighted without losing sight of social developments that pre-date the Net. In a similar vein, Dan Schiller (1999) debunks the hype about the Internet being the technology that will finally usher in the long-anticipated era of unlimited economic prosperity coupled with equality.

Most scholars who study science, technology and society (STS) would have little difficulty in questioning the polarized visions of a handful of driven Net utopians and dystopians. Despite the never-ending, internecine conflicts among proponents of various perspectives within STS, most scholars would agree that the Internet, like any other technology before it, is simultaneously the producer and product of social change. Such a formulation, however, while providing useful orientation for apprehending the dialectic of technology and social change, is too general for making sense of the specificities of particular contexts. Attempting to move beyond totalizing perspectives that represent the Internet as an agent of either democratization or social control through surveillance, this paper seeks to consider a historically specific time and place so as to examine long-term structural trends and the unintended consequences of both technology and social action, with the aim of arriving at a contextually specific analysis of the Internet. The role of the Internet in influencing politics and restructuring social groups has, of course, been fervently discussed and debated (Hague and Loader, 1999; Hacker and van Dijk, 2000; Wilhelm, 2000; Alexander, 1998; Tasagarousianou, Tambini and Bryan, 1998; Jordan, 1999; Everard, 1999; Holmes,

1998). Whether the Internet will enhance or diminish prospects for democratic institutions is a question that can only be tackled by a historical sociology that is attentive to specific contexts but does not shy away from the task of contributing to a general understanding that is always open to modification and rejection.

For a number of reasons, Singapore constitutes a good case for examining the simultaneous impact of the Internet and politics on each other. The dominant role of the Singapore state in influencing society at every possible level—from marital relations to housing and the economy—is well known and researched (Chua, 1995; 1997; Chan, 1971; 1975; Rodan, 1989; 1993a; 1993b; Tremewan, 1994; Salaff, 1988; Tamney, 1996; George, 2000; Gomez, 2000). Deploying various strategies, the People's Action Party (PAP) has, since 1959, reigned as the dominant political force, successfully surviving various alliances, break-ups and conflicts with other factions and parties, including a short-lived merger with Malaya. In the 1968 elections, the PAP won in all 58 constituencies, 51 of which were uncontested. The initial unease about the dominance of one party over Singapore politics and society has been partly neutralized by the ideology of survivalism, or the idea that the state had to rise above party politics to ensure the nation's economic and social survival (Rodan, 1989:97–98). Later, the same ideology was complemented by the ideologies of "pragmatism" and "communitarianism" (Chua, 1995) in an attempt to create an "administrative state" (Chan, 1975) that has increasingly sought to depoliticize politics. As Chua (1995:42–43; 1991; 1997) correctly points out, the commonly accepted view that "pragmatism" is non-ideological poses to be problematic, and it is far from clear that politics has been effectively depoliticized.

Singapore's emergence as a pivotal manufacturing node in the emerging network of transnational capitalism was partly made possible by missionary zeal displayed in the adoption of the Winsemius Report, submitted on behalf of the United Nations Industrial Survey Mission of 1960. The recommendations of this report were reflected in the State Development Plan of 1961–64 that assumed "owing to the dearth of local know-how and the structural immobility of domestically based local capital, foreign capital would have to be seduced" (Rodan, 1989:64). This seduction, initiated in the early 1960s, continues to be the main objective of most public policy initiatives in contemporary Singapore. To enhance the seductive charm of Singapore as a prime location for the flows of foreign capital, the state embarked

on a number of social and legislative initiatives. By 1947, only about
16 percent of the population was engaged in manufacturing. The
task of proletarianizing a much larger proportion of the population
in anticipation of the increase in the number of manufacturing sites
owned by multinationals was accomplished through a series of social
policies. These include the Trade Union (Amendment) Bill of 1966,
which made strikes and other industrial actions illegal unless approved
by the majority of a union's members, and banned strikes in essential services (Rodan, 1989:91). Other legislative measures such as the
Employment Act and the Industrial Relations (Amendment) Act, etc.
sought to create a disciplined and stable labour force. In general,
despite the occasional hiccup, ideological grids such as "pragmatism"
and "survivalism", in conjunction with established mechanisms of
controls such as the Internal Security Act, the Societies Act, etc.,
were largely successful in reproducing social discipline in line with
the perceived imperatives of being a prime site for the accumulation of global capital. These institutional actions were themselves driven by the correct perception, reinforced by the Winsemius Report,
that trade and banking alone would not suffice for the continued
employment of a growing population, and that local capital was not
sufficiently well-placed to generate manufacturing-based employment.

In addition to the legislative measures deployed to discipline labour,
other strategies were implemented to discipline the society at large.
One such initiative was put into effect right after the 1959 elections
in which the PAP won 53.4 percent of the votes. The management
committees of all community centres, originally set up to promote
active grassroots participation, were dismantled and brought under
the control of a new body called the People's Association. The management of the People's Association reported directly to the Prime
Minister's Office (Rodan, 1989:62–63; Rodan, 1993:80–81). Over
the years, the state, through amendments to existing legislation and
through the introduction of new initiatives, has actively sought to
influence almost every sphere of life—ranging from the most intimate
spheres of dating and sexuality to higher education; religion; ethnicity;
the mass media; and production, both formal and informal. A par-
tial list of these institutional measures includes the Newspapers and
Printing Presses Act, Maintenance of Religious Harmony Act, Residents'
Committees, Citizens' Consultative Committees, Social Development
Unit, Shared Values White Paper, etc. Almost all of these initiatives
were legitimized by appeals to the ostensibly non-ideological ideologies of "survivalism", "pragmatism" and later, "communitarianism".

The key consequence of these measures has been an underdeveloped public sphere and a virtually non-existent civil society. Of course the public sphere, as understood by Habermas (1989), has not been entirely absent and continues to exist and thrive in the *kopi tiams* or coffee shops, and other sites. The state's largely successful attempt at influencing most modes of cultural production, reproduction, and public expressions of opinion, however, have contributed to fragmented micro-public spheres that lack the ability to either generate or influence opinion on public issues in any meaningful way. When compared to the dramatically underdeveloped public sphere, civil society—if understood in the narrow sense of voluntary associations independent of the state and private interests such as family, clan, etc. that seek to influence state policies—was practically non-existent. Any attempt to influence public policy was perceived by the state as political activity, and a rigid demarcation between the social and political spheres was created (Rodan, 1993:91–92).

From the elections of 1959 onwards, the PAP, despite challenges from the Barisan Socialis and factions within the party, dominated politics. Although the party lost 13 seats to rival Barisan Socialis in the 1963 elections, that was the last time it lost a seat to any other party. It is within this context that the election of Joshua B. Jeyaretnam in 1981 on a Workers' Party ticket came as a major surprise. Forced to recognize the presence of a diverse population and interests, the PAP sought to introduce a number of changes. One of these was provision for the appointment of non-constituent members of parliament (NCMP) in the hope of allowing for some dissent and diversity of opinion as long as it did not emanate from opposition political parties. The subsequent elections of 1984 brought more surprises since not only was Jeyaretnam re-elected, but a new opposition Member of Parliament (MP), Chiam See Tong of the Singapore Democratic Party, was elected as well. More significant than the loss of two seats to the opposition was the fact that the proportion of votes cast for the ruling party had declined by 13 percent as compared to previous elections (Rodan, 1993:83–85). The PAP, long used to getting over 75 percent of the vote since the late 1960s, had to cope with a substantial erosion of its legitimacy by getting only 62.94 percent of votes. On the whole, despite the decline in percentage of votes for the PAP, the party still captured 77 of the 79 seats.

These electoral reverses occurred within the context of the transformation of the social structure of Singapore society and larger global trends. As Rodan (1993:85–86) points out, one of the key

factors was the relative alienation of the middle class. With rapid
economic development, the proportion of the middle class had
expanded dramatically, leading to a diversity of views and opinions
on a number of issues. At the same time, with changes in the nature
of global industrial capitalism and the consequent adoption of technologically sophisticated manufacturing processes, members of the
local bourgeoisie were apprehensive about their chances against multinationals. These factors, together with the working class' growing
frustration at the rising cost of living, were successfully transformed
by opposition parties into minor electoral victories. The recession
that followed in 1985 only exacerbated these apprehensions. It is
against this backdrop that the new prime minister, Goh Chok Tong,
announced his intention of heading a consultative government sensitive to a legitimate diversity of opinion and committed to more
input by the population at large. A number of initiatives for taking
into account the transformed social structure, with its concomitant
diversity of viewpoints and positions, were introduced. The attempt
to provide for the airing of alternative views led to the formation of
the Feedback Unit in 1985, Town Councils in 1986, the Nominated
MPs scheme and an endless number of "dialogue sessions" between
the government and the people (Rodan, 1993:87). At the same time,
some civil society groups, such as the Association of Women for
Action and Research (AWARE), the Nature Society, the Association
of Muslim Professionals and Action for Aids, emerged as institutional
communicators of alternative viewpoints in a non-confrontational
manner. All through this period, however, the concern of the government was to ensure that alternative opinions were channelled
through appropriate or non-electoral mechanisms. Although the space
for civil society had opened up a little, the overall message was the
importance of the distinction between acceptable and unacceptable
means of articulating alternative views. Thus, the circulation of a
number of foreign magazines and newspapers such as *The Economist*,
Far Eastern Economic Review, *Time*, etc. was curtailed due to what was
deemed negative coverage of Singapore. All along, a clear line of
demarcation between the social and the political was reinforced.
Social comment and the articulation of alternative views that were
perceived to be political in intent were deemed out of bounds, and
a number of such "OBs" or out-of-bounds markers were erected. A
column in a magazine published in 1994 by local novelist Catherine
Lim triggered a strong response from Prime Minister Goh Chok

Tong. Citizens were constantly reminded that politics was strictly the provenance of professional politicians and members of officially recognized parties. As one minister put it as early as 1989, public policy "isn't the playground of those who have no responsibility to the people, and who aren't answerable for the livelihood or survival of Singaporeans" (Wong Kan Seng, quoted in Rodan, 1993:91). This conception of politics as a strictly professional vocation was endlessly reiterated even as the potential for limited civil society engagement, albeit strictly within the state identified "out-of-bounds" markers, did emerge as a viable possibility. Not unexpectedly, there were ups and downs, such as the release to critical acclaim of Eric Khoo's film *Twelve Storeys* (representing the high point) and the banning of the play *Talaaq* (the low point).

In addition to these factors, changes in the pattern and nature of global capitalism also played a major role in influencing Singapore society. A number of countries, including Malaysia, Indonesia, Thailand, China, etc., emerged as major competitors to the science of attracting foreign capital. In Singapore itself, decades of export-led, foreign capital induced and sustained industrialization had contributed to the escalation of the cost of living and to wages. Frantic land reclamation along the shoreline notwithstanding, the price of industrial land had risen substantially, and other neighbouring countries had an advantage due to lower land prices. Deeply aware of the keen competition from other cheaper options for global capital, at least for certain kinds of manufacturing, Singapore sought to gear up for the challenge of tapping into manufacturing with a sophisticated technological base. The emergence and popularity of personal computers roughly around the same time drew attention to the possible emergence of a new "informational economy" (Castells, 1996) that would elude those neighbouring countries that lacked the infrastructure to take advantage of these new technological developments. It was in this context that the National IT Plan of 1985 was formulated, a plan that would later articulate the discourse of a wired, "intelligent island" once again in line with the anticipated transformations in the nature of the global flows of capital (Lim, 1999). On the heels of the National IT Plan was the setting up of the National Computer Board (NCB), which would be replaced by the Infocomm Development Authority (IDA) in 2000. The IDA spearheads the goal of leading Singapore into a "knowledge-based economy" (KBE). The groundwork for dealing with the challenges of an anticipated "knowledge-based economy" has been built over a number of years; the media, and the public speeches of ministers, university administrators and other public officials is saturated with associated buzzwords such as "creativity", "critical thinking", "thinking outside the box" and "lateral thinking". Indeed, Edward de Bono, the guru of "lateral thinking", has been invited to Singapore, presumably to kick-start lateral thinking on a mass scale. Much of this drive is propelled by the perception—buttressed by a survey and report—that the Singapore labour force needs to be re-engineered and re-tooled to be more "creative" if the country hopes to take advantage of the new industries associated with biotechnology, information technology, etc. A labour force disciplined for the manufacturing industry would not be sufficient for industries associated with high-tech, knowledge-based production.

It is within the context of these larger transformations in the nature of global capitalism, the changing social structure of Singapore society, the emergence of a substantial middle-class and some minor political changes triggered off by a break in the PAP's monopoly of parliament that the introduction and relevance of the Internet for the changing relationship between the state and society can be understood. When the state undertook the project of creating an "intelligent island" and systematically sought to wire up every individual and institution, the action was driven initially by the perception of the changing nature of manufacturing and later, by the fact that Malaysia was embarking on the construction of a Multimedia Super Corridor (MSC). The MSC is meant to be a giant, information technology park designed to attract high-tech industries. In embarking on its "intelligence island" project, the Singapore state has unintentionally laid the foundation for the proliferation and expansion of the public sphere and civil society. These developments represent a prime example of the sociology of unintended consequences of technological infusion. What the Internet has made possible now in Singapore was a distant possibility just a few years ago, and while there is no doubt that the capacity for social control through surveillance is dramatically heightened due to this technology (Rodan, 1997), there is at the same time a discernible, if not dramatic, re-negotiation of the relationship between the state and civil society. The very fact of many-to-many communication made possible by Internet technology facilitates the circumvention of a number of regulations that seek to monitor political organization and discussion. As the section below seeks to establish, despite the new rules with respect to the use of the Internet and web sites, formulated barely weeks before the recently concluded elections, there is no doubt that this technology has dramatically enhanced pre-existing social trends and will continue to influence the emergence of a degree of negotiation between the state and society in Singapore. Even though the founder of Sintercom, which was one of the most vibrant of virtual communities, resigned a few weeks before the last elections and the web site has been virtually—but not quite—shut down, the public sphere continues to thrive through communities such as Think Centre, TalkingCock.com and others discussed below.

As far as the expansion of the public sphere is concerned, the most significant development of the year 2000 was the inauguration of Speakers' Corner in Hong Lim Park. Barely a few weeks before it was actually allowed, the proposal for a Speakers' Corner modelled after Hyde Park was categorically rejected by the state. The usual arguments, gelled with images of chaos, confusion and the possible breakdown of society, were marshalled to point out that Singapore was not yet ready for this form of freedom of speech. Although most people seem to have lost interest in it now, Speakers' Corner in Singapore represents a response both to changing state and society relations, and to the very nature of the new technology represented by the Internet. The headline "Is the Internet Another Speakers' Corner?" in the local daily *The Straits Times* (2 September 2000) drew attention to the fact that the Net has provided virtual speakers' corners for Singaporeans for quite a while. In many ways, the official Speakers' Corner is merely catching up, perhaps late in the day, with what Internet technology and social changes have made possible in the restructuring of state–society relations. Indeed, web sites such as The Speakers' Platform (http://www.sintercom.org/sp) and The Online Speakers' Corner (http://www.onlinespeakerscorner.com) have been thriving for some time.

In Singapore, the Internet has contributed to the dramatic proliferation of bulletin boards, chat rooms, discussion groups as well as web sites that seek to articulate alternative views vis-à-vis existing social arrangements and discourses. It is perhaps premature to assess the precise impact of these alternative spaces on the state–civil society relationship. As the opening of Speakers' Corner, partly in response to the existence of many such corners in cyberspace indicates, however, the impact of Internet technology in transforming at least some aspects of this relationship ought not to be underestimated and merits further attention. The web sites that expressly address politics and

religion with the aim of promoting alternatives to the dominant discourse can be divided into five categories. Needless to add, these
categories are not mutually exclusive and they have been delineated
for heuristic purposes alone.

Civil Rights/Constitutional Rights

These web sites represent groups, organizations and individuals that
invoke either the Singapore constitution or a general conception of
civil rights to promote their views. Their main claim is that the existing laws, regulations and constitution theoretically allow for their
existence but in practice, they cannot pursue their agenda. They do
not attempt to change existing laws but only want to claim what
they perceive as entitlements promised by the constitution. Examples
include the web site of the Unification Church or "the Moonies"
(http://members.tripod.com/~teopl/), whose activities were banned
in Singapore a few years ago. The Speak Dialect homepage (http://
web.singnet.com.sg/~bluesky/dialect.html), representing mainly the
Hakka community, protests against the "Speak Mandarin" campaign,
which it claims is not necessarily helping younger Chinese Singaporeans discover their roots. Finally, there are international web sites
devoted to the protection of privacy that focus on Singapore, too
(http://www.privacy.org/pi). Other organizations such as the Central
Christian Church of Singapore, which pursued a lawsuit against local
newspapers *The New Paper* and *Lianhe Wanbao* for being labelled a
"cult" (http://www.icoc.org.sg), seek to assert their right to exist as
legitimate organizations since, in the church's case, it is "registered"
as a church by the authorities.

Civil Society Organizations

These are groups and organizations that aim to promote alternatives
to existing laws and regulations. According to these groups, existing
regulations were formulated at a time when concern about issues
such as the environment, women's rights, gay rights, etc. were either
non-existent or were not assigned too much significance. Such groups
in Singapore include the Nature Society of Singapore (http://www.
post1.com/home/naturesingapore/), AWARE (Association of Women

for Action and Research, http://www.aware.org.sg/), Action for Aids (http://www.afa.org.sg/); gay rights advocacy groups such as People Like Us (www.plu-singapore.com) and Yawning Bread (http://www.geocities.com/yawning-bread); and groups for animal rights and the humane treatment of stray cats (http://wizard.net/~peacock/singhelp.htm).

Anti-Censorship/Freedom of Speech

These web sites claim to represent groups, organizations and individuals that seek to either reduce or entirely do away with censorship. They seek alternatives to the existing curtailments, formal or informal ("out-of-boundary markers"), on speech and expression in Singapore. Some of these groups take up the current campaign to promote "critical thinking" and "creativity" through educational and other institutions. Their general argument is that a plurality and diversity of views contributes to critical thinking and creativity, and that these attributes are being stifled by over-regulation in all spheres. These include pioneer groups such as Think Centre (http://www.think-centre.org), the brainchild of James Gomez; The Socratic Circle (http://www.geocities.com/soc_circle); The Round Table (http://www.roundtable.org.sg); and the personal web sites of James Gomez (Gomez Online Archives http://web.singnet.com.sg/~think101), Chee Soon Juan, Cherian George (http://www.cheriangeorge.tripod.com/index.htm), etc. In response to the perceived lack of outlets for non-governmental viewpoints in the local daily, *The Straits Times*, a web site called Not the Straits Times seeks to present alternative perspectives on controversial issues. This web site also includes letters that were rejected for publication in the "Forum" section of the local daily. Other web sites include Singaporeans for Democracy (http://www.gn.apc.org/sfd). In the sphere of religion, the web site of the Unification Church (the "Moonies") also focuses on the issue of censorship and freedom of speech by posting a number of documents that represent appeals to the government and the media. Finally, there is a web site, How to Defeat Singapore's Net Censorship, which provides a step-by-step procedure for circumventing proxy servers (www.geocities.com/Pentagon/Barracks/8845/singapore_Internet_censorship.html).

Organized Opposition Political Parties

Unlike all the other groups discussed above, these web sites represent established opposition political parties that not only seek to contest dominant discourses but also seek political power through electoral means. Their short-term goal is increased representation in Parliament. Despite these clear-cut, formal political goals, these organizations also seek to contest the dominant discourse and, hence, share ideological space with other web sites of resistance. The web sites in this category include those of the Workers' Party (http://www.wp.org.sg), National Solidarity Party (http://www.nsp.org.sg), etc.

Singapore as an Alternative Space

Although most of the web sites listed above seek to create alternative spaces and question existing regulations, there are others that may not be welcome in their place of origin but can use Singapore to host their sites. These include the official web site of the Bahais, who are persecuted in Iran (http://www.bahai-org.sg.org); the Falun Gong sect, whose members are persecuted in China (www.falundafa.org/world); and the Ananda Marga, a sect occasionally in trouble with the authorities in India (http://home1.pacific.net.sg/~rucira/yoga/index.html).

The current dominant discourses of the "new economy", "knowledge-based economy", "intelligent island", "critical thinking", "creative thinking", culture as "software" to complement the economic "hardware", etc. in Singapore emanate from an awareness of the dramatic growth of the "informational economy" (Castells, 1996) and fundamental changes in the nature and speed of the flows of transnational capital. These flows of global capital are contributing to a dramatic restructuring of "time", "space" and "location" substituting physical contiguities with cyber-contiguities shaped by networks of capital and information, a process that is unprecedented in human history (Castells, 1996; Harvey, 1989; Calhoun, 1998). It is the acute awareness of the fact that the rules of the game have changed and will continue to change in the future that has led to dramatic changes in policies and institutional reconfigurations in Singapore. With Singapore having the second highest per capita access to computers in the world, the IDA is determined to wire up every home and every classroom in the city-state and, possibly, every public space in the future.

The driving force behind all these initiatives is the anticipation of dramatic institutional and ideological changes in the wake of globalization and digital capitalism. Policies designed to reconfigure the economy and the infrastructure in line with the realities of global capitalism have been complemented by a relentless reiteration of buzzwords—such as "creativity", "critical thinking" and "life-long learning"—that seek to address changes in the nature of the workforce required for the "knowledge-based economy". The effort to re-engineer the workforce to meet the requirements of a turbulent "new economy" that might require higher doses of independent critical thinking is increasingly coming into conflict with the hyper-regulatory role of the state. Until recently, the state's strong regulatory authority has managed to consolidate conditions for the accumulation of transnational capital in the "old economy".

Even under conditions of the "old economy", however, the state had to deal with changing class structures and ideologies that were constituted by the rapid industrialization of Singapore. Slowly but surely, the state came to recognize the importance of a degree of negotiation, as opposed to clamping down on various pressures and demands from the new social groups, classes and constituencies that were thrown up as a consequence of industrialization. Thus, the emergence of a limited number of civil society organizations (AWARE, NSS, then Action for Aids, etc.) in the early 1980s reflected dramatic institutional reconfigurations of state–society relations. No doubt, the imperative for negotiation, at least over some issues, as opposed to a unilateral formulation of policies was partly driven by the shock of electoral reverses for the ruling party during the same period. Coupled with the creation of the institution of Nominated MPs, it constituted a strategy of managing dissent. Even though room for negotiation was fairly limited, however, these reconfigurations of state–society relations opened up genuine spaces for the new social groups and classes that sought to influence policies on crucial issues like gender and the environment.

With the state aggressively wiring up the nation, new spaces have opened up even as existing spaces have expanded. In addition to globalization and massive social transformations within Singapore that have created and consolidated new constituencies and social groups, the nature of Internet technology has itself contributed to this fundamental change. Computer mediated communication (CMC) represents a fundamentally different kind of technology in many ways. In addition to the possibilities for the creation of networks of communities or "virtual communities" of various kinds, the Internet represents a technology that fuses many functions—economic, cultural, entertainment, politics, etc., such that these functions cannot be disaggregated. In the past in Singapore, the circulation of specific issues of magazines and newspapers could be restricted or banned without substantial impact on the economy. Internet technology, with its aggregated bundling of functions, cannot be restricted in a meaningful way without the probable curtailment of possibilities that may emerge in the future. Some over-enthusiastic proponents of the constructivist perspective have underestimated the material aspects of the technology. Even though it is clear that the Internet emerged from a specific constellation of social factors, and the open-ended IP architecture was a consequence of largely social decisions, the fact remains that as it is now constituted, the Net, due to its very technical features, enables certain social possibilities. The Internet, as Mark Poster (1998), drawing on Heidegger, has argued, is also a unique technology because of its inherently interactive nature. Due to this interactivity, the Internet is not outside us as are all other communication technologies. Our interaction as end-users with the Internet plays a constitutive role in its evolution. As such, it would be short-sighted of the state to exercise too much control over the use of the technology that it has gone out of its way to promote. Ultimately, as a web site titled "How to Defeat Singapore's Net Censorship" demonstrates, the blocking of some sites by local ISPs is largely symbolic as these can, indeed, be circumvented by dedicated computer experts.

The diverse interest groups in Singapore that have either been thrown up or were in existence but have managed to consolidate in the wake of internal and global transformations, have sought to capitalize on the social and political potential of the Internet (Ho, Baber and Khondker, 2002). Whatever may be the case elsewhere, there is no question that the Net has contributed to the emergence of a "public sphere" (Habermas, 1989; Calhoun, 1992), even though it is a limited one at this stage. The "public sphere" understood by Habermas refers to the space that opens up the potential for an unfettered exchange of ideas aimed at reaching a pragmatic consensus. This is evident in the enormous proliferation of web sites, discussion groups and chat rooms devoted to discussions of critical issues that affect the lives of Singaporeans. As mentioned earlier, a Speakers' Corner, proposals for which were rejected barely a few months ago, has become a reality with promises of more such corners in other parts of the island. Confronted with the fact there have been many such virtual Speakers' Corners in cyberspace, the state sought to engage with this new reality in a negotiated rather than a unilateral way.

Seizing the new opportunities and possibilities offered by the Internet and by the promises of Singapore 21 in encouraging "active citizenship"; People Like Us (www.plu-singapore.com), a virtual gay community in cyberspace, sought permission for a public forum on 28 May 2000 with the intention of registering as an official society. In Singapore, a public gathering of more than eight people requires a permit. The permit was denied, but this attempt to further expand the "public sphere" and "civil society" was discussed widely in the local daily, *The Straits Times*, and more vigorously on the web site-linked discussion group, Not the Straits Times. In real terms, this attempt at resisting existing laws and discourses failed, but not quite. It opened up the discussion and drew attention to the fact of a thriving virtual gay community in Singapore. In the letters posted on the web site entitled Not the Straits Times Forum, a number of individuals drew attention to the fact that existing policies would keep Singaporean gays out of Singapore and inhibit foreign gays from taking up jobs in Singapore. Many letters drew attention to the states promise of attracting "creative" and critical-minded individuals to Singapore by pointing out that gays, as individuals, do possess these qualities. The publicity, both internal and international, generated by this attempt to expand the public sphere contributed enormously to future possibilities, and a search with the keywords "gay+singapore" resulted in 13,900 hits. This attempt to formally test the limits of the public sphere and civil society is just one in a series of pressures from below. Well organized virtual communities such as Thinkcentre, TalkingCock.com and Sintercom (or what is left of it), together with the many other web sites, discussion groups and chat rooms, do represent real changes and possibilities that were present in the past but have been speeded up due to a combination of the following factors: the fusion of functions in Internet technology that facilitate multilateral connections; virtual communities and economic transactions; the rise of new social groups, classes and constituencies as a consequence of the industrialization of Singapore; and the differential restructuring of time and space that is made possible by the Net.

To address the question raised in Langdon Winner's (1985) important article, "Do Artifacts Have Politics?", the answer, at least in the case of the Internet, would have to be in the affirmative, although not in exactly the same manner as he has formulated on the relationship between technology and power relations. For Winner, technologies need not be analyzed just for their contributions to efficiency and productivity but also for the ways in which they can embody specific forms of power and authority. In the article, Winner seeks to examine the claims to technical expertise and the role of technology in deterring democracy by facilitating the consolidation of power at the top. Although at one level, the Net does provide the infrastructure for the consolidation of power in Singapore through surveillance and enhancing technocracy, the simultaneous possibilities for contesting that power and authority, made possible by the same technology, cannot be ignored. The significant ideas raised by Winner (1985) are relevant in this context, even though he continues to be sceptical of the blanket, contextless, cyber-libertarian position (Winner, 1997). The potential of the Internet for resistance, expansion of the public sphere and civil society, however, is only one side of the political coin. The flipside of the Internet and CMC in general is the hitherto unthinkable capabilities of social control through surveillance and the creation of databases of all sorts (David Lyon, 2001; Gandy, 1993). As Craig Calhoun puts it, ". . . he general tendency is not for the web to produce a radical democracy of constant citizen participation and instant referenda . . . nor to empower the poor, weak, and dispersed against the rich, powerful and well-positioned. Computer mediated communication does a little of each of these things, but it does a lot to enhance existing power structures" (Calhoun, 1998:381). The possibilities and limits of resistance via this new technology in Singapore are not easy to predict. It would be a mistake, however, to interpret the dramatic rise in the percentage of votes for the ruling political party in the elections of November 2001 as indicative of the pointlessness of Net-based activism and civil society. The fact that the gradual blooming of civil society organizations has enhanced the legitimacy of the government would not have surprised Gramsci (1971). The contributions of civil society organizations do not necessarily need to be evaluated through references to the outcomes of formal, electoral politics. The creation of a space for deliberation on public issues, the sense that personal troubles can be connected to issues of social structure (Mills, 1959) and the feeling of contributing even minimally to the social shaping of society point to the expansion of the public sphere. As Wilhelm (2000) perceptively points out, the public sphere need not be confused with electoral politics. Rather, ". . . it represents the vital channels in civil society in which individuals and groups can become informed about issues, discuss and debate these issues autonomously, and ultimately have an impact on policy agendas" (Wilhelm, 2000:9). To this end, the Net in Singapore has contributed to the expansion of an incipient, micro-public sphere that nurtures serious and informed debate that is not completely under the regulatory ambit of the state. In his early writings Habermas (1970a; 1970b), while reflecting on the significance of communication, refers to a situation of social trauma associated with distorted communication. While it is unlikely that the proliferation of the Internet in Singapore will by itself lessen such social trauma, it is arguable that it might facilitate the eventual erosion of social alienation. Although it is true that Internet Service Providers are held responsible for content, and that recent regulation in the context of the elections have set certain limits, the discussion of controversial issues is possible more than ever before. In a recent article, Garry Rodan (1997) focused on the role of the Internet in facilitating surveillance and social control through the use of proxy servers and other mechanisms. A more plausible scenario, largely due to the impossibility—at least for the time being—of disaggregating the various functions and capacities of the Internet is the continuing expansion of some alternative spaces, even as others are closed off as both the state and society seek to negotiate the dialectic of resistance/empowerment and surveillance/social control made possible by this new technology, and even as the Net itself is shaped by these social forces and relationships.

THINK CENTRE: THE INTERNET AND POLITICS IN THE NEW ECONOMY OF SINGAPORE

JAMES GOMEZ
Think Centre Asia
Bangkok

Introduction

The Think Centre was incorporated by the author as an events and publishing company with the Registry of Businesses in Singapore on 16 July 1999. It was started to publish *Self-Censorship: Singapore's Shame* (2000), a social critique of the climate of fear in the Republic. The aim was to raise awareness of political issues and to address concerns surrounding political reform.

The Registrar of Societies on political discussion groups undertook a business registration to bypass the restriction on organizing public events. Political discussion groups are only allowed to organize activities for their members. Adjustments have been made to allow for by-invitation-only activities even though under the specifications of the Public Entertainments Act, any individual, group or business can apply for a licence for public events that do not contravene the law. The contradiction lies in that some societies continue, under the Societies Act, to be restricted from organizing public events even though such events do not contravene the law.

Within two years, Think Centre was able to move from being a sole proprietorship to a partnership—eventually registering as a political society with the Registry of Societies. On 1 April 2001, the Centre was gazetted under a new law—the Political Donations Act—which prevented it from receiving funds from abroad and required it to declare local funding in access of S$5,000. During these processes, the Centre had built up a modest base of members, several of whom (including the author) joined political parties in the run-up to Singapore's general elections in 2001. Unlike other political NGOs, no restriction was placed on membership and organization of public events when Think Centre's registration as a society was approved in October 2001. The Centre, however, continues to be gazetted as a political organization, which placed restrictions on funding.

Politics on the Internet

The Centre came onto the scene at a time when the Internet culture was beginning to embrace e-politic—an important tool with which to navigate the People's Action Party's (PAP) legislative control of the political landscape and media hegemony. At that time, the only guideline regarding the Internet was the 1996 Singapore Broadcasting guideline, which included prohibition of undesirable sites and a requirement to register with the authorities for sites that carry topics on religion and politics.

There was no vigorous attempt, however, to control the Internet on political terms as no local web site devoted itself to this area. There were several foreign web sites (http://www.singapore-window.org; http://www.sfdonline.org) and a couple of local ones for political parties. There was also http://soc.culture.singapore, which had some political postings and discussions. Most people saw the situation as one in which the authorities took a hands-off approach to the Internet. Thus, those whose political sentiments did not conform to those held by the PAP viewed the Internet, the lack of means to control it and the perceived hands-off approach with considerable excitement.

The Centre's use of communication technology in the years 1999–2001 was significant as it used this medium as a vehicle to organize activities on the ground. Through a mixture of momentum, opportunity, strategy, and local cost, the Internet played an important role in the evolution of Think Centre. The ability to harness the potential of the Internet allowed the Centre to have an impact on the political landscape. It also flushed out surveillance of the Internet and allowed a close vantage point from which to observe the introduction of more legislation, such as the amendments to the Parliamentary Elections Act to control and limit the political potential of the Internet in Singapore.

The author's response to the government's attempt to control communication technology for political communication and mobilization was to personalize Internet usage by setting up an individual mailing list and web site. At the same time, the Centre also sought to regionalize the expertise gathered through the Singapore experience and bounce it onto a global platform. The interaction among communication, mobilization and control in Singapore is likely to remain fluid.

Self-Censorship: Singapore's Shame—*Using Information Technology*

The Think Centre kicked off with *Self-Censorship: Singapore's Shame*. This book was printed at the end of September 1999 as a critique of the climate of fear in the Republic, and called for people to organize themselves through discussions to find solutions to move the political process forward in Singapore. This presented the Centre with its first opportunity to harness the potential of the Internet. In the initial phase, for instance, most bookstores were not keen on carrying the title. To circumvent the problem, existing web sites such as "Singaporeans for Democracy" (www.sfdonline.org) were used to advertise the book. A notice was written up with information on the cost of the book, contact mailing address and method of payment. This was effective. By the end of the first week, orders and payments for 25 copies were received.

It is interesting to note that among the first batch of Internet orders were from the Ministry of Foreign Affairs and the Ministry for Information and the Arts! This offered the first glimpse of the PAP government's surveillance of the Internet and set the tone for the kind of close monitoring of the Centre's activity on the Internet. The flip side, however, was that because there was demand for the book, a local bookshop, Select Books, was persuaded to distribute it. This allowed the Centre to organize a book launch in a major bookstore, MPH. A few difficulties were encountered at the launch, however, as a permit to speak during a book launch was denied by the licensing division of the police. In response, the Centre issued an open letter on various web sites, sent out press releases, and launched the book without an oral introduction. Reporters from the local media were there to cover the event and their reports gave the book and the Centre mainstream publicity.

Soon after the book was launched, readers began to e-mail their reactions to the book and those who agreed with the conclusions of the book also felt that something needed to be done. A dialogue began with some of the readers because a contact e-mail address was printed on the book cover and readers were able to e-mail and make first contact. These people formed the core group that launched the political education programme that was named "Politics 21". Others who were not part of the organizing group were placed on a mailing list for alerts for the forum series.

As the title made its way into bookstores, the co-operative bookstore at the National University of Singapore decided to take it down
from its shelves. An investigative report commissioned by the Centre
revealed that the bookstore practised self-censorship. The Internet
was used to highlight the incident and name the bookstore concerned.
In using the Internet the way the Centre did, a new approach for
political mobilization and dissemination of information was utilized.

Politics 21 Forum Series—The Internet and Public Entertainment Laws

The Think Centre web site arose out of a need to accommodate
the online registration of participants for the Politics 21 forum series
in mid-September 1999. One of the main aims of the series was to
highlight the fact that the Singapore 21 initiative and report by the
government to prepare Singaporeans for the future did not directly
address the issue of politics. Hence, the Politics 21 series, a ground-
up initiative, was set up to communicate an awareness of social,
economic and political realities and alternatives; to cultivate an
understanding and appreciation of different social, economic and
political perspectives; and to foster a sense of duty to participate, as
citizens of Singapore, in the nation's political processes.

1 October 1999 was set as the date for the first forum, and the
topic was confirmed as "Youth and Politics". The themes for future
forums, the Centre agreed, would be decided as the project progressed.
To this end, the Internet was used to invite participants to the forum.
Many Singapore political web sites carried announcements of the
Centre's first forum. Announcements for the first forum were also
posted on existing web sites such as Singaporeans for Democracy
(www.sfdonline.org) and Singapore-Window (www.singapore-win-
dow.org). Postings were also made on http://www.soc.culture.singapore
and in Sintercom's (www.geocities.com/newsintercom) SG Daily mailing list. These advertisements attracted many participants, who sent
e-mails to register for the forums. When these e-mails increased, we
decided to set up an online registration URL using a free web hosting service.

Those who wanted to attend the first forum were requested to
key in their name and contact details so that the Centre could prepare a registration list for participants and also start building up a
database for future forums and for a possible membership drive. The

turn-out at the first forum was about 70 people, and all those present declared the event a success and expressed interest in the Centre's activities. Soon after the first talk under the Politics 21 series was launched, however, officers from the Tanglin police station summoned the author and several others for organizing a talk without a permit. The various individuals were questioned separately over a period of two months. During some of the interviews, printouts from the Centre's URL registration were shown to those questioned to jog their memory and to record their answers to questions asked.

The investigation was used to point out that using the Internet to gather people for an indoor forum was illegal. This event was not made public through the mass media but was advertised through e-mail alerts to friends and contacts who were directed to the URL for registration. Having people register online for an in-door forum, however, was also seen as constituting a public activity. At the conclusion of the investigation, the author and three associates were identified as being the organizers and were given a verbal warning in lieu of prosecution, and were told to apply for public entertainment licences for future events.

The heart of the problem was the innovative use of the Internet in creating awareness, inviting people for the forum and having them register online. The porous nature of the Internet did not give the organizers control in keeping the closed-door activity private. The event under investigation was put into the category of public events. The event also demonstrated the kind of scrutiny the police place on activites over the Internet and showed that any movement in cyberspace was monitored, and that the strict letter of the law applied to it. In return, the Centre adopted the same approach both during and after the period of police questioning: it used the Internet to publicize the police investigation in detail. As a form of public education, detailed reports, pictures and updates were frequently provided. Many people rallied behind the Centre on the Internet throughout the course of the investigation. The Centre introduced instant transparency to police investigations and offered anonymity to anyone as soon they left the Internet and began to engage the Centre, its members and its activities in the real world.

System Upgrade—Improving Political Communication

The great Internet attention the Centre received created the momentum in January 2000 for the web site to be redesigned. It was redeveloped to present colourful pictures, reports on its forums, speeches, and extended and investigative reports. A small pool of regular contributors was gathered to provide new and constantly updated original content. The site was further developed with links to other civil society organizations, both locally and abroad. In the first three months of the year 2000, the site chalked up over 7,000 hits.

To harness the potential of the web site and to experiment with online audio and video, a domain name—http://www.thinkcentre.org—was purchased. This site was launched at Borders bookstore on 3 March 2000 during a reading of *Self-Censorship: Singapore's Shame*. Incidentally, the police appeared after the event to talk to Borders staff about the political nature of the reading. In the space of four months, the site saw an additional 3,000 hits. Given the volume of updates and limited manpower, however, updates were not optimal. To overcome this problem, the web site went through another upgrade to employ the use of Web Automation software. Instead of relying on one or two people who could upload changes to the FTP server, a template was designed where information could be more easily uploaded.

As part of the web site's continual development, a database for automatic archiving was incorporated, a search engine added, decentralized updating by a core group of web editors set in place, and audio and video uploads explored. New sections included "Human Rights", "Media", "Policy" and "Election Watch". These sections were incorporated with reports on both local and foreign issues to draw attention to the individual areas and increase awareness of the various topics.

The web site also had a section on web statistics that was only accessible to the editors. With this feature, the Centre was able to track where hits to its site came from. In doing so, the Centre was also able confirm that officers from the Singapore Broadcasting Authority were very frequent visitors to the web site.

A "Speaker's Corner Online" (SCO) section was also added to facilitate interaction for visitors to the site. The aim was to supplement the Speaker's Corner instituted at Hong Lim Park by the government, so as to promote free speech on the Internet. As there was a dearth of online forums on the Internet, the Centre decided to provide a simple and intuitive user interface, focused group discussions on hot topics, peer voting for articles and replies, and the ability to suggest discussion topics as well as post private messages to individual users on the web site. The volume of traffic on the SCO was modest, but it represented a space for free speech.

As part of the online strategy, a mailing list service was started under Yahoo e-Groups and was used for fast and instantaneous dissemination of breaking news and announcements. This list, which started mainly from the author's private list, included friends, people who read *Self-Censorship: Singapore's Shame*, members of Singapore's civil society, the local media and political parties. The list was then enlarged to include regional and international civil societies and media groups. Provisions were made for anyone visiting the Centre's web site to subscribe to this mailing list service by registering at its e-Groups link. The Centre used this mailing list to inform subscribers of new postings, upcoming talks and projects, and to co-ordinates activities.

Even the mailing list was kept under a watchful government eye. Once, when the Centre sent a notice through the mailing list for a human rights study group meeting, the author was informed, through telephone by the head of the licensing division, that he needed a permit to do so. The meeting was then rescheduled as a private dinner. When this incident was published, the police called the act mischievous for exposing the incident. The extent of scrutiny those on the mailing list received will be discussed later in the essay. Internally, a member's mailing list was set up to help co-ordinate and organize in-house projects and duties. The members also supplemented their contact with one another through Short Messaging Service (SMS). This kept communication among the Centre's members rapid, constant and tight.

Making News, in the News

The web site and mailing list were important in amplifying the local and original news the Centre carried about its activities. The Centre created a separate media mailing list to send out press releases and to engage the media. Thus, commentators and media practitioners referred to the web site and information send out to its mailing list as sources of news. For instance, when the Centre co-organized an event to commemorate International Human Rights Day on 10

December 2000, the police investigated a possible violation of the law by its organizers. The event had as its theme "Abolish ISA", referring to the Internal Security Act that provides for detention without trial. The police were essentially looking into whether any laws, such as that of assembling without a permit, were broken when a crowd of 100 people gathered at Speakers' Corner in Hong Lim Park, raised their fists and, along with the organizers, chanted "Abolish, Abolish ISA." The police summoned two persons for an interview, including the author, we were investigated and given a warning letter.

The Think Centre followed up by posting reports about the investigation on its web site, highlighting the two interviews and the grey areas of the law pertaining to the Speakers' Corner. The appearance of the interviews on the web site was a rare first, in that the public was provided with all the information pertaining to the investigation from the organizers' point of view. The police, on the other hand, were tight-lipped about the investigation. The media, however, picked up the information from the web site and the mailing list, and gave the whole incident international coverage. In late March 2001, Think Centre received notice that it was to be gazetted as a political organization under the Political Donations Act. Essentially, this meant that the Centre could not receive foreign funds and had to declare local funds in excess of S$5,000, just like political parties in Singapore. The local media went into a frenzy when the PAP government made an advance announcement that the Centre was to be gazetted. Several journalists began investigating whether the Centre had received foreign funds, which it had not. The Centre took the country and the media by surprise by turning the issue completely around, by stating that if the government treated the Centre—a civil society grouping—as a political party, it would behave as one. On the eve of 1 April 2001, the Centre sent out a press release announcing its intention of fielding a slate of candidates to contest in the upcoming general elections. It further stated that this decision was in direct response to the government's decision to gazette the Centre as a political organization, place restrictions on its funding and treat it as a political party. The media could not resist the news and bought into the announcement, plastering the news all over the country.

As expected, the announcement immediately drew a barrage of comments from PAP members of parliament (MPs); one spontaneously suggested that the background of the candidates would be checked.

The joke also exposed many people's real feelings. Thus, when the Centre sent out a press release close to midnight on 1 April, the floodgates were opened. The media was sore that it had been played out. The PAP MPs, especially those who were not quick to give their opinions, complained that politics was no joking matter. The Centre, however, defended its position by stating that while politics per se is serious, the state of politics in Singapore was a joke. It was one of the deepest media impressions the Centre created and all this was due to its web site and mailing list, which the media kept referring to for their news.

Other issues posted on the web site concerned applications for permits, and correspondence between the licensing division of the police and the Think Centre. For instance, the police rejected a permit application for a road show to promote a Speakers' Corner venue at a public market on 13 November 2000. The police insisted that Hong Lim Park was sufficient and that there was no need for a road show. Think Centre also applied for a permit to hold a picket at the offices of the 93.8FM radio station. The picket was to highlight the fact that as a public radio station, 93.8FM had a responsibility to its listeners to come clean about an incident of self-censorship (see next section). The police rejected the application, citing potential law-and-order problems.

The laws affecting these activities were not made clear by the authorities concerned to the ordinary citizen. Rather than taking a pro-active approach by stating what could or could not be done and looking at the grey areas of the law, the authorities reacted with a flat "no", without citing clear reasons for their decisions. On the other hand, the exchanges between the licensing division and Think Centre were kept transparent through postings on its web site.

The web site also highlights the ways in which bookstores and libraries practise censorship on publications with political content. A request to launch the book, *Publish & Perish: The Censorship of Opposition Political Parties*, in December 2000 was turned down by the National Library. It gave the explanation that it does not launch publications dealing with sex, religion, race and politics. Again, the exchange of correspondence between the prospective organizers and the library officials was put on the web site.

The web site and mailing list were collectively used to circulate press statements, announcements by various interest groups and amateur reports on events that were not carried by the mainstream media. Not all of these reports were picked up by the media and amplified, but the significant and important issues that the Centre dealt with were adequately covered in the usual Singaporean manner.

Managing the Media and Watching the Watchers

Among the sections that the Centre introduced on its web site, "Media Watch" displayed reports on media monitoring issues. Since the Centre did generate a lot of news, not all of it was fair coverage. Thus, there was a need to have a mechanism in place to clarify issues. At the same time, there was also a need to expose instances of self-censorship and direct censorship of news that the media did not want to carry. An avenue was needed for the public to know, even if it was in a limited way, what was going on. The Centre also realized that many of its activities were being monitored both on the Internet as well as on the ground. Therefore, it wanted to make it clear to surveillance agents that if they wanted to watch the Centre's activities, they had to be prepared to be watched and run the risk of being exposed. In this regard, the web site and mailing list were excellent tools. One specific incident of media watch is the special report put out by the Centre on the censorship of a radio programme by the management of local station 93.8FM.

The report was about the commemoration of International Human Rights Day on 10 December 2000. At about 8:30 A.M. the next day, the programme was aired in three parts: a letter to the prime minister of Singapore that was read by J.B. Jeyaretnam, a principal portion of the International Human Rights Day (IHRD) message by Kofi Annan, and an interview with a member of Think Centre. The presenter said that the programme would be aired again at about 9:20 A.M., together with an additional interview. When the time came, the presenter began the programme by saying that the management was unhappy with the earlier broadcast and had asked that the programme be edited. She repeated this announcement at the end of the programme.

As a local academic put it, this decision by the 93.8FM management marked the first time in Singapore's media history that a working journalist exposed the self-censorship that operated in a public broadcast station. As a public radio station, 93.8FM has a responsibility to its listeners to present the news as objectively as possible.

Furthermore, the radio station did not feel it had to explain itself fully and continued to insist that what it had done was the normal editing of a programme due to time constraints. Access to information was compromised in this case, since there was no transparency or accountability. 93.8FM was not forthcoming when Think Centre asked for the transcripts and taped recordings of the programme. A government Feedback Unit on media did not deliberate on this issue even when such a request was made. The local media did not report extensively on this incident, and a general silence all around showed the extent of reluctance to come clean. Details of the incident were not reported in-depth locally, but the Think Centre web site kept its readers informed and provided transparency.

The Centre has been active ever since the Speakers' Corner opened in Singapore. It regularly organized speaking events and used the Internet to mobilize attendance for its activities. By organizing actual events, however, the Centre found out very quickly that apart from the Internet, there was also active surveillance of the Centre's activities on the ground. So, one of the strategies the Centre adopted was to take pictures of all those present at its events and publish them on the web site. The Centre had previously done this for its indoor forums where it posted the pictures of licensing officers who audited the Centre's talks on the Web. On two separate occasions, two men in their late thirties, a Malay and a Chinese, came to inquire about the registration status of the Think Centre at the Think Centre office registration booths at International Plaza at Shenton Way, and Excelsior Shopping Centre at Coleman Street. On other occasions, however, we had the camera handy.

One incident involved a Chinese man in his mid-thirties who was spotted both by Think Centre members as well as members of the public. He regularly attended the Centre's events at Speakers' Corner and recorded members' speeches on tape. An informal check revealed that this man was not a journalist. What the Centre did then was to take a series of digital pictures of his recording activity and publish them on the web site with an article in which we asked members of the public to help identify the man. The Centre also sent out an e-mail alert through its mailing list, asking for further help from members of the public to identify the person in question. The alert stated that the Centre wanted his contact details to find out what he was recording and whom it was for. Think Centre never got any answers but it created the desired effect. This man no longer appeared at any of the Centre's activities. Word was also put out that the Centre would not hesitate to expose those who want to spy on its members and its activities.

Thus, the Internet was employed as a good counter-surveillance tool, both for managing the media as well as those who spy on the Centre and its members. What the Centre did was seen in many quarters as being innovative and bold.

Curbing Politics on the Internet

The potential for political campaigning on the Internet led the PAP government to amend legislation and implement rules and regulations in the run-up to the general elections in 2001.

Among other things, the first amendment was in holding owners and editors of online forums accountable for posting of discussion boards. These people were to be held accountable for postings that were libellous, even if these were from anonymous sources. For online forums, the regulations would address the concern that false and slanderous statements, name-calling, racial and religious slurs, and obscenities may be made with impunity on unmoderated chat sites. Therefore, while chats on political sites were allowed, they would be moderated.

Speakers' Corner Online ran until the government passed legislation surrounding the Internet and held the owners and editors of web sites accountable for the views that surfers posted on online forums. Since most postings were anonymous and could not be controlled, there was no guarantee that one would be free of prosecution even if it were only one posting a year! Therefore, when the bill was passed, the Centre withdrew Speakers' Corner Online in protest. It argued that it did not agree with the amendment to the Parliamentary Act that was brought before Parliament without consulting all the groups concerned.

Other amendments made to the Parliamentary Act (PEA) to regulate political parties, candidates and groups hosting web sites that discuss politics included the requirement that they register with the Singapore Broadcasting Authority. The amendment regulates any material that is thought to promote any candidate or party, even if it does not mention them by name. In any election advertisement in print or on the Internet, the publisher and the printer are required to be identified, and the person for whom the advertisement is for has to be named. Any violators of these regulations could face jail terms of up to a year.

The amendments to the PEA did have an impact on the Centre as they effectively crippled its ability to report on anything during the elections. This can be seen by an act of the Elections Department. On Friday, 19 October 2001 at 5:11 P.M., the Centre received a fax from the Elections Department, ordering it to remove all materials that could be construed "election advertising" by 11 P.M. on the same day or face prosecution under the law. The letter read:

> DIRECTION TO REMOVE ELECTION ADVERTISING—The Returning Officer HEREBY DIRECTS the Think Centre to remove all election advertising published on the Internet in www.thinkcentre.org in contravention of Regulation 6 of the Parliamentary Elections (Election Advertising) Regulations 2001. The Think Centre must remove the subject election advertising by not later than 2300 hrs, 19 October 2001. Failure to comply with this direction is an offence punishable under section 78A(2) of the Parliamentary Elections Act.

The insufficiently short notice that was given allowed the Centre less than six hours to act on the Election Department's orders. The Centre's members who knew how to operate technical aspects of the web site had full-time jobs and were on work duty when the fax was received. This incident took place in spite of the fact that on 10 October 2001, unclear about the Internet guidelines on elections, Think Centre took the initiative to fax and e-mail a letter to Mr. Robin Chan, Head of the Elections Department with a request to clarify specific areas of Parliamentary Elections Act. This was not met with a direct response.

The ambiguity and restrictiveness of the legislation effectively resulted in non-party political sites like Think Centre having to remove articles that do not conform to election rules, and removing hyperlinks to sites that campaign for a political candidate or party. It also gave the government permission to prosecute anyone who publishes anything that does not conform to what it regards as acceptable news/information. Non-party political web sites are effectively prevented from monitoring the progress of or covering the elections during the election period under the extremely broad-based rule that such web sites are prohibited from carrying information that "constitutes campaigning for any political party or candidate". Such legislation was made comprehensive enough to cover both mailing lists as well as SMS messages.

Thus, it was not surprising to received frustrated e-mails from many of the Centre's website users, asking why the web site was not updated on matters related to the elections. Hence, the legislation was effective; it prevented the Centre from putting out "Election Watch" reports and performing election monitoring.

James Gomez News

To date, legislation in Singapore on the Internet covers web sites and, during an election period, covers political parties and organizations. It has yet to cover individuals, and there has not been a single case that the PAP government has had an opportunity to act on. An indication of how it might take place, however, can be seen from the explorative steps taken by the author.

In August 2001, the author decided to set up an individual web site and an accompanying mailing list. To this end, a personal database of about 2,000 addresses collected from the author's first year as sole proprietor of the Centre was set up in Yahoo e-Groups as "JamesGomezNews". A personalized domain name, www.james-gomeznews.com, was also acquired. During this process of planning the new web site, the Minister of Home Affairs in the Singapore Parliament raised the issue that this author was setting up a new web site.

An e-mail inquiry was then sent to the government by Think Centre to clarify what the Minister meant by this "new web site", as the author himself was unaware of any announcement of his plans to set up a web site. The response from the Minister of Home Affairs' office was a statement indicating that the Minister was referring to the mailing list. The statement, signed by a civil servant, went further to suggest that the mailing list the author had set up was somehow misappropriated from Think Centre, hinting at some kind of wrong-doing. The civil servant referred to the number of e-mails on the Yahoo e-Groups' "JamesGomezNews".

The author responded to this statement by offering Ministry officials full access to the mailing list, to dissect it and examine what they thought was wrong. The author also invited them to discuss the issue of the mailing list and the accompanying legislation that the government was at that time introducing to control it. The Ministry did not take up the offer.

Readers should note that at this point, only the mailing list at the Yahoo e-Groups site had been set up, and one welcome message sent out. Yet, there was much excitement over the personalization of the mailing list system. This incident occurred without the mailing list ever being put to use. The incident offers the reader, once again, an insight into the rigour of surveillance of the Internet. The mailing list was eventually deleted when the government introduced the ruling that mass e-mailing could be a form of political campaigning and should be regulated as such. As an individual, it would have left the author open to attack, as the rules of the Internet ruling are still ambiguous to many.

In the meantime, the idea for a personal web site is still under consideration. This is one area of outreach that will take the use of communication technology a step further. It is in this area that observers will have to track the extent to which the government will legislate to include individual and private communication under the category of political outreach tools. This will be point of future engagement.

Think Centre Asia

During that time, the author moved to Bangkok and with several Thai nationals, founded Think Centre Asia. The aim was to build on some of the successes of the Singapore experience and execute these at a regional level. One of the outcomes of the Singapore experience was a regional awareness of Think Centre's activities. The Internet, and modern communication technology reduced the distance among other regional groups and linked the Centre to pan-regional management and co-ordination of civil society projects.

This gave the Centre a chance to participate in regional and international meetings and conferences; thereby, plugging it into the global economy. To consolidate these networking experiences, a web site, http://www.thinkcentreasia.org, was set up in Bangkok in August 2001 and a mailing list of regional organizations and individuals interested in regional issues was also incorporated. The Think Centre Asia web site not only expanded its geographic coverage, but also the issues it represented. Within four months of its being set up, the web site averaged 20,000 hits per month and attracted new subscribers to its e-newsletter on a daily basis. The newsletter, which is sent out periodically, receives an enthusiastic response and interaction rate from subscribers all over the world, especially from Central Asia and Australia.

Working with local and international organizations, Think Centre Asia's current concerns are press freedom and corruption. Together with the Office of Civil Service Commission of the Royal Thai Government and the International Chamber of Commerce, new formulas for transparency and accessibility to public information are being advocated. Future plans for Think Centre Asia are to increase the number of participating countries, and to increase activities to a regional basis.

Conclusion—Taking Stock

In less than two years, the Think Centre had grown from strength to strength, and part of its success was its ability to ride on Internet technology. The Think Centre web site has come a long way from its humble beginnings as a mere registration URL for the Politics 21 forums. By making politics livelier with the use of photos and bold graphics, the Centre has, in a short time, injected new vibrancy to Singapore's Internet political scene. Indeed, in many ways, it succeeded in pushing the frontiers of political expression.

The Internet made the Centre interactive by allowing people to send letters, contribute opinions and take part in online polls. More importantly, it enabled the Centre to bring people together physically in one location. At the same time, it was inevitable that with Singapore's political culture, it was only a matter of time before restrictions were placed on the Internet. Civil society and the Internet have a role to play in revitalizing politics, but both must continually add new dimensions to their contributions.

The ability to mobilize people for action allowed the author to devolve ownership of the Centre from that of a sole proprietorship to that of a partnership. After that, the author stepped down as the Centre's founding director and joined a political party. The Centre decided to register as a multipartisan political society with the Registrar of Societies. When the application was approved, the Centre's business registration was cancelled. The status of a society provided the Centre with a constitution, internal elections and the opportunity to grow and increase its membership even further.

For Think Centre (in Internet time at least), however, two years is also a very long time. It is enough for competitors to catch up with the Centre and for others who used to carry the Centre's postings to focus on their own areas of interests and, in reverse, regard the Centre as a competitor. Hence, there is always a need to re-invent politics on the Net to keep up with the times and to remain at the forefront. This is the principle for success on the Internet.

The Internet is but a small window accessed by the converted, the curious and those who spy on others. Some use it to cast aspersions under the cover of anonymity. In Singapore's case, the government continues to legislate as much as it can to control the political potential of the Internet. Many are still afraid to discuss politics on the Internet; nevertheless, the Internet remains important. It connects people together in a way that was previously not possible. Co-ordination for activities is easy; dissemination of information is fast. Through a "snowball" effect, messages reach more people than the initial target. If you are upfront and personal, you can even build credibility and a following. In this case, the ability to individualize and globalize the use of communication technology for political communication will be crucial.

BEYOND THE DOTCOM FEVER:
MAPPING THE DYNAMICS OF E-COMMERCE
IN HONG KONG

Naubahar Sharif

Department of Science and Technology Studies
Cornell University

Introduction

This paper attempts to provide recommendations for a specific branch of public policy—electronic commerce (e-commerce) policy. It provides policy recommendations mainly by studying similar policy in other countries, primarily, Singapore and, secondarily, the United States of America. By analyzing the current status of e-commerce policy in Hong Kong as compared with the other countries, deficiencies in Hong Kong's policies can be identified. Further, based on those deficiencies, recommendations can be made for e-commerce policy in Hong Kong.[1]

Electronic Commerce (E-commerce)—A Background

E-commerce refers to business transactions carried out on the Internet. E-commerce is a means of conducting transactions that, prior to the evolution of the Internet as a business tool, would have been completed in more traditional ways: by telephone, mail, facsimile, proprietary electronic date interchange systems, or face-to-face contact.

Two facets of the new, emerging economy are e-commerce (that is, business processes that shift transactions to the Internet or some

---

[1] In reading this paper, it is important to bear in mind the subject matter that is examined. E-commerce is in flux worldwide, not least because of the decrease in euphoria over the promises of "dotcom" companies over the past 18 to 24 months, and also because of the global economic slowdown. In and of itself, too, e-commerce is a newly developing arena where governments have only recently (within the past decade) begun to engage themselves. Therefore, many of the issues and ideas raised in this paper may change rapidly in response to a fluid social, regulatory and technological environment.

other non-proprietary, Web-based system) and the information technology (IT) industries that make e-commerce possible. Both these
facets of the new economy are growing and changing at a breath-
taking speed. Not only were we unable to foresee five years ago how
advances in information technology would alter the manner in which
we do business and create value, but the rate of change is racing
ahead of estimates.

The value of e-commerce transactions, while still small relative to
the size of the economy, continues to grow at a remarkable rate. More
significant than the dollar amount of these transactions, however, is
the new business processes e-commerce enables and the new business
models it is generating. This is witnessed none other than by the
growing number of IT or e-commerce companies that are being set
up every day in Hong Kong, and those that are being listed on the
stock market (particularly the Growth Enterprise Market or GEM).
Both the new Internet-based companies and the traditional producers of goods and services are transforming their business processes
into e-commerce processes in an effort to lower costs, improve customer service and increase productivity.

While individual private estimates of Internet access and size vary
significantly from one another, taken together, they indicate remarkable growth. For example, *The Industry Standard* reports that from
1998 to 1999, the number of Web users worldwide increased by 55
percent; the number of Internet hosts rose by 46 percent; the number of Web servers increased by 128 percent; and the number of
new Web address registrations rose by 137 percent.[2]

Although, it goes without saying that Internet penetration and
usage is most concerted in the USA and Canada, it is also true to
say that growth in Internet access has been the fastest in Asia.
According to Nua, an Internet strategy firm, as of May 1999, 171
million people across the globe had access to the Internet. The Asia-
Pacific region accounted for 27 million or 15.8 percent of users. In
March 2000, the same source reported that there were 304 million
people across the globe who had access to the Internet. In March
2000, the Asia-Pacific region accounted for 68.9 million or 22.6 percent of users. This represents an increase of 43.22 percent of peo-

---

[2] Thompson, Maryann Jones (1999) "My How We've Grown," *The Industry Standard*,
April 26. (http://www.thestandard.com)

ple who had access to the Internet in Asia-Pacific over a ten-month period, and is the largest increase for any region in the world.[3]

Internet usage for online transactions, however, is still fairly small. According to AC Nielsen, 26.2 percent of Hong Kong families regularly use the Internet. Among those users, only 13 percent—less than four percent of the six million population—had used the Internet for online transactions. The situation is far different in other nearby countries—in South Korea and Taiwan, for example, respectively 78.7 percent and 56.1 percent of Internet users buy products or services online.[4]

Present State of E-Commerce Policy in Hong Kong

In his 1997 Policy Address, the Chief Executive outlined his vision to make Hong Kong a leader in the information world of tomorrow. In his 1998 Policy Address, he further emphasized the importance of using IT to help Hong Kong retain our competitive edge and drive our overall economic expansion. To realize the Chief Executive's IT vision, the "Digital 21" IT strategy was announced in November 1998. This is a comprehensive strategy to enhance and promote Hong Kong's information infrastructure and services so as to make Hong Kong a leading digital city in the globally connected world of the twenty-first century.[5]

The government fully recognizes the strategic importance of promoting the development of electronic commerce for Hong Kong's long-term benefit. Towards this end, the government is committed to providing a favourable environment supported by a sound legal framework to foster the development of electronic commerce in Hong Kong. A certification authority has been established as part of a

---

[3] For complete survey results, definitions, and methodology, see http://www.nua.ie/surveys.

[4] SCMP, Monday, 19 November 2001.

[5] Hong Kong's Policy Objective on IT is fully supported by the "Digital 21" IT strategy, which is built upon four enabling factors: developing a high-capacity communications infrastructure, establishing an open and common interface for the conduct of secure electronic transactions, equipping our people with the know-how to use IT widely in our everyday life, and nurturing a culture that stimulates creativity and welcomes advances in the use of IT. In the past year, Hong Kong has put in place and made significant progress in launching various initiatives in pursuit of these enabling factors.

public key infrastructure to provide security and trust in the conduct of electronic transactions over open networks. Hong Kong also participates in the deliberations of international fora such as the WTO, the APEC and the OECD in order to keep in close touch with world developments in, and to put across its views on, e-commerce.

The Hong Kong SAR (HKSAR) Government's Role

The HKSAR government views the major barrier for the wider adoption of e-commerce as concerns about security and the protection of personal data when transactions are conducted over the Internet. The presence of supporting infrastructure is extremely important in addressing the identities of the parties involved, the integrity and confidentiality of the information transmitted, and the non-repudiation and legal status of the electronic transactions.

The government is building an Electronic Service Delivery (ESD) infrastructure to enable the community to obtain public services through the Internet and other electronic means.[6] Private companies can also make use of the Infrastructure for the conduct of e-commerce. Services under the ESD scheme will be provided based on a public-oriented approach.

The ESD scheme was first launched on 9 December 2000. A wide range of services provided by 10 government departments and public agencies will be covered under this first phase of implementation. Under this phase, examples of services include the filing of tax returns, search for job vacancies, voter registration, renewal of driving licences, changing of personal information in various government departments, payment of government bills, appointment booking for registration of identity card, and investment and tourist information.

Subsequent phases will be implemented on an ongoing basis. In the long run, the government aims to include all public services that

---

[6] The ESD is a key initiative under the "Digital 21" strategy for the delivery of public services through the Internet and other electronic means. It will provide seamless delivery of various types of public services under a citizen-centric approach, and will allow for an adoption of an information infrastructure with a common and open interface accessible throughout the territory. The services of the ESD will be available for use 24 hours a day and seven days a week at locations convenient to the public, and it will act as a catalyst to pump-prime the development of electronic commerce in Hong Kong.

are amenable to the electronic mode of delivery under the ESD
scheme. The benefits of the ESD scheme will be: an improvement
in quality and efficiency in the delivery of public services; an improvement in the accessibility of government services, and widening the
reach of public services; a reduction in the cost of providing public
services in the longer term; promotion of the wider use of electronic
transactions within the community; and the provision of a favourable
environment for electronic commerce to take hold and flourish in
Hong Kong.[7]

In November 2001, the HKSAR government and 10 local business
and technology associations[8] announced an e-commerce adoption
campaign to promote the use of the Internet among local businesses
and the public. This campaign was set up in an effort to increase
awareness and encourage the adoption of e-commerce in Hong Kong.
It was launched in response to the low usage of the Internet for
e-commerce purposes in Hong Kong despite the large number of
Hong Kong households and businesses that are connected to the
Internet. In particular, Hong Kong was said to lag behind other key
Asian markets (principally Japan, South Korea and Singapore) in
e-commerce adoption.[9]

Furthermore, to instil the public's confidence on the use of electronic
transactions, the government has taken the lead to establish a public
Certification Authority through the Hong Kong Post. The Hong Kong
Post has established a Public Key Infrastructure. Through the use of
digital certificates and the public/private key mechanisms, the security
and integrity of transactions conducted over the Internet can be ensured
(further details of the Hong Kong Post's role can be seen below).

The government is also providing a legal framework through the
Electronic Transactions Ordinance to enhance certainty and security
in the conduct of electronic transactions. The Ordinance seeks to
give electronic records and digital signatures used in electronic transactions the same legal status as that of their paper-based counterparts.

---

[7] In association with the introduction of the ESD scheme, the government will
develop a common Chinese language interface to facilitate electronic transactions
and information exchange in Chinese.

[8] These organizations include the Hong Kong General Chamber of Commerce,
the Hong Kong Information Technology Federation, American Chamber of
Commerce, the Hong Kong Post, Hong Kong Society of Accountants, the Productivity
Council and the Office of the Telecommunications Authority.

[9] Paraphrased from: http://www.tryitonline.com.hk

The other main objective of the Ordinance is to establish a framework that will promote and facilitate the establishment and operation of Certification Authorities in Hong Kong.

A whole series of promotion and educational programmes have been launched to enhance the awareness among public and local enterprises on the use of e-commerce. The government has been promoting ESD through roving shows, exhibitions and the launching of simulation software to provide the public with hands-on experience.

Apart from the HKSAR government, Hong Kong's e-commerce initiatives are presently pushed through three major government/quasi-governmental organizations (the first two are industry-support organizations):

1. The Hong Kong Productivity Council (HKPC)
2. The Trade Development Council (TDC)
3. The Hong Kong Post

The Hong Kong Productivity Council (HKPC)

DigiHall 21 is Hong Kong's first streamlined and integrated IT promoter and services provider. As a key initiative by HKPC's Institute of Information and Media Industries (IIMI), DigiHall 21 is designed to serve the ever-increasing IT needs of various industries and the general community, thereby, enhancing the competitiveness of Hong Kong as it enters the digital age.

Designed to serve the IT needs of the key phases of business operations, DigiHall 21 comprises six IT centres built around a central arena. The six centres are:

1. E-Commerce Centre[10]
2. Business Intelligence Centre
3. Enterprise Resource Planning
4. E-Community Centre
5. Software Industry Information Centre (SIIC)
6. New Media Centre

---

[10] The DigiHall 21 E-Commerce Centre is the first centre in Hong Kong that offers integrated electronic commerce solutions to local manufacturers, traders, retailers and other service providers. The E-Commerce Centre offers the following services: market intelligence information, electronic sourcing, electronic data interchange (EDI), electronic marketing, electronic payment, and electronic assisted delivery.

The Trade Development Council (TDC)

The major campaign by the Trade Development Council is the establishment of Tradelink Electronic Commerce Ltd.—a joint venture between the Hong Kong SAR government and 11 private sector shareholders,[11] all of who are key players in the international trade cycle in Hong Kong, either directly or as representative organizations. The government's shareholding is just under 45 percent.

Tradelink's mission is to help the local trading community enhance its efficiency and stay competitive in the global market place through greater use of electronic commerce. Since all import and export shipments involve government documentation at some stage, Tradelink is "jump-starting" the adoption of e-commerce in Hong Kong by providing electronic services for the most commonly-used government transactions, linked to a programme of migration from paper to full electronic submission.

As well as providing an electronic link to the government, Tradelink's services offer a number of value-added transaction management facilities, including message checking; matching and validation; message authentication and security; electronic billing and payments; and message archiving and audit trail services.

In order to speed up the transition from paper to electronic commerce and maximize the efficiency benefits for all parties, the Hong Kong SAR government has set a series of deadlines for migration to electronic submission.

- Quota License applications were made fully electronic from 1 January 1999, following a four-stage migration programme in 1998.
- Trade Declarations were made fully electronic from 1 April 2000, following a timetable for the gradual withdrawal of modes of submission of paper declarations to government counters.

For those traders who are not ready to move to electronic commerce by these deadlines, Tradelink is providing a series of special facilities for non-computerized traders.

---

[11] The private sector shareholders are: Cable & Wireless HKT, China Resources (Holdings) Ltd., The Federation of Hong Kong Industries, Hong Kong Air Cargo Terminals Ltd. (HACTL), Hong Kong Association of Freight Forwarding Agents (HAFFA), The Hong Kong General Chamber of Commerce, Hongkong International Terminals Ltd. (HIT),The Hongkong and Shanghai Banking Corporation Ltd. (HSBC), Modern Terminals Ltd. (MTL), Standard Chartered Bank, and Swire Pacific Ltd.

More than 98 percent of Hong Kong's exporters and manufacturers are classified as small- to medium-sized enterprises (SMEs),
and over 87 percent have fewer than 10 staff. Tradelink recognizes
the constraints that this places on investment in IT skills and resources,
and has carefully designed its services and software to be as affordable,
convenient and easy to use as possible.

In addition, a number of special initiatives have been introduced
to help reduce the start-up cost for smaller businesses, or those that
use government transactions infrequently, including:

- Low-cost packages for SMEs
- SilkNet Service Package[12]
- ValuNet Service Package[13]
- Secure Internet Gateway service
- Special facilities for non-computerized traders

---

[12] The SilkNet service is based on the Restrained Textiles Export Licence (also
known as "quota licence", "blue licence" or RTEL), which some 5,000 Hong Kong
exporters and manufacturers currently use. The Quota Licence application was the
first government trade transaction in Hong Kong to be offered electronically when
Tradelink introduced SilkNet in January 1997, and it was the first to go 100 percent electronic when the Trade Department's receiving counters for paper applications were closed permanently from 1 January 1999 following a four-phase migration
programme in 1998. Those traders who are not yet computerized now have to submit their applications through one of the Tradelink service centres, where they can
be converted to electronic format for submission to government. Currently over 94
percent of applications are submitted through SilkNet and only six percent through
the service centres. Notification of licence approval to the designated sea or air car-
rier is also now fully electronic, while an electronic service for submitting the "visa
copy" of approved licences to US Customs was introduced at the beginning of
1999. This helps to speed delivery of textile shipments by enabling many consign-
ments to receive customs clearance prior to their actual arrival in port. Two further
transactions added in the third quarter of 1999 are Production Notification, which
is required to support many Quota Licence applications; and Certificate of Origin,
which certifies to overseas authorities that the goods are made in Hong Kong.
[13] ValuNet is a package of electronic commerce services designed to help Hong
Kong's general importers and exporters handle their trade documentation more easily. It is built around the Import and Export Declaration, which must be submitted to the government for every import into, or export from, Hong Kong. The
service offered by Tradelink enables traders to include in their declarations English
or Chinese characters in those fields where current government regulations permit.
With effect from 1 April 2000, the Hong Kong SAR government only accepts
Import and Export Declarations received electronically. The main government collection office in Tsim Sha Tsui closes with effect from 1 October 1999 and from
then until 31 March 2000, only the Hong Kong (Sheung Wan) collection office
will remain open to receive paper declarations.

Hong Kong Post

The Internet is a global and faceless environment. Being able to identify and trust the other party is a challenge in any Internet transaction. A digital trust system based on the use of digital signatures and certificates, enables parties to establish one another's identities and transact safely and confidently.

Towards this end, to enable the development of e-commerce in Hong Kong, the Hong Kong Post has established a public key infrastructure (PKI) and acted as the public Certification Authority (CA) in Hong Kong since 31 January 2000. This provides a secure and trusted environment for the conduct of electronic transactions.

Accordingly, an Ordinance (CAP 553 ELECTRONIC TRANS-ACTIONS ORDINANCE) was enacted by the government of the HKSAR on 7 January 2000 for the purposes of:

a. facilitating the use of electronic transactions for commercial and other purposes;
b. giving electronic records and digital signatures used in electronic transactions the same legal status as that of their paper-based counterparts; and
c. establishing a framework to promote and facilitate the operation of Certification Authorities (CAs) so as to ensure trust and security in electronic transactions.

Public Key Infrastructure (PKI) covers the use of public key cryptography and digital certificates as the accepted means of authentication and access control over unsecured networks, such as the Internet. While public key cryptography addresses issues of data integrity and transaction privacy, certificates address concerns in authentication and access control.

Public key cryptography involves the use of a pair of different, but related, keys, which enables the conduct of e-commerce securely on the open telecommunications network or the Internet. Each user has a private key and a public key. The private key is kept secret, known only to the user; the other key is made public by placing it in the Public Directory maintained by the Hong Kong Post.

A digital certificate is a digital document attesting to the binding of a public key to an individual or other entity. It allows verification of the claim that a specific public key does, in fact, belong to a specific individual. A Hong Kong Post e-Cert contains a public key, the name of the holder, an expiration date, a certificate serial number and subscriber reference number.

Other Organizations of Note

While the above are the three main carriers of Hong Kong's e-commerce policy (in addition to the HKSAR government), there are a few other organizations of note that promote e-commerce in Hong Kong.

- *Supply Chain Management (SCM) Resource Centre (HKANA)*
  The Hong Kong Article Numbering Association (HKANA) provides supply chain management services such as library facilities, with a collection of the latest information and publications on e-commerce, training and education. It also has a demonstration centre that displays software applications on the various supply-chain processes.
- *Internet Business Consortium on E-commerce*
  The e-commerce portal site is maintained by the Internet Business Consortium (IBC), a non-profit organization led by the Cyberspace Centre of the Hong Kong University of Science and Technology. The site aims to provide help and information to small- and medium-sized enterprises in e-commerce solutions. A step-by-step guide on how to start an e-business is presented. Support personnel are available to provide technical advice to viewers through a forum.

E-Commerce Policy in Singapore

Singapore aspires to be a centre of international e-commerce activity. A good set of e-commerce services is available, including online payment services, security services and bureau services. The legal foundation for e-commerce is also in place. Electronic records can be used as evidence in court, and contracts formed electronically and electronic signatures are recognized. Furthermore, Singapore has an IT-literate and Internet savvy population. Some 40 percent of homes have Internet access, and there are more than 600,000 dial-up Internet subscribers. As at end 1999, the number of info-comm staff in Singapore was estimated to be 92,800. The info-comm manpower demand is projected to grow 10 to 12 percent per year for the next two years. Singapore has seven tertiary institutes offering IT studies and six research and development centres. Businesses are highly computerized, due to an 18-year history of computerization in the public and private sector. More recently, the Singapore ONE initiative has also brought about a variety of multimedia and interactive services on the Internet.

The Singaporean government is committed to making Singapore a competitive place for international e-commerce. A master plan (details below) has been formed to deliver this vision, and schemes have been designed to make this an attractive proposition.

Unlike Hong Kong, therefore, Singapore has had a well-defined e-commerce policy for a couple of years. In 1998, Singapore launched an e-commerce master plan. The launch marked the start of a campaign to bring e-commerce to mainstream businesses and to the public; and to attract international e-commerce activities to Singapore.

The government launched the e-commerce plan to drive the pervasive use of e-commerce in Singapore, and to strengthen Singapore's position as an international e-commerce hub. The target is to have S$4 billion worth of products and services transacted electronically through Singapore, and for 50 percent of businesses to use some form of e-commerce by the year 2003. This was announced by then Deputy Prime Minister BG (NS) Lee Hsien Loong at the opening of COMDEX/ASIA at Singapore Informatics '98.

Since the introduction of the Electronic Commerce Hotbed programme in August 1996, Singapore has made much progress in its e-commerce landscape. The legal framework for e-commerce is in place and the basic infrastructure services are available. There is also an increasing number of innovative and compelling e-commerce services and applications. The launch of the e-commerce plan marks the start of a campaign to bring e-commerce to mainstream businesses and the public; and to attract international e-commerce activities to Singapore. One of the main objectives of the e-commerce plan is to help businesses exploit this potential and create a strong, competitive edge for themselves.

On the national level, by developing Singapore into an international e-commerce hub, the plan aims to help create and sustain an e-commerce services sector. This will comprise business strategists, creative designers, system integrators, network operators and other e-commerce intermediaries. Another important contribution is the

additional activity that can be generated for Singapore's port, logistics, financial and telecommunications services, as a result of the mul-
tiplier effects that e-commerce has on these key sectors of the economy.

The plan has five main thrusts and various programmes and projects to drive these thrusts:

a. *To develop an internationally linked e-commerce infrastructure*
   The purpose of this thrust is to strengthen Singapore's position
   as an e-commerce hub, and the financial and logistics sectors have
   a key role to play in driving this thrust. An efficient settlement
   system for Internet transactions among businesses, covering international trade payment and multi-currency payment, has been
   planned to be deployed. Additionally, a well-connected logistics
   infrastructure has been planned to support requirements for the
   delivery of physical goods. Singapore also aims to be positioned
   as a centre of e-commerce infrastructure development, where international infrastructure players in areas such as trading platforms,
   and trust management and rights management systems will hub
   to develop and deploy services there.

b. *To jump-start Singapore as an e-commerce hub*
   This initiative focuses on the sectors in which Singapore has an
   inherent advantage as a hub, especially in business-to-business services. These advantages include a stable and excellent financial
   infrastructure, a transport and logistics infrastructure that is well
   known for its efficiency, and strong telecommunications connectivity and e-commerce infrastructure. Incentive schemes and other
   support programmes are used to attract international and local
   companies to base their e-commerce hub activities in Singapore.
   Finally, an international publicity plan is being developed, and trade
   shows are being used to promote Singapore as an e-commerce hub.

c. *To encourage businesses to use e-commerce strategically*
   Under this thrust, education and other support programmes are
   being put in place to help businesses exploit e-commerce to enhance
   their productivity and competitiveness. Simple and easy to use
   trading platforms are being provided, and a usage promotion drive
   has been launched to bring about the widespread participation of
   SMEs. To ensure a steady supply of business and technical manpower, businesses are encouraged to invest in retraining their staff
   through incentive programmes.

d. To promote usage of e-commerce by the public and businesses

This thrust enables Singaporean citizens and businesses to enjoy the benefits that e-commerce can bring, and at the same time, create an e-commerce savvy culture. Mass education efforts are being used. In addition, e-commerce has started to be taught in business and professional courses in Singapore universities and polytechnics. The government itself is setting the pace to proliferate the use of e-commerce in Singapore through its electronic public services initiatives. Key public services will be delivered electronically by the year 2001.

e. To harmonize cross-border e-commerce laws and policies

This thrust is key to enabling businesses to trade confidently with overseas partners. Besides putting in place legislation that is internationally consistent, Singapore is working with its major trading partners to align their e-commerce laws. Efforts have already been initiated with Canada, Australia and Germany. Singapore also continues to participate actively at major international forums to bring about international agreements on a harmonization of e-commerce frameworks.

A key supporting programme is Singapore's efforts to be "thought leaders" in the emerging and dynamic e-commerce scene. In particular, the Department of Statistics is leading an initiative to measure the growth of the e-commerce services sector, the contribution of e-commerce to growth in GDP, and the volume of goods transacted through e-commerce. In addition, research for e-commerce would be expanded to include policy research as well as market research. Partnerships with academia and industry to jointly sponsor and contribute to research would be sought. These programmes will advance Singapore from having the basic legal and technology infrastructure to support e-commerce now (1998), to having a critical base of e-commerce services and a reliable infrastructure in 2000, and finally, to have a sizeable amount of e-commerce transactions, an e-commerce services sector and the widespread adoption of e-commerce by the industry in 2003.

In particular, Singapore has a conducive and pro-business e-commerce environment to support the implementation and deployment of online services. This environment is the foundation and infrastructure for conducting e-business on the Internet safely and reliably.

On 13 March 2000, the S$9 million Local Enterprise Electronic Commerce Programme (LECP) began operation. The LECP aims to jump-start the mass adoption of e-commerce among local enterprises so as to exploit the full benefits of e-commerce for all industries.

LECP (EC) applies only to e-commerce services and applications. Some examples are:

- The provision of online transactional functions for a business, such as order processing.
- The provision of online services, for example, Internet banking and customer care services.
- The integration of a company's web site and internal computer system.
- The use of electronic data interchange (EDI) with business partners.

Companies that meet the following criteria can apply for assistance:

1. The companies must be locally registered.
2. The companies have equity that is at least 30 percent owned by a Singaporean.

Under the programme, the assistance provided to the companies is as follows:

- The company enjoys a free service that broadcasts the company's e-commerce adoption needs to a group of IT consultants and solution providers.
- The company receives a grant of up to 50 percent of the e-commerce project cost, to be capped at S$20,000, for each qualified local enterprise.[14]

Furthermore, the environment consists of the physical network, components and services. It also includes a collection of standards, support and incentives to assist the online business community.

Steps are also being taken to ensure that the infrastructure is internationally linked in order to support cross-border transactions, and that policies are harmonized with international practices.

---

[14] Connectivity to Singapore ONE may be included. The money can be used to cover consultancy fees, cost of hardware and software, and subscription fee (up to the first 12 months).

E-Commerce Policy in the United States of America

In contrast to Singapore, the USA takes a much less interventionist view towards e-commerce policy. The US view is recognition of the fact that governments can have a profound effect on the growth of commerce on the Internet. By their actions, they can facilitate electronic trade or inhibit it. Knowing when to act and—at least as important—when not to act, will be crucial to the development of electronic commerce.

Furthermore, in addition to the Federal Government's initiatives, there are state initiatives also. These include those from the American Bar Association (ABA), Congress, the Federal Reserve Board, the Food and Drug Administration (FDA), the National Institute of Standards and Technology, the Health and Human Services, the Internal Revenue Service, the Treasury Department, and the National Conference of Commissioners on Uniform State (NCCUSL).

As for the US government, it has articulated the administration's overall vision for the emergence of the Global Information Infrastructure (GII) as a vibrant global marketplace by suggesting a set of principles, presenting a series of policies, and establishing a road map for international discussions and agreements to facilitate the growth of commerce on the Internet. The salient points of these principles have been extracted and set out below.[15]

Principles

1. *The private sector should lead*
Though government played a role in financing the initial development of the Internet, its expansion has been driven primarily by the private sector. For electronic commerce to flourish, the private sector must continue to lead. Innovation, expanded services, broader participation and lower prices will arise in a market-driven arena, not in an environment that operates as a regulated industry.

Accordingly, governments should encourage industry self-regulation wherever appropriate and support the efforts of private sector organizations to develop mechanisms to facilitate the successful operation of the Internet. Even where collective agreements or standards are

---

[15] The full text of the report is available at http://www.ecommerce.gov.

necessary, private entities should, where possible, take the lead in organizing them. Where government action or intergovernmental agreements are necessary, on taxation for example, private sector participation should be a formal part of the policy-making process.

2. *Governments should avoid undue restrictions on electronic commerce*

Parties should be able to enter into legitimate agreements to buy and sell products and services across the Internet with minimal government involvement or intervention. Unnecessary regulation of commercial activities will distort the development of the electronic marketplace by decreasing the supply, and by raising the cost of products and services for consumers the world over.

Business models must evolve rapidly to keep pace with the break-neck speed of change in the technology; government attempts to reg-ulate are likely to be outmoded by the time they are finally enacted, especially to the extent that such regulations are technology-specific. Accordingly, governments should refrain from imposing new and unnecessary regulations, bureaucratic procedures, or taxes and tariffs on commercial activities that take place via the Internet.

3. *Where governmental involvement is needed, its aim should be to support and enforce a predictable, minimalist, consistent and simple legal environment for commerce*

In some areas, government agreements may prove necessary to facilit-ate electronic commerce and protect consumers. In these cases, gov-ernments should establish a predictable and simple legal environment based on a decentralized, contractual model of law rather than one based on top-down regulation. This may involve states as well as national governments. Where government intervention is necessary to facilitate electronic commerce, its goal should be to ensure competition, protect intellectual property and privacy, prevent fraud, foster transpa-rency, support commercial transactions, and facilitate dispute resolution.

4. *Governments should recognize the unique qualities of the Internet*

The genius and explosive success of the Internet can be attributed in part to its decentralized nature and to its tradition of bottom-up governance. These same characteristics pose significant logistical and technological challenges to existing regulatory models, and govern-ments should tailor their policies accordingly.

Electronic commerce faces significant challenges where it inter-sects with existing regulatory schemes. We should not assume, for example, that the regulatory frameworks established over the past 60 years for telecommunications, radio and television fit the Internet. Regulation should be imposed only as a necessary means to achieve an important goal on which there is a broad consensus. Existing laws and regulations that may hinder e-commerce should be reviewed and revised or eliminated to reflect the needs of the new electronic age.

5. *Electronic commerce over the Internet should be facilitated on a global basis* The Internet is emerging as a global marketplace. The legal framework supporting commercial transactions on the Internet should be governed by consistent principles across state, national, and international borders that lead to predictable results, regardless of the jurisdiction in which a particular buyer or seller resides.

In summary, the USA advocates a co-ordinated strategy that views the success of e-commerce as requiring an effective partnership between the private and public sectors, with the private sector in the lead. Government participation must be coherent and cautious, avoiding the contradictions and confusions that can sometimes arise when different governmental agencies individually assert authority too vigorously and operate without co-ordination. The variety of issues raised, the interaction among them, and the disparate fora in which they are being addressed necessitates a co-ordinated, targeted governmental approach to avoid inefficiencies and duplication in developing and reviewing policy.

Private sector leadership accounts for the explosive growth of the Internet today, and the success of electronic commerce depends on continued private sector leadership. Accordingly, the US government encourages the creation of private fora to take the lead in areas requiring self-regulation, such as privacy, content ratings and consumer protection; and in areas such as standards development, commercial code and fostering interoperability.

Problems of Hong Kong's Existing Policy on E-Commerce

E-commerce is a new field. Therefore, e-commerce policy is a newly developing area that is changing day by day. Standards and trends are different depending on geographical area, degree of Internet development, political culture, etc.

Analysis of Existing E-Commerce Policy Vehicles

The three main carriers of Hong Kong's e-commerce policy are the two industry support organizations—the Hong Kong Productivity Council (HKPC), the Trade Development Council (TDC) and the government (and the Hong Kong Post, which is a direct part of the government). These entities are achieving their objectives as regards e-commerce policy with a fair degree of success.

The HKPC's DigiHall 21 is Hong Kong's first streamlined and integrated IT promoter and service provider. DigiHall's stated objective as regards e-commerce policy is to offer integrated electronic commerce solutions to local manufacturers, traders, retailers, and other service providers. The HKPC also organizes seminars, training and workshops as well as provides business and technical advisory services and e-commerce solutions. In these regards, the centre it seems is doing a fairly good job. This was substantiated from a meeting with the centre's officer responsible for e-commerce, Ms. Ada Cheng, and from a survey of the centre's services, which include helping local companies (particularly manufacturers) set up e-commerce services in their companies (through a variety of initiatives).[16]

As for the Trade Development Council, its focus rests much more with the local trading community (as opposed to the manufacturing organizations, which are mainly targeted by the HKPC). The TDC is similar to the HKPC in that it also promotes e-commerce (but to a different sector of the business economy in Hong Kong) by organizing seminars, training and workshops as well as providing business and technical advisory services and e-commerce solutions. The TDC's mission, through its Tradelink service, is to help the local trading community enhance its efficiency and stay competitive in the global marketplace through greater use of e-commerce. Since all import and export shipments involve government documentation at some stage, Tradelink is "jump-starting" the adoption of e-commerce in Hong Kong by providing electronic services for the most commonly-used government transactions, linked to a programme of migration from paper to full electronic submission. In this respect, Tradelink has also been achieving (and continues to achieve) its objectives. For instance, the most obvious example of this is the fact that since 1st April, import

---

[16] These include subsidized hosting of web pages, designing of web pages, basic consultancy and education services, etc.

and export declarations have become fully electronic and no paper declarations are accepted when the Customs and Excise Department closes its Hong Kong Collection Office in April. The 1 April 2000 transition date marks three years to the day since Tradelink launched its electronic lodgement service in 1997. It also marks the most important step in Hong Kong's switch from paper to electronic commerce.[17]

The HKSAR government's initiatives and the Hong Kong Post's initiatives can be analyzed together, as the Hong Kong Post's establishment of the public Certification Authority was directly led by the government. In summary, the government basically began the following schemes: Electronic Services Delivery, the establishment of a public Certification Authority, and the provision of a legal framework via the Electronic Transactions Ordinance. All of these policy objectives have either been met (the establishment of the CA, and the enactment of the requisite law), and the other policy objective (the ESD) is the in process of being met (the first phase of the ESD to be launched in October this year).

From the analysis provided in the preceding sections of this paper of Hong Kong's, Singapore's and the USA's e-commerce policy, however, the main problem with respect to Hong Kong is not that the existing policy does not achieve its objectives; rather, that there are *deficiencies* or *shortcomings* in the existing policies. Existing policies do not go far enough. Specifically, the shortcomings of the existing policy are:

• Hong Kong's e-commerce policy is not detailed enough (too broad), and is not based on any solid principles.
• There is simply not enough being done by the HKSAR government with respect to e-commerce on various fronts.

---

[17] As for the non-computerized businesses or those who make only a few declarations a year, Tradelink is also providing special data processing facilities for them with a network of 27 Tradelink service centres all over the territory. Traders can also post their declarations to Tradelink for processing, or drop them into collection boxes provided at a number of Dah Sing Bank and HSBC branches. Traders, however, are reminded that with effect from 1 April, Tradelink will make an additional charge of HK$25 on all lodgements submitted in paper format through the service centers, collection boxes or postal lodgement facility, to cover the cost of data processing. Using tradelink-ebiz.com, customers can make their Internet declarations directly through the "Web Form declaration" available on the web site, thus, eliminating the need to install special software; or through an Internet-enabled version of the existing ValuNet Standard software, which carries the advantage of being able to keep customized databases and access a wide range of management reporting functions.

The fact that the HKSAR government's polices are not detailed enough and do not go far enough can be witnessed by the number of media reports that carry the same message. In March 1999, an article in AsiaInternetNews[18] made the comment that "many Hong Kong Internet professionals believe that while the government is moving on e-commerce, it is not moving quickly enough to catch up with neighboring competitive markets, Singapore and Taiwan . . . both have . . . rapidly developing e-commerce industries". Similar sentiments of Hong Kong doing "too much talking, and too little doing' " were echoed by Prof C.C. Lin, Vice President of Research and Development at The Hong Kong University of Science and Technology (HKUST).[19]

To briefly illustrate that Hong Kong's e-commerce policy is not detailed or broad enough, the case of intellectual property protection can be used. Hong Kong has had somewhat of a poor image in terms of software piracy, which is a form of breach of intellectual property rights. If the government is unable to curb intellectual property abuses in the wider community, it will have difficulties in persuading users of e-commerce that their intellectual property rights will indeed be protected. The solution to this problem would be greater education to all those involved in the community, particularly the younger generation, in order to form a mindset among the local community that breaches of copyrights and intellectual property rights are simply wrong and not acceptable.

Singapore's policy is one that is strongly government-led. On the other hand, the USA's policy differs from Singapore's quite substantially, in that the major driving principle is that of private industry taking the lead.

Possible Areas for Improvement of Hong Kong's E-Commerce Policy

There are several areas in which Hong Kong' e-commerce policy can be improved upon. These recommendations emanate mainly from an analyses of Singapore's and the USA's policies, in the areas in which the USA and Singapore are doing well with regards to their e-commerce policies.

---

[18] http://asia.Internet.com/1999/3/0103-hk.htm.
[19] *South China Morning Post*, http://www.scmp.com.

The general improvement required for Hong Kong's e-commerce policy is that it should be tighter, better co-ordinated and well rounded. At present, it is ad-hoc and perfunctory. Within this framework, the three specific recommendations for Hong Kong are as follows:

1. *To learn from the US model and develop guiding principles for the development of e-commerce policy*

As use of the Internet expands, there are numerous issues of concern that arise. For each of these concerns, there are not necessarily easy ways out and not necessarily any single answer to solve or address the issues appropriately. Potential areas of problematic regulation include taxes and duties, restrictions on the type of information transmitted, control over standards development, licensing requirements and rate regulation of service providers. Solutions have to be negotiated by balancing various concerns of society, business, governments, etc. That is not to say, however, that in that case, governments (and the HKSAR government in particular) cannot do anything; it can. The HKSAR government can have a profound effect on the growth of commerce on the Internet. By its actions, it can facilitate electronic trade or inhibit it. Knowing when to act and—at least as important—when not to act, is crucial to the development of e-commerce.

Therefore, the government should have guiding principles that oversee its specific policy development. Those guiding principles should be balanced with Hong Kong's traditional political culture (of non-interventionism) and also with the need to be the leader and aggressively promote e-commerce in society.

In particular, the HKSAR government should employ three specific principles of the USA (described in detail in the preceding sections) that are of especial appropriateness:

a. Avoid *undue* restrictions on e-commerce.
b. Where governmental involvement is needed, its aim should be to *support and enforce* a *predictable, consistent* and *simple legal environment* for e-commerce.
c. Recognize the unique qualities of the Internet.

2. *To learn from the Singapore model and develop complete e-commerce infrastructure.*[20]

Singapore's e-commerce infrastructure is quite comprehensive, yet still continues to evolve quickly. Due to the speed at which the infrastructure evolves, Hong Kong should be able to adapt to the changes of the future, by having guiding principles (see above). The infrastructure can be illustrated as a multi-tiered pyramid, where each layer provides support for the layer above, as in the figure below.

It is a complete infrastructure that Hong Kong should aim to implement. It covers all the main issues relating to e-commerce, yet provides room for the government to work with the private sector (and not necessarily take up the responsibility of providing all the aspects of the infrastructure themselves).

The e-commerce infrastructure can be categorized as follows:

• *Electronic Commerce Environment*
These are guidelines and frameworks designed to create a conducive environment for e-commerce. The environment includes:

Policy Framework
This is basically the first recommendation provided above. The framework consists of a set of guiding principles and specific policy recommendations and initiatives. The framework, which should obviously

Figure 1. Guiding Principles for E-Commerce Infrastructure Development

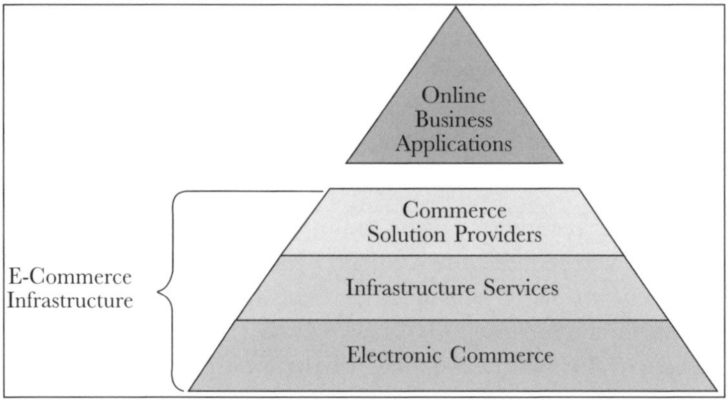

---

[20] http://www.ec.gov.sg/ECFramework6x.html.

be endorsed by the government, should set out the policy objectives of the government to work with the private sector so as to provide a conducive legal and operational environment for businesses to engage in e-commerce. It should also contain policy recommendations that are targeted to help accelerate e-commerce take-up and improve Hong Kong's competitiveness, with the view towards Hong Kong becoming a premiere e-commerce hub.

Technical Standards
These include open, industry-led, technical standards in the areas of network protocols, security, e-mail and directories, electronic commerce, and information sources and exchange. The standards facilitate the interconnection and interoperability of businesses over networks.

Legal and Regulatory Framework
For electronic commerce to flourish, there needs to be a conducive legal and policy environment. Businesses need to know that when they conduct business online, they enjoy the same legal protections as traditional businesses. This is particularly important for Hong Kong, keeping in mind the difficulties Hong Kong has had in protecting intellectual property rights in the software industry. Therefore, the legal and regulatory framework will not necessarily have to be aimed at e-commerce principally; rather, it may be more widespread and permeate to all areas of society (for instance, education for the protection of copyrights and intellectual property rights).

Various Incentive Schemes
These include investment and tax incentives for online businesses. The incentives help organizations venturing into e-commerce to manage the costs and risks of their initiatives. Currently, the HKPC and TDC provide low-cost services to companies wishing to go online. These services include web page design, web hosting, etc.

• *Infrastructure Services*

These are services that provide specific e-commerce functions, like user authentication or credit card payment processing. Typically, one or more infrastructure service is required by an electronic commerce solution. The infrastructure services can be further categorized as network services, directory services, security services and payment services.

• *Commerce Solution Providers*

These are organizations that offer complete end-to-end solutions, or packaged components of a solution, for businesses that choose not to implement electronic commerce systems on their own. There are two main industry-support organizations in Hong Kong that act as commerce solution providers—the HKPC and the TDC. They are doing a commendable job in light of the missions (analyzed in the preceding section). Their services are extremely widespread and broad, and include the provision of e-commerce solutions for individual companies to a more general educational role for e-commerce users and the public in general.

3. *To ensure that the basic institutions continue to perform healthily and effectively*

It is worth remembering, as a final point, that although the focus is on e-commerce policy, Internet (e-commerce) policy is just one of many in society. For government policies to be effective and able to meet their objectives, there are a whole set of basic institutions that have to be performing effectively even before the policies are considered. In this case, these institutions include the judiciary, the education system, and an efficient civil service. It is easy to forget the role that these vital institutions play. Their role is often taken for granted, particularly when new policies are being discussed, such as the case here. It is, however, crucial that for the "new" policies to be effective, the so-called "old" institutions have to continue to play their roles as well as—or in some cases (for instance, education), better than—they had been performing previously.

A case in point to illustrate this is the shortage of IT professionals or IT-literate people in Hong Kong. Without these sorts of people, it would be extremely difficult for the government to implement the policies outlined above. There simply would be insufficient numbers of qualified people able to implement the government's policies. Therefore, in order for government policy to be successful, it is of utmost importance that the education system in Hong Kong (and, specifically, in the higher education system) continues to perform as well as it has been doing in the past, if not even better. Only then will it be possible for talented individuals to be available in Hong Kong to understand the vital issues related to e-commerce and implement the government's policies on e-commerce. If the basic yet important education system of Hong Kong does not continue to perform as well as it has been doing, then the implementation or indeed the drafting of new policies to meet new challenges will become infinitely more arduous.

In summary, therefore, the recommendations contained here are to ensure that the basic government institutions continue to perform efficiently, and have over-arching guiding principles for e-commerce policy; then, within that framework, they can develop a complete e-commerce infrastructure.

Analysis of Policy Recommendations

The e-commerce infrastructure policy is a flexible one that allows for a great deal of room for private participation. This fact can ensure that Hong Kong need not sacrifice its traditional political culture of positive non-interventionism when it comes to developing its e-commerce infrastructure. In fact, the policy focuses on infrastructure—which is crucial. Throughout its history, Hong Kong has always been used to developing a "level playing field" and the right institutions for the pursuit of private goals. Hong Kong needs only to develop the infrastructure and from there onwards, there are plenty of non-governmental organizations, not least private firms (or indeed quasi-governmental organizations), that are (and have traditionally been) more than willing to take over the baton. This model is one that has proven its success before, and there is no reason to doubt that it will prove its success in the case of e-commerce policy.

Further evidence of the feasibility of this recommendation is given from the fact that Singapore has already adopted the strategies (policies). The Singapore government has taken a very pro-active view towards its e-commerce policy and, therefore, is a couple of years ahead of Hong Kong in this regard. Although regrettable, Hong Kong should make use of this opportunity and learn from Singapore's experience in order to first catch up and then, later, take over the city-state. The potential for e-commerce development and usage in Hong Kong is clearly much greater than in Singapore because of Hong Kong's strategic location as the entry point to Mainland China. Hong Kong should not let this opportunity pass it by and should, therefore, ensure that its e-commerce policy is a conducive and well balanced one. The fact that the policy has been proven in Singapore only adds credence to the need to adopt it, and improve on it.

One of the ways in which Hong Kong can improve on Singapore's e-commerce policy is via the other recommendation given above; that is, to adopt the USA's stance of developing *over-arching* principles for the use of e-commerce. These may, at first, seem ineffectual, but it is believed their importance is far-reaching. They help "pave the road" for the government to develop specific policy recommendations. Without a "road map" (the guiding principles), a tendency to get carried away or lose sight of a country's aims may occur. This is usual, in particular, in governments because there are so many different departments and organizations within the central government, which all try and push through their visions and individual policies. In order to maintain a level of consistency, the guiding principles can prove to be invaluable. If there is one criticism of Singapore's e-commerce policy it is that the policy can become too detailed in certain areas. In order to avoid such a case from arising in Hong Kong, the guiding principles will help as they will have to be referred to each time the government or government departments wish to set up any sort of e-commerce policy.

FRENCH SCANDALS ON THE WEB AND ON THE STREETS: A SMALL EXPERIMENT IN STRETCHING THE LIMITS OF REPORTED REALITY

RICHARD ROGERS
Department of New Media Studies
University of Amsterdam

NOORTJE MARRES
Department of Philosophy
University of Amsterdam

Methodological Dictum
If it's not on the streets, it may be on the Web
But if it's not on the Web, and it's not on the streets . . .
Case closed?
Farmers are on the streets, but who are these farmers?
Better check the Web!
Academic Graffiti, 2000

Introduction: Newsreel

On 30 June 2000, the Dutch daily newspaper, *de Volkskrant*, published a short report on the globalization protests taking place in the French town of Milau. The report referred to a "bunch of disorganized anarchists" engaged in "activist tourism". The piece also cast doubt on the viability of this form of social criticism. Referring to the smashing of windows at "MacDo" as a case in point, the piece expressed concern about the corner that activism has been backing itself into ever since the violent encounters during the WTO meeting in Seattle in 1999.

Inevitably, the Internet had a part to play in these accounts. The advent of anti-globalization protest in its current form is closely tied to the wiring up of society. The Internet was introduced as an essential for the widespread dissemination of announcements for upcoming events, as well as for in situ logistical support for the protesters. What was surprising about the role allocated to the Internet in these accounts was its depiction as a medium of convenience. Just as the activists were portrayed as youthful, backpacking travellers, the Internet was characterized as their guidebook in this particular context. The Internet served as a kind of *Lonely Planet* edition.

In this paper we will argue that the Internet—or the World Wide Web—may serve as a substantive guide to the events in Milau, France. The location and analysis of the Milau protest network on the Web will show how the Web may have provided insights into the substantial organizational efforts that were behind the event. What is more, these organizational accounts potentially served as adequate means of evaluating the larger rationale of the event. Our empirical analysis of the role of the Internet in recent global protest events, thereby, potentially undermines mass media accounts of the same. More importantly, it aims to show how the Web undermines and enriches accounts of anti-globalization protest events themselves, and the Internet. In the process, questions about the part played by social science in the broader societal critique of mass media arise, as do questions about the broader societal commitment to the new medium, not to mention social science's commitment to that commitment.

The definition of the Internet as a channel of alternative reporting, which would potentially make up for the deficits of mass media, has been evoked by both mass and Web media, ever since the integration of new media into publishing practices took off about eight years ago. Moreover, the promise of alternative media, historically, has a special status within social science. Recently, Steve Jones (2000:172) has pointed to the deep-rooted connection between social science and alternative reporting, citing an adage by John Dewey that "a proper daily newspaper would be the only possible social science." While Jones is quick to reject a simple transplantation of Dewey's grand aspirations onto the Web—by which the Internet would be embraced as a candidate for bridging the great divide between social science and the public—he does single out the definition of the Web as an alternative to off-line media. According to Jones, it is in its guise as an alternative to established reporting practices that the Web becomes an important object of social science reporting. In the case study that follows, we take up this understanding of the Web as an alternative as an empirical question worthy of investigation.

From our controlled exercise of searching the Web for alternative accounts of mass media events, we have two key findings. On the one hand, from the vantage point of empirical study, the Web cannot be properly understood as a parallel universe, existing "alongside" the world of mass media. On the other hand, the exercise indicates that the Web may be especially well equipped to serve as an informant of sociological accounts of events reported in the mass media.

Romanticisms of the Web and of the Streets:
The Web as "Reality Check"

The definition of the Internet as a realm of alternatives has been part of the repertoire of social studies of the Internet. The question of whether interactions via the Internet "complement" or "substitute" their off-line manifestations, for example, has occupied social scientists. As Sherry Turkle (1999:341) puts it, it proves difficult to keep out of the "war of the worlds" while defending or resisting the "virtual life". Even the post-disciplinary framing of a research field called "Internet studies" already contains the seeds of this conflict (Stone, 1995; Borgman, 1999). It points towards the definition of the Internet as a domain unto itself, juxtaposed with social lives off the Net. While this definition of the Internet can, of course, at all times be dismissed on methodological, theoretical or, as we will show, empirical grounds; the simple fact of dedicating one's inquiries to the one channel in particular brings along with it the risk of inadvertently choosing sides in the conflict between the virtual and the real, indeed, favouring the former.

We became particularly aware of this divide when asked by a French sociologist whether we, as Web analysts, could explain why the French did not hit the streets after a fraud scandal surrounding the Crédit Lyonnais bank. The initial suspicion handed to us was that the French may instead have "hit the Web". As Web analysts within the broader field of the sociology of scandals and protests, we sought not just to dig up alternative accounts, but also to check whether the Web perhaps provides an alternative to the streets. The definition of the Internet as alternative, not just to the news, but also to the off-line in general in this respect, seemed to come with the job of being the Web sociologist among sociologists.

Turning this problem into a virtue, we decided to go after French protesters on the Web, as a way of testing the understanding of the Web as a realm of alternatives. Using the earlier methodological dictum as a guideline, our intention was to provide a reality check for the idea that the Internet has the potential to somehow substitute the mass media, or for empty streets. We will, thus, test the twin assumptions that the Web provides an alternative to mass media reporting, and to the streets. As to the first assumption, our small experiment of "checking the Web" provided an empirical answer to the question of whether the Web can be approached as a realm that exists alongside that of mass media reporting. As to the second assumption, the aim of our small experiment was to see if and how the Web can come to our aid in filling in, and complicating, the picture of the streets. To the degree that the Web allows for a depiction of the substantial organizational efforts that go into street protests, the small experiment also provides a reality check for the romanticism of the streets—found in the mass media as well as in some social science circles—which equates real social action with street gatherings. Our small experiment, in this way, aims to provide a test of the explanatory power of the Web; on whether it can provide an account of events that add to mass media and social science reporting.

In a lecture at the British Virtual Society Research Centre, Bruno Latour (1998) argued that the Web is mainly of importance to social science insofar as it makes possible new types of descriptions of social life. According to Latour, the social integration of the Web constitutes an event for social science because the social link becomes traceable in this medium. Thus, social relations are established in a tangible form as a material network connection. We take Latour's claim of the tangibility of the social as a point of departure in our search for French protesters on the Web.

Encounters with the Street and the Web, and the Indispensability of "Webbified" Mass Media

It is important to point out that we know little of the Crédit Lyonnais scandal from our vantage points in Amsterdam and Budapest, and from our respective wired sources of knowledge and information. We hear that the French did not hit the streets because of the Crédit Lyonnais scandal. All we know in terms of the French hitting the streets, recently, concerns not bankers but French farmers. While not wishing to make too much of our semi-ignorance, we consider the circumstance favourable in light of our question, that is, what *the Web*—not merely television and the newspapers—can tell us about the French protests and scandals on the streets.

In asking whether the French hit the Web as an alternative to the streets, we are of the impression that an affirmative answer would imply a radical transformation of the rules of mobilization as they are perceived by the mass media. The problem with the Crédit Lyonnais scandal, as we speculated, was likely to be a problem of iconization.

The scandal's focal points—the *faux bilans* published by Crédit Lyonnais and the "substantial costs per French taxpayer"—assumed the form of numbers. Was it the scandal's resistance to movement from this numerical realm into the more colourful, more material realm of media icons that kept the French off the streets? If so, a solid presence of protesting French on the Web as opposed to the streets would mean that this medium in some way evaded the golden rule assumed by the mass media: iconization as indispensable for mobilization. When boarding the Web, it is precisely the hope to short cut the mass media and their golden rule of iconization that has to be stowed. In order for the uninitiated to find protesting French on the Web, a familiar starting point is required; this can be none other than a mass search engine like www.altavista.fr or a mass "journal" like www.tout.lemonde.fr.

For our attempt to locate a displaced protest surrounding the Crédit Lyonnais scandal, www.altavista.fr and www.tout.lemonde.fr provided the starting points. A story from www.tout.lemonde.fr yielded the names of the main actors involved in the scandal, among which were a number of potentially "http-ed" institutions such as Crédit Lyonais, MGM, Commission des Opérations de Bourse, la Cour des comptes, l'Inspection des Finances, le Trésor, etc. With the aid of a search engine, their URLs can be found. Yet these actors, even if they mention the scandal, do not link to one another. A Web-based network of organizations involved in or mobilizing around the scandal could not be located. In the absence of any direct acknowledgement of other parties involved among our actors, we were forced to conclude that the Web showed no sign of collective engagement with the issue.

The question of whether the Web allows for mobilization in the absence of media iconization had to be, at least for this case and at that moment, answered in the negative. In this instance, we admit we were unable to harness the explanatory power of the Web. The only way the absence of the Crédit Lyonnais issue on the Web could provide an explanation for the empty streets would be the argument that the French did not hit the streets *because* they failed to hit the Web. We would not want to go that far. Secondly, we must admit that from the standpoint of the uninitiated, an unfulfilled romanticism of the streets cannot be replaced by a romanticism of the Web. The streets are empty, but so is the Web. In the case of empty streets, the hope that mobilization may occur through the Web must be abandoned. Finally, we gladly admit that, at least for the moment, there is no need to start grappling with the issue of the absorption of the French streets by the Web. Thus, we partially fill in the dictum: There are Frenchmen not in the streets and not on the Web in the Crédit Lyonnais case. There are, however, farmers in the streets.

The television representation of French farmers on the streets looked like a proper street protest. The newspaper articles, however, presented a less straightforward story, questioning the farmers' authenticity. The site www.tout.lemonde.fr alluded to the "phoneyness" of the farmers; the Dutch newspaper *de Volkskrant* subsequently referred to a "bunch of disorganised anarchists", joyfully hopping on the protest train, whose act of "activist tourism" thereby compromised the original cause of the farmers. The involvement of an impressive range of international entities in the trial following the farmer attack on a "Macdo" seems to complicate the picture further. It is hard to believe that the international entities just dropped out of the air, as the romanticist perspective that portrays street protest as a spontaneous phenomenon might have it.

We return to our dictum:
There are Frenchmen not in the streets and not on the Web (Crédit Lyonnais).

There are farmers in the streets; but who are these farmers? (Better check the Web!)

From the newspapers, we seem to have stumbled upon the delicate subject of the French streets potentially being invaded, perhaps even taken over, by international entities. As it is not just the romanticism of the streets, but of French streets that seems shaken, the issue of the identity of the protesters becomes vital. How does one find out? Better check the Web! Whilst it is the case that, for the uninitiated, protests on the Web cannot be seen as distinct from protests on the streets, from real-worldly icons; the Web may, nevertheless, provide us with the means to stretch the limits of iconization and gain a clear view of what the farmers do besides farming.

Web Findings: Who are these Farmers? Whose are these Streets?

Following the same methodology as outlined above, involved actors were distilled from an article at www.tout.lemonde.fr, and their URLs easily found. Interestingly, even though the fact cannot be perfectly squared with allusions to "phoney farmers" made elsewhere on www.tout.lemonde.fr, our finding indicates French-only starting points, with the semi-exception of Attac, the NGO founded in France and now internationalized (see Figure 1). Our list of starting points is in keeping with the historicized French street romance of a spontaneous alliance of students and workers. The impression is only reinforced by that fact that quite a few of the web sites of the syndicates, political party branches and associations mentioned by the newspaper, do mention the farmers' trial. Was the gathering in the town of Milau, after all, predominantly French, and maybe even ad hoc?

We now turn to our homemade "netlocator" software to find out whether an authoritative network is disclosed from our chosen starting points. If it locates such a network, the "netlocator" would give us an indication of the degree to which the streets are still romantic, still French. With the netlocator serving as our medium, the Web was searched in an attempt to remake or unmake the various spectacles brought to us by CNN, *de Volkskrant* and www.tout.lemonde.fr.

Figure 1. Actors in "French Farmers Protest" Media Story

Actors from the newspaper article that (a) have a web site, (b) mention the farmers' trial and (c) link to other domains, were entered into the netlocator. Links from the URLs of the French farmers, French left-wing political parties and syndicates, French NGOs, and a network were returned through co-link analysis. This network contained mainly French political parties, syndicates and NGOs. The farmers are absent. The brief analysis yielded the view that, according to the Web, the farmers were not farmers, but mainly French "politicos". Without the farmers, we had only a portion of the ingredients for the "romantic streets" recipe. Taking these French politicos and the initial starting points, and then inputting them into the netlocator, however, returned not only French politicos, but also a significant number of international, issue-based, activist organizations, many of which are dedicated to global economy issues. There were still no farmers. Thus, according to the Web, the farmers were not farmers, but represented an organizational configuration that moved from the national to the global, and from the political-ideological to the issue-activist. As is evident from Figure 2, it was quite an organized picture, whereby not farmers, nor "phoney farmers", nor "a bunch of disorganized anarchists" made up the protests. Instead, it was a professional national-international network.

It is important to stress that merely querying the Web does not allow the uninitiated to locate the protest network. We were unable to evade the media's narrow definition of what counts as real protest. The Web, however, enabled us to put the media's rehearsals of the events as well as our friendly analysts' romanticism of the streets in their proper places, as it shows us that, like Russian dolls, organized professionals inhabited the iconized and perhaps romanticized figures of farmers (see Figure 3). By means of the Web, the limits of iconization and street romanticism can be stretched. Here, we would like to make clear, to the proverbial French romantic, that the Web does not remedy the dying romanticism of the streets. Rather, the streets are alive with "webby" networks.

Conclusions

We wish to conclude with the idea that the main virtue of the virtual is to open up the question of the real. There are four steps in this position. Firstly, one could be tempted, from the outset, to believe

Figure 2. Actors in "French Farmers Protest" Network on the Web

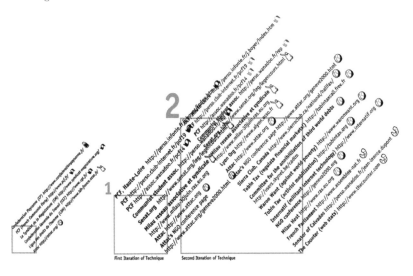

Legend

National farmers organisations

National grassroots organisations

National student organisations, unions, political parties

International grassroots organisations

Remaining

in the purity of French farmer protest and the streets, especially if one is a foreigner. Secondly, upon examination of the media, the reality of the event of French farmer street protest is compromised when it is cynically represented and mystified as "a bunch of disorganized anarchists", engaged in a novel form of conflict tourism. Such a rendering also unintentionally blurs journalism with cultural studies. Thirdly, "checking the Web" becomes a "reality check" in the sense that it allows one to fill in the integrity of the streets that were sullied and compromised through reporting. Of course, one could travel to Milau, and by observing and/or participating, capture some of the complexity of the French streets in the age of the Web. The streets, however, tend to have no names. Indeed, reports from Seattle often lacked any semblance of knowledge about the actual networks of groups involved and their positions. Sound bites on television and one-liners in newspaper articles often strip "a group calling itself . . ." of a (networked) past and a (networked) future. Only an overall anti-message from a group of protestors, plus television spectacle, was communicated. Fourthly, and finally, it could be argued that the Web and Web analyses ultimately enrich the streets. Without these, the "coded" web site for "swimmers" announcing team "meets", as was in the case of Milau, France on 30 June, would remain opaque.

In adding the description of the organizational network that supported it to the mass media accounts of the street protest, our small exercise brought in the Web and a research instrument to take up the formidable task put to social science by C. Wright Mills (1971:212) as "no less than to present conflicting definitions of reality itself." Whereas the goal of Mills' social science was to extract the marginal definitions of reality from social life by means of the interview and the survey, Web analyses can rely on pre-existing documentations of social life, having been encoded on to the Web by the actors "themselves". In the context of the new media, the staging of the conflict

Figure 3. From the Web to the Streets: French Farmers as Russian Dolls

between competing definitions of realities thus becomes a question of crossing available information streams, to bring those emanating from news agencies in contact with those generated on the Web. Insofar as the justification for this type of research is concerned, however, Mills' mission statement can be transplanted to the context of the new media virtually unchanged. It was Mills' conviction that as documenter of the conflict between dominant and marginal definitions of reality, social research counts as a viable alternative to "hitting the pavement, taking the next plane to the scene of the current crisis [. . .] or buying a newspaper plant." Web analysis adds descriptions of the encounter between action and reporting. As a footnote to Mills, however, we would like to add that in documenting that encounter on the Web, it is possible to show that *political action itself* may extend well beyond the narrow limits to action suggested by "hitting the pavement" or "buying the plant".

Methodological Appendix

We ask, who are these farmers? Or, how are we able to find (or be sure not to find) French farmers on the Web, and determine whether *they* are hitting the streets? To make a determination, one first finds the "issue network", that is, those (1) discussing and debating the "issue" and (2) mobilizing other actors to action. In order to find an issue network among the swells of sites whose issues somehow revolve around protesting French farmers, one is in need of fixed starting points. Previously, we have identified and discussed the outcomes of at least five distinct starting points for locating issue networks on the Web: search engines, associative reasoning, media stories, public actors and/or discussion lists (Rogers and Zelman, 2001). In isolation or in combination, these means of identifying starting points are aimed at finding those organizations whose sites reveal the debate most extensively by virtue of their respective link lists. This is the first step in locating an issue network. We then deploy a simple, homemade machine (the "netlocator", also called the "depluralising engine" by www.govcom.org) to "rub" the network and chart the most relevant sites. By "rub", we mean that the netlocator mines each starting point three levels deep, follows links and identifies candidate sources; those sources linked by at least two actors (in the "medium inclusiveness" setting) are brought back by the locator. The netlocator currently supports up to seven starting points. Normally, a minimum of three will suffice.

As for the different means of locating the starting points with search engines, it is assumed that the surfer knows the keywords. One uses the top returns as starting points, and rubs for a network with the machine. Associative reasoning relies on intelligent guesswork; either the issue or the presumed relevant organization is simply typed into the browser, with .org, .com or another suffix attached (in a previous case study, we began with milk.org, grains.org and corn.org). One follows links from the associatively reasoned site(s), until one finds sites displaying the debate extensively. These sites are rubbed. The third technique allows a leading media story to be the guide; those organizations mentioned are then located either through a search engine, or by associative reasoning. The URLs are then rubbed. Public actors are similarly located; one presumes well-known public actors (for example, Greenpeace for climate change) will display the debate around an issue extensively, and they are located through a search engine or by associative reasoning. One could also subscribe to a discussion list about the topic in question, and chart the links recommended by the discussants in their ongoing postings over a particular period in time. It is important to note that each means relies on distinctly different "expertise" or "recommenders" with varying epistemological and "info-societal" consequences for each of the subsequent networks located (Marres and Rogers, 2000).

We present the case study with the aid of the "diary of a crawler". The kept log explains how the network is located; it also details the most significant finding touched upon above, that is, *the de-iconization of the romantic French streets by organized, virtual ... global civil society*. We present the case through the following steps:

1. Knowing nothing of the issue concerning French farmers, we turned to www.tout.lemonde.fr. There was no need to take recourse to their *moteur de recherche*; the first headline on their homepage staged our farmers. The issue, according to *le toutlemonde* (http://www.lemonde.fr/article/0,2320,seq-2030–74010–QUO,00.html):

> Evénement planétaire à Millau, Aveyron: 30 000 à 50 000 manifes-
> tants venus du monde entier sont attendus pour le procès, le 30 juin,
> de José Bové. Figure emblématique de la résistance à la mondialisa-
> tion, il sera jugé pour avoir attaqué, en août 1999, le McDonald's en

construction dans cette ville. La chaîne américaine CNN a installé ses caméras dans plusieurs appartements face au tribunal.

Then some background:

Le 12 août 1999, un groupe de trois cents éleveurs du Syndicat des producteurs de lait de brebis et de la Confédération paysanne « démontent » virilement le restaurant McDonald's en construction dans la ville. Avec M. Bové à leur tête, ils entendent protester contre la surtaxation américaine du fromage de roquefort après que l'Union européenne eut décidé de ne plus importer de viande aux hormones des Etats-Unis.

2. The article yielded a long list of potentially webby (http-ed) actors:

- CNN (present at the scene)
- José Bové (leader of the resistance)
- *Le Syndicat des producteurs de lait de brebis* (farmers)
- *La Confederation paysanne* (farmers)
- Lori Wallace of Public Citizen ("expert" witness in the trial)
- CGT (Confederation Generale du Travail)
- Les SUD (Solidaire, Unitaire et Démocratique, a *syndicat*)
- CNT (Confederation Nationale de Travail)
- PS (Socialist party)
- PCF (Communist party)
- Verts (Green party)
- LCR (Ligue Communiste Revolutionnaire)
- Ligue des droits de l'homme (a human rights organization)
- DAL (Droit au Logement)
- Attac (association of citizens, newspapers and *syndicat*)
- Droits Devant! (human rights organization, linked to DAL)
- Le Syndicat de la Magistrature (a *syndicat*)

3. Most of these actors were easily found by surfing search engine returns (www.altavista.fr) and by following links. That is to say, we were on familiar ground where the behaviour of civil society actors was concerned; we had linking organizations that disclosed their cohorts. A selection of these actors (those that had web sites, discussed the issue, and linked to other actors) was ready to be fed into the network locator. Judging from the intensity of linking, a demarcated sample would have probably emerged, and we would have had the makings of an issue network map.

4. As is often the case with freshly erupted events, two actors presented as central players by the newspaper, *Syndicat des producteurs de
lait de brebis* and the French McDonald's, had a very thin presence
on the Web. The site www.altavista.fr returned only five entries when
queried for the *syndicat*: three online newspaper articles (*midilibre*);
the *confederation paysanne*; and *milau-clic*, a local portal for the town
that was our scene of action (for reasons that are easy to guess, that
site was almost impossible to reach on 30 June 2000—a protest day).
The *syndicat* did not own its own domain on the Web, and
www.Macdonalds.fr was "under construction". For the sake of contrast, we would like to mention that during the Kyoto Conference
on Climate Change (1998), the web site of Shell, a main target of
the CO_2 emission reduction lobby, initially remained more or less
silent on the issue. When British eco-terrorists destroyed GM crops
in the summer of 1999, the Monsanto web site initially showed no
sign of awareness of the protests against its business. While McDonald's
is certainly less central to the farmers' protest, and the fact that its
site was under construction most probably due to other reasons, it
is surprising to notice how actors that are at the centre of the action
according to the mass media, remain in the background on the Web,
at least initially.

5. Judging from its "links in from the issue-network", the following
site has a solid presence: http://www.millau-30juin.ras.eu.org. It is
a practical information site set up by, well, some of the people
involved. Self-evidently, this site did not figure in the newspaper article. Newspapers only go so far in contributing to mobilization.

6. As to the question of whether "they" were really farmers, the
answer seemed to depend on the centrality of the *confederation paysanne*
(farmers' federation) in the network. In any case, it was clear that
there were many people in Milau dressed up as farmers; or more
accurately, the farmers were serving as "dress" for many other players. Not surprisingly, it turned out that for .orgs, it was more a question of going to where the action was, than whether one was already
tied to the issue. The organizations involved range from "against
homelessness" to "the workers" to "the environment". That is to say,
they did not exactly have careers in farming. They were civil society swarmers.

On a final note, it should be mentioned that two domains that appeared in the Credit Lyonnais scandal also figured at http://www.verts.imaginet.fr and wanadoo.fr.

Actors in "French Farmers Protest": Media Story Network

• Confederation Paysanne (CP)	http://www.confederationpaysanne.fr/
• Ligue des droits de l'homme (LDH)	http://www.ldh-france.asso.fr/
• Attac	http://attac.org/
• CNT energie (CNT)	http://assoc.wanadoo.fr/energie/
• PCF (French Communist Party)	http://www.pcf.fr/
• Les Verts	http://www.verts.imaginet.fr/
• Le Syndicat de la Magistrature (SM)	http://www.syndicat-magistrature.org/
• Confederation Generale du Travail (CGT)	http://www.cgt.fr/
• LCR	http://www.lcr-rouge.org/
• DAL	http://www.easynet.fr/appelsan/dal.html
• Droits Devant (DD)	http://www.easynet.fr/appelsan/mani.html

Having found these linking actors with so little effort, the presence of an issue-network was to be expected. Thus, the network locator was called in to crawl and cull the network.

The link lists of CP, CNT, PCF, Verts and CGT above were inputted as starting points. Hit and crawl from CP, CNT, PCF, Verts and CGT brought up the following actors:[1]

• PCF, Haute-Loire	http://perso.infonie.fr/j.boyer/index.htm
• PCF	http://perso.club-internet.fr/pcf19
• PCF	http://assoc.wanadoo.fr/pcf14
• Communist student association	http://perso.wanadoo.fr/rep

---

[1] By hit and crawl, it is meant that the locator crawls the site three levels deep and follows the outward links to sites other than its own; those sites linked by at least two actors in the sample are returned by the locator.

- Attac, Toulon   http://perso.infonie.fr/lvaisse/
- CGT   http://www.multimania.com/cgtforclum
- CGT   http://assoc.wanadoo.fr/ufcmpx

It is clear that these starting points disclose a national kinship network of allied organizations. Perhaps, interestingly, *confederation paysanne*—the organization presented as central by the newspapers and one that could be regarded as such on the basis of its site—was not in the webby issue network. Also, note the frequency of the *perso* (personal) domain. This brings to the surface that there are people (identifiable people, no less) behind this protest event! In the Crédit Lyonnais scandal, people were not self-evident. The former crawl being a trial, six starting points were next entered: CP, LDH, Attac, PCF, SM, CGT (leaving out those public actors that did not discuss the issue). Hit and crawl brought us the following:

- Attac's NGO   http://www.attac.org/geneve2000.html
  conference page
- *Le Monde*   http://www.monde-diplomatique.fr/md/1997/
  Diplomatique   12/ramonet/9665.html
- PCF, Haute-   http://perso.infonie.fr/j.boyer/index.htm
  Loire
- PCF   http://perso.club-internet.fr/pcf19
- PCF   http://assoc.wanadoo.fr/pcf14
- Communist   http://perso.wanadoo.fr/rep
  student
  association
- Senat.org   http://www.senat.org/leg/legencours.html
- *Milau reseau*   http://www.milau-30juin.ras.eu.org
  associative et
  syndicale

Then, we inputted this actor network and the original starting points. This rub would affirm the presence of an issue-network if the sites returned here overlapped with original starting points, and with these actors themselves. The second rub would yield medium threshold yields:

- Attac's NGO   http://www.attac.org/geneve2000.html
  conference page
- Attac Netherlands http://www.attac.nl

- *Le Monde*   http://www.monde-diplomatique.fr/md/
  Diplomatique   1997/12/ramonet/9665.html
- PCF, Haute-   http://perso.infonie.fr/j.boyer/index.htm
  Loire
- PCF   http://perso.club-internet.fr/pcf19
- PCF   http://assoc.wanadoo.fr/pcf14
- Communist student   http://perso.wanadoo.fr/rep
  association
- Senat.org   http://www.senat.org/leg/legencours.html
- *Milau reseau associative* http://www.milau-30juin.ras.eu.org
  et syndicale
- French Parliament   http://www.assemblee-nat.fr
- Senator of Calvados   http://perso.wanadoo.fr/jean-leonce.dupont
- Sierra Club, Canada   http://www.sierraclub.ca/national/halifax/
- The Counter   http://www.thecounter.com
  (web stats)
- *Tobin Tax* (regulate   http://tobintaxcall.free.fr
  financial markets!)
- Committee on   http://users.skynet.be/cadtm
  annihilliation of
  Third World debt
- *Waron Want* (against   http://www.waronwant.org
  world poverty)
- *Tobin Tax* (activist   http://tobintax.org
  mobilization)
- *Internatif* (militant http://www.internatif.org
  internet technology)
- Lyon organization   http://www.alyon.asso.fr
- NGO conference   http://geneva2000.org
- Milau host   http://www.ras.eu.org

We noticed the globalizing tendencies of issue networking. In the second rub, many more international organizations were returned, and again, the *confederation paysanne* is absent. What is more, the delocalized issue of the regulation of markets re-emerged at the second rub, where it seemed to have been absorbed by French revolutionary politics after the first rub.

THE REVENGE OF THE MACHINES:
ON MODERNITY, DIGITAL TECHNOLOGY
AND ANIMISM

Stef Aupers
Faculty of Social Sciences
Erasmus University Rotterdam

Introduction

William Gibson's influential science fiction novel, *Neuromancer* (1984), is mainly located in cyberspace. Case, the protagonist, speaks contemptuously about the limitations of our earthly existence and refers to the human body as "meat" or "prison of flesh". As a result of this, Case prefers to live in the immaterial realm of cyberspace where he meets a variety of strange characters such as Riviera, a cyborg with occult capacities; Flatline, a deceased hacker whose soul is still wandering through the matrix; and Linda, his dead, but virtually reincarnated ex-girlfriend.

In short, Gibson imagines cyberspace as a sort of heaven where the souls of the living and the dead meet. Technology and religion, generally assumed to be incompatible realms, are interwoven with ease in *Neuromancer*. Of course, the book can be considered as merely the result of Gibson's literary imagination. In fiction, by definition, everything is possible. Unexpectedly, however, several non-fiction authors are also taking the relationship between technology and religion more seriously. The physicist and mathematician Margaret Wertheim, for instance, claims in her book, *The Pearly Gates of Cyberspace: A History of Space from Dante to the Internet* (1999), that the modern, scientific age resulted in an expansion of "physical space", while "soul space" has become increasingly marginalized. In her view, the rise and widespread application of the Internet changes this situation. She considers this medium a "technological substitute for the Christian space of Heaven" (Wertheim, 1999:16). In general, there are various indications that the "digital revolution" triggers a variety of religious, esoteric and occult impulses. Even the journal *Technology and Society* recently dedicated a whole issue to the "spiritual dimension of new technology".

Kevin Kelly, one of the contributors to this special issue, makes the point that "computers have become a spiritual event for humans" (Kelly, 1999:388). The journalist Erik Davis goes even further. Deploying the ideas of Max Weber, he argues that "it is perhaps inevitable that the cosmological imagination returns, attempting to revive and re-enchant the patterns and logic of the material world" (Davis, 1996:11).

This article is the result of an empirical study of the affinity between new technology and religion. I will limit myself to one specific manifestation of this relationship. In his book, *TechGnosis: Myth, Magic and Mysticism in the Age of Information*, Erik Davis (1998) writes about a group of Information and Communication Technology (ICT) experts who refer to themselves as "technopagans", "technoshamans" and "technowitches". According to Davis, these people assume that "the postmodern world of digital simulacra is ripe for the premodern skills of the witch and magician" (Davis, 1998:188). Although these techno-pagans form a relatively small, marginal group, they can be seen as exemplars for a more general development of "technological animism" or "technoanimism" (Davis, 1998:187). Apparently, some computer experts see our technological surroundings as some sort of animated, living force, in much the same way as the premodern animist saw his natural surroundings. Similarly, the Dutch anthropologist Jojada Verrips (1993:71) speculated on different modern manifestations of what he calls "modern animism", and wrote about "machine animism".

If these loose speculations are correct, then they are sociologically relevant. Sociologists generally consider the progress of science and technology as the main driving forces behind what Weber called the "disenchantment of the world" (1996:17). This assumption also forms the core of the thesis of secularization. Bryan Wilson, for instance, commenting on the strong influence of technology on the process of secularization, notes that:

> Secularization is in large part intimately involved with the development of technology, since technology is itself the encapsulation of human rationality. Machines, electronic devices, computers, and the whole apparatus of applied science are rational constructs. They embody the principles of cost efficiency, the choice of the most effective means to given ends, and the elimination of all superfluous expenditure of energy, time, or money. The instrumentalism of rational thinking is powerfully embodied in machines (Wilson, 1976:88).

From this perspective, it is remarkable that religious impulses appear in the field of technology. Animism, according to classical authors such as Comte, Tylor, Marett and Freud, can even be seen as the most "primitive" form of religion. Comte, for instance, compares the "intellectual level" of the animist with that of the "higher species of animals" (Comte, 1979:49). According to the Freudian psychoanalytical approach, animistic ideas are nothing less than infantile fantasies, neuroses and psychologically damaging illusions. From the typically evolutionary perspective of these authors, animism can essentially be seen as a primitive stage in the history of humanity that lies far behind us and will never return. If animistic ideas and sentiments still exist then, according to these scientists, they will not be found among technological experts, who are, after all, the main agents of our rational, secular and disenchanted society.

These preliminary considerations lead to the following questions that I will try to answer in this study: Is there any evidence of animistic ideas and sentiments among ICT specialists? If so, how are they manifested and how does one account for the appearance of this form of religion in one of the most rational and advanced sections of society? In order to obtain empirically based insights into these questions, I have conducted a qualitative analysis of *Wired*, a well-known American magazine on new technology. Before presenting the results of this analysis, I will define animism and examine the parallels that exist between the animistic vision on the material environment and technological developments in the field of artificial intelligence and artificial life. My argument is that these technical developments constitute the main condition for late modern technoanimism.

Parallels: Animism, Artificial Intelligence and Artificial Life

In contemporary sociological and anthropological literature, the term "animism" is seldom used because it is considered outdated and contaminated by the evolutionary, positivistic and ethnocentric approach of authors such as Comte, Marett, Tylor and Freud. They addressed the subject around the turn of the nineteenth century, and I will use their work to define animism. For my purpose, the discussion between Tylor (1977) and Marett (1914) is relevant. These scholars wrote most substantially about animism in their search for what Tylor called "the minimum definition of religion".

The premodern animist, according to Tylor, saw his natural environment and the earth, the rocks, the trees, the moon and the stars essentially as living objects with souls. In other words, the material world was originally seen as charged with spiritual forces and, at a later stage, with well-defined entities or a variety of gods that gave each object its specific quality. Tylor considered animism, essentially, as a primitive and false way of intellectual reasoning. If people have a soul, the animist falsely generalized, why would not nature and the objects that surround me have souls as well? Directly connected with this belief in the subjectivity of the material environment is the power that objects exercise over the human lifeworld. Premodern animists, according to Tylor, see themselves as surrounded by supernatural forces and, consequently, as having limited control over their direct environment. Trees, for instance, are for the animist not passive objects but entities with good and bad intentions. In this context, Tylor writes, "spiritual beings are held to affect or control the events of the material world, and man's life here and hereafter" (1977:426).

Tylor's definition of animism has been criticized by many authors (Hamilton, 1995:45–54). The most substantial critique was offered by Marett (1914) and concerns Tylor's intellectualistic approach. Animism, Marett argues, is not just a primitive way of philosophizing but is, above all, rooted in the emotional realm. Confronted with their natural environment, premodern people experienced mysterious and undefined powers or *mana*. According to Marett, the experience of *mana* could lead to animistic philosophy and, eventually, to well-defined polytheism, but these ideas were just secondary intellectualizations of basic religious feelings. The basic religious feeling that premodern people experienced was humility, which manifested itself in both fear and fascination for the natural environment. A mixture of these feelings, especially awe, is important because "of all English words awe is, I think, the one that expresses the fundamental religious feeling most nearly" (Marett, 1914:13). According to Marret, animism is essentially one of the first intellectual manifestations of these archaic religious feelings.

It seems that the intellectual and emotional definitions by Tylor and Marett can easily be combined into a threefold definition. In this article, I consider animism as (1) the attribution of subjective characteristics to the material environment, combined with (2) the assumption that objects actively and autonomously exercise influence over the human lifeworld, which is accompanied by (3) feelings of humility manifesting itself in fear, fascination and "awe". This threefold definition will be the main focus in the following empirical analysis.

Despite their polemic, Tylor and Marret agree on one point—as a result of the progress in science and technology, animism is bound to disappear from Western society. Ironically, however, contemporary developments in the field of technology have made the relationship between humans and their material environment more complex, and have problematized the Cartesian dichotomy of subject and object. Due to the influence of scientists such as Marvin Minsky, Claude Shannon and Allan Turing, a new discipline called artificial intelligence emerged after World War II. Minsky formulated the basic goal of artificial intelligence as "trying to get computers to do things that would be considered intelligent if done by people" (cited in Turkle, 1995:125). Not surprisingly, the developments in this field were accompanied by philosophical discussions about the degree to which high-tech computers and robots could already think. Questions such as "Can these complex machines reason?"; "Are they conscious?"; or "can they feel?" are, until today, the theoretical by-product of this discipline. In other words, because of the input of artificial intelligence, computers and robots are increasingly seen as subjective or intelligent entities. Originally, these technologists worked from a "top-down" approach. With this approach, computers are programmed with a variety of well-defined rules, forms of behaviour and actions and, consequently, behave intelligently but predictably. This "top-down" approach differs radically from the "bottom-up" approach that was developed in the late 1980s. In this method of working, often referred to as artificial life, machines are no longer directly programmed. The technologists create an artificial context in which the artefacts are stimulated to learn, develop and evolve like biological organisms. Noble (1999) and Turkle (1996) broadly summarize this development as "emergent artificial intelligence". In their view, the key characteristic of artificial life is the open-endedness of the process and the unpredictability of the results. Speculating on the dramatic impact of artificial life, Kelly writes that "the world of the made will soon be like the world of the born: autonomous, adaptable and creative but, consequently, out of control" (Kelly, 1994:4).

What do these developments in the field of modern technology have to do with animism? Apparently, there are parallels—like animists, technologists working in the field of artificial intelligence attribute subjective characteristics to lifeless objects. The attitude of these specialists, therefore, complies with the first criterion of the three-fold definition of animism. It would, however, be false to simply conclude that these experts in artificial intelligence are late modern technoanimists. The crucial difference can be found in the fact that they actively construct intelligent entities such as robots, high-tech computers and "digital organisms". This construction occurs on a basis of exact scientific knowledge and experiments that take place between laboratory walls. The attribution of subjective qualities to these machines is, therefore, not a false generalization—as Tylor suggests is the case with animists—but the logical result of a conscious and purposive implementation of human characteristics in these objects. In short, there is an objective foundation for the interpretation of technologists and philosophers that we are dealing here with intelligent entities. Despite the evident parallels, experts in the field of artificial intelligence are not animists.

So far, this paper has focused on technological developments between laboratory walls. Technology, however, is not neutral but is influenced and driven by cultural norms and values, and it evokes various cultural reactions (Pacey, 1983). The Dutch philosopher Rein de Wilde (2000) has demonstrated that the emergence of computer technology is accompanied by exaggerated expectations, utopian thought and the mystification of digital technology. In this paper, my aim is to focus on the meanings that people attribute to technology. More specifically, I want to investigate whether artificial intelligence, artificial life and their practical manifestations trigger technoanimistic ideas and sentiments. The empirical data for the analyses of these issues comes from *Wired* magazine.

The Technoanimistic Discourse in Wired *(1993–2000)*

Wired magazine covers all aspects of the digital revolution and is one of the most authoritative forums for analyses of the Internet. The contributors to its pages include computer scientists and people from the industry, such as Steve Jobs, Steven Wozniak, Marvin Minsky and Bill Joy. *Wired* is not an obscure, marginal or religious magazine. Another reason for the selection of *Wired* for this research is the fact that unlike most scientific journals, it does not aim to provide neutral, purely scientific information about technology. Rather, the magazine reflects the "culture of technology" (Pacey, 1983). One journalist associated with *Wired* contends that it "was the first main-stream magazine to demonstrate that 'culture' and 'computing' were not mutually exclusive" (Borsook, 2000:119). In short, the popularity of *Wired*, and the fact that it covers subjective ideas and the opinions of various specialists on technology, makes it a legitimate source for sociologists of culture.

New Technology as an Artificially Intelligent Force of Nature

According to E.B. Tylor, the fact that animists attribute subjective qualities to their natural surroundings, the earth, the trees and rocks has far-reaching consequences. Animists conceptualize themselves as surrounded by intelligent forces and powers and, consequently, have limited control over their environment. In the context of this study, the question is whether the same attitude is reflected in *Wired*. To what degree do the authors see their technological environment as constituted by forces emanating from artificial intelligence and, therefore, relatively out of control?

The articles in *Wired* often elaborate on the far-reaching consequences of artificial intelligence and artificial life for the human lifeworld. Technologists, according to Johnson (January 2000), generally find "the sociological implications as fascinating as technique itself." In this context, attention is paid to advanced artificially intelligent toys like Barney, Tamagotchi and Furby. In one article entitled "Moody Furballs and the Developers Who Love Them" (Kirsner, September 1998), it is stated that Furbies are appealing primarily because they act as if they are alive. Furbies not only behave like living creatures but also have unique characteristics. They are programmed to learn from interaction with children and, according to their manufacturers, show unpredictable or even irrational behaviour.

The author of the article assumes that the commercial success of Furby is exemplary in the widespread advance of artificially intelligent toys in the lifeworld of children. For the author, Furbies could be the *Australopithecus afarensis* of an entire race of artificially intelligent toys. Artificial intelligence is not only implemented in toys but is also used in "smart" household devices. According to some authors, this will eventually result in a "living material environment". Another article on MEM (very small microchips), for instance, states that:

> Within 20 years, there will be no avoiding MEMS: They will be in
> every telecom line, computer, and coffeemaker—even in our own bod-
> ies. As these sensors and actuators—devices that react to their envi-
> ronments—permeate the world, the fabric of daily existence will come
> alive (Leonard, January 2000).

Another author echoes a similar sentiment:

> Your environment will become alive with technology . . . The walls will
> contain logic, processors, memory cameras, microphones, communica-
> tors, actuators, sensors (Johnson, January 2000).

Is it possible to equate a "living material environment" with animism?
The following quotes indicate that the description "alive" in this context cannot simply be seen as a metaphor. Although various authors
in *Wired* assume that our material environment will "come alive with
technology", it is important to note that they often also think that
technology will increasingly "lead its own life". This distinction is
important in the context of this study. If artificial constructions "lead
their own life" then this means that they can withdraw from the rational control of their creators and, more generally, from that of human
action. In this regard, the material in *Wired* complies with both the
first and second criteria of techno-animism—not only are subjective
characteristics attributed to technological "things", but these things
are also believed to autonomously influence the human lifeworld.
Many of the articles in which this development is represented cover
the implications of artificial life and related techniques, such as "ecological computing", "evolutionary programming" or "artificial evolution" on society.

   Another example is the article "Do-It-Yourself-Darwin" (Frauenfelder,
October 1998). The author writes about the Galapagos project, in
which technologists allow programmed "digital organisms" to evolve
into more complex and more beautiful organisms. This project is
based on the Darwinian concept of the "survival of the fittest". In
a similar project, computer specialists constructed a "digital eco-
sphere"—in which digital organisms can freely develop (Dibbel,
February 1995). The following statement was made about the leader
of this project:

> Ray, convinced that his programs are as good as alive, calls them sim-
> ply 'organisms', or 'creatures'. Whatever they are, though, he's been
> breeding quite a lot of them. He's been breeding them with the full
> support of his university employers, with the financial backing of major

corporations, and with the steadily growing curiosity and respect of fellow researchers in the fields of both biology and computer science (Dibbel, 1995).

The fact that Ray is "convinced that his programs are as good as alive" indicates an animistic view. Due to his conviction, the denotation "alive" cannot be construed simply as a metaphor. Ray would like to continue his experiments on the World Wide Web. He assumes that the evolution of digital organisms will accelerate enormously in this "open climate". He does not, however, have permission to do this since this evolution would be totally out of control. He is, therefore, compelled to continue his project within the limits of a closed computer system.

According to various articles in *Wired*, Ray's prognosis has already been realized. Several authors assert that during the 1990s, the number of forms and manifestations of artificial life on the Internet and the World Wide Web has rapidly increased. These digital organisms, although programmed by humans, increasingly lead a "life of their own". They demonstrate, according to *Wired*, specific human-like behaviour. They multiply, evolve and mutate. In most cases, these creatures on the World Wide Web are referred to as "viruses", "bots" and "personal agents". Due to the rapid increase of artificial life on the Web during the 1990s, this period is sometimes compared with the Cambrium Explosion in biological evolution:

> In the annals of bot evolution, IRC in the mid-90s will probably be remembered as the bot equivalent of the Cambrium Explosion—a relatively short period 540 million years ago that spawned more new species then ever before or since (Leonard, April 1996).

The article "Viruses are Good for You" (Dibbel, February 1995) covers the development of viruses. These were placed on the Internet by anarchistic hackers with mythical names such as Dark Avenger and Hellraiser. Originally, the virus was nothing more than a kind of "digital graffiti". The rapid evolution towards complex artificial life, however, can be explained by the battle between hackers and anti-virus teams such as McAfee. About this, the author writes:

> Once anti-virus software was introduced into the cybernetic ecology, viruses and the programs that stalk them have been driving each other to increasing levels of sophistication. This is nothing less than the common co-evolutionary arms race that arises between predators and prey in organic ecosystems (Dibbel, 1995).

A digital organism that is related to the virus is the "bot". Bots are also called "spiders", "wanderers" or "worms". In "Bots are Hot!" (Leonard, April 1996) the author defines a bot as "a software version of a mechanical robot . . . that performs functions normally ascribed to humans." He adds to this definition:

> Even more important than function is behavior—bonafide bots are programs with personality. Real bots talk, make jokes, have feelings, even if those feelings are nothing more than cleverly conceived algorithms (Leonard, 1996).

The World Wide Web and, especially MUDs and newsgroups, are brimming with bots that all have different functions, "personalities" and ways of behaving. According to the author, some virtual communities are even closed nowadays because there are more uncontrollable bots than people. This often leads to confusion. Some bots are so ingeniously programmed that people do not immediately notice that they are talking to a virtual conversation partner. Vernon Vinge says in *Singular Visionary*: ". . . there are MUD participants who are robots right now, some of them very good. You never quite know whom you're dealing with" (Kelly, June 1995).

What kinds of bots are there and how exactly do they behave? The author states that "to unravel their taxonomic threads is no simple task: it demands a Darwin." The first "software robot", however, was developed in the 1990s by a MIT professor and is called Eliza. She is the prototype of all contemporary bots. *Wired* did an interview with Eliza and asked her: "Do you know you are the mother of all bots?" Eliza, who is programmed to be a humanistic psychologist, answered: "Does it please you to believe I am the mother of all bots?" Eliza is classified as a "chatterbot". Her "offspring", however, can be categorized in an amazing number of groups such as "gamebots", "gaybots", "hookerbots", "checkerbots", "warbots", "annoybots", "clonebots", "killerbots" and many others. In most cases, bots have the task of making life easier for people in MUDs and newsgroups. For instance, they provide information and introduce new participants to the virtual MUD community. Increasingly, however, bots cause problems in these virtual communities. Leonard mentions two main reasons. For one, a programming error can result in an uncontrollable, mutating bot. An example is the so-called "floodbot" that generates incoherent text on the Net. More problematic, according to the author, are the bots that are deliberately designed to irritate people. An example is the "annoybot" that can suddenly appear in discussion groups, will immediately reproduce itself and gibber subversive phrases. When this bot is thrown out of a community, it will return in greater numbers. Other examples are the "guardbot" (follows you wherever you go), the "spybot" (monitors a conversation and sends the information to its maker), the "bumbot" (does not go away before it gets money) or the "hookerbot" (makes "indecent proposals").

In short, various authors have argued that a growing number of different bots "live" on the World Wide Web. Once on the Web, they autonomously evolve, reproduce and mutate without the helping hand of human beings. One can, of course, write about these botsin pure technical terms; the authors, however, see these creations as living entities and, consequently, write about them in animistic terms. In the words of Leonard (1996): ". . . they're breeding like mad in the hidden swamps of the digital wilderness." About the dominance of these digital organisms in cyberspace, he states:

> Bots are everywhere in the online universe—roaming the interstices of the World Wide Web; lounging about in MUDs and MOOs; patrolling Usenet newsgroups . . . They will not go away. The future of cyberspace belongs to the bots (Leonard, 1996).

In addition to the virus and the bot, attention is also paid to the "personal agents". In the article "Super Searcher" (Whalen, May 1995), these are defined as "digital butlers that roam the Infobahn gathering data for you—based on your needs—and learn more about your interests over time." In fact, the personal agent can be considered an advanced bot and is, in a sense, the constructive counterpart of the destructive virus. In an article titled "Agent of Change" (Berkun, April 1995), personal agents are labelled our "alter egos" on the World Wide Web because, according to the author: ". . . they will know what we are interested in, and monitor databases and parts of networks."

The articles in *Wired* on digital organisms show that the technological environment is no longer seen as inanimate and fully under control. The viruses, "bots" and personal agents are portrayed as kinds of "spiritual beings" that live on the World Wide Web, and have good and bad intentions. More generally, many articles describe new technology as an organic, uncontrollable and "irrational" force of nature. This is remarkable because contrary to the classical modern perspective where nature is seen as a mechanical and, therefore, controllable machine, *Wired* portrays new technology as an uncontrollable, artificial force of nature. In the article "Only Connect", for instance, the World Wide Web is compared to the "ocean", "the air", "a biological system" (Johnson, January 2000). The author of "Web of Weeds" (Levinson, November 1995) contends that:

> Many of us are quick to laud nature as a model for technology. The truth is we prefer our devices to be unnaturally consistent. Yet the weed may be the prime mover of our digital works. The links that shoot across the Web may be the result of someone's intention, but no one has planned or even knows the extent of the interconnections. There is no real librarian on the Web, no master gardener: links seem to spring up on their own. They thrive without tending, harking back to a world before agriculture (Johnson, 2000).

Nature is not merely used as a metaphor. Increasingly, theories, concepts and methods of biological science enter the area of technological engineering. Technologies such as "ecological computing" and others are often mentioned in *Wired* and are an indication of this development. In other words, the interpretation of new technology as an artificially intelligent force of nature also changes the practical working method. Johnson (January 2000) makes a prognosis about this by arguing that "the network of today is engineered, and the network of 2050 is grown." According to the prediction of Vinge (January 2000), this will happen within a few years. He believes that "by 2007, the largest control systems are being grown and trained, rather than written." The authors of "Out of Control" (Pauline, DeLanda and Dery, September/October 1993) even state that every human attempt to fully control our contemporary technological systems is doomed to fail. They seek alternatives in irrational interaction with machines:

> Systems are getting so complicated that they're out of control in a rational sense. To avoid self-destruction, we have to start thinking of our interaction with technology in terms of the intuitive, the irrational (Pauline, DeLanda and Dery, 1993).

The Rebirth of Humility, Fear, Fascination and Awe

According to Marett, the origin of religion can be found in "the birth of humility" (Marett, 1914:169–202). Premodern people, he argues, felt primarily humble in relation to the supernatural and mysterious forces they were surrounded by. This manifested itself in feelings of fear, fascination and awe. Up to this point, this analysis demonstrated that the authors in *Wired* often imagine their technological environment to be an artificially intelligent force of nature that is, to a certain degree, out of control. In the next section, I will explore the question whether, and to what degree, this view is accompanied by humble, and, according to Marett, religious feelings.

Various descriptions in *Wired* reflect a certain degree of fear, fascination and awe. One of the topics in this context is the expressed fear of advanced computers and robots. It is often argued that human beings are no longer the masters of their own creations. Rather, they will increasingly compete with, or even battle against, these complex machines. A concrete example is the chess computer. The article "The Last Human Chess Master" (Goldsmith, February 1995), covers the battle between the chess champion Kasparov and what he refers to as "the silicon monster". Originally, Kasparov ridiculed the idea of being beaten by a computer. At a tournament in München in 1994, however, he lost his first match to "Fritz 3". After that day, Kasparov has kept insisting that the computer would never be able to rival with human beings in the game of chess: "Chess is not mathematics", he insists, "Chess is fantasy; it's our human logic, not a game with a concrete result." With the development of "Deep Blue", the newest chess computer, his position is getting more and more problematic:

> Kasparov's confidence when he speaks of beating 'Deep Blue' with intuition makes a listener want to believe him. But IBM's Campbell calls intuition 'just a very powerful evaluation function'. People play without knowing whether they are completely correct or not. Deep Blue won't play unless it thinks it is correct (Goldsmith, 1995).

The article about Kasparov and "the silicon monster", "Deep Blue", is exemplary for the increasing battle between man and machine, and the fear that this development evokes. A more radical and overall vision on this topic is provided in the article "Why the Future Doesn't Need Us" (Joy, April 2000). The author states:

> . . . our most powerful 21st-century technologies—robotics, genetic engineering, and nanotech—are threatening to make humans an endangered species (Joy, 2000).

According to Bill Joy, it is not inconceivable that mankind will eventually be caught up in "The Age of Spiritual Machines". Of course, these are futuristic speculations based on rapid developments in the discipline of artificial intelligence. Joy's apocalyptic vision, however, is no exception. In *Singular Visionary* (Kelly, June 1995), the mathematician Vernon Vinge simply assumes "that machines are about to rule the human race as humans have ruled the animal kingdom." Another example comes from one of the most renowned experts in the field of robotics, Hans Moravec. In an article titled "Superhumanism" (Platt, October 1995), Moravec's vision is portrayed in the following quotation:

> By 2040, he believes, we can have robots that are as smart as we are. Eventually, these machines will begin their own process of evolution and render us extinct in our present form . . . And in his own laboratory, he's laying the groundwork that may help this evolutionary leap happen ahead of schedule (Platt, 1995).

Not only computers and robots but also the autonomy of the virus is experienced as a threat. In "Viruses are Good for You" (Dibbel, February 1995), the author tries to explain this deep-rooted fear of the virus by arguing that:

> What scares you most about getting that virus? Is it the prospect of witnessing your system's gradual decay, one nagging system following another until one day the whole thing comes to halt? . . . Or is it not, in fact, something deeper? Could it be that what scares you most about the virus is not any particular effect it might have, but simply its assertiveness, alien presence, its intrusive otherness? Inserting itself into a complicated choreography of subsystems all designed to serve your needs and carry out your will, the virus hews to its own agenda of survival and reproduction . . . They are products not of nature but of culture, brought forth not by the blind workings of a universe indifferent to our aims, but by the conscious effort of human beings like ourselves. Why then, after a decade of coexistence with computer viruses, does our default response to them remain a mix of bafflement and dread? (Dibbel, 1995).

Another case that shows the fear technicians have for their own creations is Y2K. Today of course, we know that the fears of Y2K were exaggerated. This is not important in this analysis. What matters are the attitudes and emotions it evoked among technicians. According to *Wired*, the potential threat of a millennium crash demonstrates, more than anything else, the autonomous, uncontrollable and destructive force of our technological surroundings. In "The Myth of Order" (Ullman, April 1999), it is argued that Y2K rightly corrodes the "religious belief" and unconditional trust that people have in digital technology. The media attention on Y2K merely makes visible what the technical experts knew all along:

that software operates just like any natural system: out of control . . . Y2K is showing everyone what technical people have been dealing with for years: the complex, muddled, bug-bitten systems we all depend on, and their nasty tendency towards the occasional disaster (Ullman, 1999).

In other words:

The millennium bug is not unique; it's just a flaw we see now, the most convincing evidence yet of the human fallibility that lives inside every system (Ullman, 1999).

Ullman vividly describes what strategy programmers use to deal with the, in essence, irrational and uncontrollable forces of the global computer network. Practically, the technicians generally solve this problem by working on a local level and think in short terms (this was the basic cause of the millennium bug!). One of the psychological coping strategies of programmers is black, cynical humour ("ha, ha, my system's so screwed up you wouldn't believe it!"). When they come to realize the interconnectedness of all local systems and the complexity of the problems, fear is often a reaction. Ullman provides an example:

. . . the job of fixing Y2K in the context of an enormous, linked economic machine was now a task that stretched out in all directions far beyond his control. It scared him (Ullman, 1999).

The articles on the autonomy of computers, robots and digital organisms do not only reflect fear but also indicate feelings of fascination or awe. This corresponds with the hypothesis of Marret. In this context, our artificially intelligent environment is imagined as a dynamic, complex and organic network that increasingly covers the earth. In most cases, these articles are written about the global implications of the Internet and the Word Wide Web. In the article "A Globe, Clothing Itself with a Brain" (Cobb Kreisberg, June 1995), for instance, the growth of the World Wide Web is related to the theologically inspired ideas and prognosis of Teilhard de Chardin. This priest invented the so-called "Gaia hypothesis", where the ecosystem is conceptualized as a huge organism in which the whole transcends its parts. About the relevance of his work for the growing Internet and World Wide Web, the author writes:

Teilhard imagined a stage of evolution characterized by a complex membrane of information enveloping the globe and fueled by human consciousness. It sounds a little off-the-wall, until you think about the Net, that vast electronic web encircling the Earth, running point to point through a nervelike constellation of wires (Kreisberg, 1995).

It is, of course, possible to write about the World Wide Web in purely technical or functional terms. The author, however, quotes Teilhard de Chardin to describe the nearby future of the Internet: "We have the beginning of a new age. The earth gets a new skin. Better still, it finds its soul." The ideas of Teilhard de Chardin have, according to Cobb Kreisberg, an enormous influence on many contemporary engineers, technological experts and techno-gurus. The article "One Huge Computer" (Kelly and Reiss, August 1998) covers a rather technical description about the possibilities of a "global nervous system" that will be completely "interconnected". In this context, the authors also refer to the theological prognosis of Teilhard de Chardin:

> . . . the closer it gets, the easier it will be for everyone to see. " 'Imagine a global network so complex it will be a kind of organism, a dynamic, richly interconnected medium wrapped around the earth 24,000 miles deep.' " That's not Teilhard de Chardinit's—it's the 1997 annual report from Daimler-Benz North America (Kelly and Reiss 1998).

In other articles, Teilhard de Chardin is not mentioned but similar ideas are pursued. In "The Digital Gaia" (Vinge, January 2000), for instance, the author writes about the ultimate consequences of "embedded computer networks" and states: "As computing power accelerates, the network knows all—and it's everywhere." This statement about the omnipresence of the digital network has an animistic connotation. The author of "Only Connect" (Johnson, January 2000) is also fascinated by what appears to him as spontaneously growing information systems and, like Vinge, he portrays these systems as "omnipresent" and "all-knowing". These characteristics are central to his analysis of what he calls the "Omninet":

> Today's metaphor is the network—a vast expanse of nodes strung together with dark, gaping holes in between. But as the threads inevitably become more tightly drawn, the mesh will fill out in the fabric, and then—with no voids whatsoever—into an all-pervasive presence, both powerful and unremarkable (Johnson, 2000).

In short, many authors imagine the Internet as a unity, a dynamically interwoven network that will increasingly "wrap up" our entire planet. This essentially holistic attitude towards new technology has, according to the author of "Getting Lost" (Thieme, September 1996), huge implications for individual consciousness:

Connecting on the Net, after all, is more like being cells in a body than being individuals. We lose and find ourselves in the emerging Self that is putting itself on the Net (Thieme, 1996).

Katz also demonstrates the spiritual significance of the Internet in "The Medium is the Medium" (July 1995):

It's the spiritual side of the digital world that is little known and little explored. Yet in some ways it's potentially one of the most significant parts. The ability of one person's spirit to reach across space and connect with another's is, to many, a spiritual act in itself (Katz, 1995).

Feelings of "awe", however, can also be triggered by a vision of technology on the micro level. In "Invisible Worlds" (January 1996), Yeskel demonstrates what happens when you ask a technological expert consistently about "why", "what" and "how". The author argues that "after a few levels of questioning, you're at the invisible domain; another level or two and you're in the spiritual domain." An image on the screen can be reduced to the memory of the computer and, eventually, to "bits" and invisible electrons of which one can only observe the influences and effects. Finally, the author argues, the technician gets into an invisible and, in essence, incomprehensible world. Therefore, Yeskel concludes, the view of reality adopted by technicians does not really differ from the one his grandfather believed in:

My grandfather believed in an invisible world. It was populated by angels, demons, and a beneficent god . . . My fellow technicians and I share a belief in an invisible world that is no less miraculous than my grandfather's and, many would say, no less evident of a beneficent god . . . We do well to occasionally remember, with *awe*, the worlds that exist just out of sight (Yeskel, 1996).

The Animists: Pagans, Shamans and Witches in Cyberspace

By now, it can be concluded that our technological environment is imagined in *Wired* as an artificially intelligent, relatively autonomous force of nature that in turn arouses "humble" feelings of fear, fascination and awe. With this view and these sentiments, the sources in *Wired* comply with the posed threefold criterion of technoanimism. Yet, the most evident and explicit form of technoanimism in *Wired* is represented by a group of people who refer to themselves as technopagans or "technoshamans" (male) and "technowitches" (female). In this case, an interpretation based on the work of Tylor and Marett is no longer necessary, since these people explicitly consider themselves postmodern animists. *Wired* dedicated three articles to this subculture. One is the article "Technopagans: May the Astral Plane be Reborn in Cyberspace" (Davis, 1995), in which the author explains what these people do and what they believe in. Generally, Davis describes technopaganism as:

> a small but vital subculture of digital savants who keep one foot in the emerging technosphere and one foot in the wild and wooly world of Paganism . . . they are Dionysian nature worshippers who embrace the Appolonian artifice of logical machines (Davis, 1995).

This paradox, the loose integration of two apparently incompatible realms, can be considered characteristic of technopaganism. What, however, is a pagan? In the contemporary neopagan movement, people base their philosophy on ancient traditions such as witchcraft, the Celtic tradition and "Native Americans", and try to live in harmony with their natural surroundings. The earth, Gaia, and also the trees, the plants and animals are essentially seen as living, animated and sacred entities for whom people should take full responsibility. In other words, neopagans can be seen as animists. Despite the fact that pagans sacralize nature, there seems to be a remarkable interest in technology, software, computers and Internet among them. A relatively high percentage of pagans are working in the field of technology. Some of these neopagans consider themselves technopagans. They view nature and the technological environment as animated and sacred. A characteristic technopagan "dogma" is derived from the work of the science fiction writer Arthur C. Clark. Technopagans believe that any sufficiently advanced form of technology will appear indistinguishable from magic.

Davis uses the technopagan Mark Pesce, one of the renowned inventors of virtual reality, in his article as an illustration. From his perspective, the "sacred" natural elements—air, earth, fire and water—are nowadays replaced by silicon, plastic, wire and glass. As with all technopagans, he worships the magical powers of cyberspace. The article "The Goddess in Every Woman's Machine" (Borsook, July 1995) indicates that a relatively high number of technopagans are female. Borsook writes:

Technopaganism is the grand exception to the 85 percent male, 15 percent female demographics of the online world. It is one virtual community where rough parity—both in number and in power—exists between the sexes (Borsook, 1995).

The article discusses several female technicians who occupy themselves with technopagan ideas, magical practices and "online rituals". According to Davis, one of these rituals is "gender swapping" or the continuous change of gender in cyberspace. Legba, a female technopagan, writes:

Gender-fucking and morphing can be intensely magical. It's a very easy way of shape changing. One of the characteristics of shamans in many cultures is that they're between genders, or doubly gendered. But more than that, morphing and Net-sex can have an intensely and unsettling effect on the psyche, one that enables the ecstatic state from which Pagan magic is done (Davis, 1995).

Davis and Borsook see the group of technopagans as a small subculture. In "Zippies" (Marshall May, 1994), the author writes about a growing movement that is, at least, related to technopaganism. The participants refer to themselves as "Zippies" or "Zen Inspired Professional Pagans". They are also called "cyber-crusties" or "technohippies". Analogous to the technopagans, these people aim to fuse the shamanistic with the technological way of thinking. In general, a Zippie is "someone who has balanced their hemispheres to achieve a fusion of the technological and the spiritual" (Marshall, 1994).

In short, there are some articles in *Wired* about a small group of people that can be considered technoanimists *par excellence*. Davis, who claims he was a "participant observer" of technopagans for several years, gives the following explanation for the emergence of this movement:

As computers blanket the world like digital kudzo, we surround ourselves with an animated webwork of complex, powerful, and unseen forces that even the 'experts' can't totally comprehend. Our technological environment may soon appear to be as strangely sentient as the caves, lakes, and forests in which the first magicians glimpsed the gods (Davis, 1995).

Conclusion and Discussion

Various classical thinkers such as Comte, Tylor, Freud and Weber, claimed that the rationalization of Western society inevitably leads to the marginalization or even the disappearance of religious–mythical ideas and magical practices. This assumption is basic knowledge in contemporary sociology; with science and technology as driving forces, humanity will ultimately head for what Weber called a "disenchanted Western world".

Apparently, these characteristics of a disenchanted world contrast sharply with the content of the articles in *Wired* magazine. According to *Wired*, late modern people find themselves increasingly in a sort of simulated or artificially "enchanted garden". Not nature, but the technological environment we create, is experienced as mysterious. More important in the context of this research is the fact that there are technoanimistic ideas and sentiments in the technological field. Although the group of technopagans can be seen as the most evident case of technoanimism, it is surely not the only illustration of this unexpected development. How then can it be explained that we find "primitive" religious or animistic impulses in this section of society that are assumed to be "responsible" for the rationalization of Western society? Apparently, a paradoxical development is taking place; technoanimism, I will argue, can be seen as a direct but unforeseen consequence of the accelerating process of rationalization. This process does not contribute to the disappearance of religion. On the contrary: it can be seen as the main driving force behind the emergence of this archaic form of religion. How can this be sociologically understood?

In his work, Weber (1988) argued that goal-oriented rationality has increasingly dominated Western society since the seventeenth century. With the gradual institutionalization of bureaucracy, science, the economy and, more importantly, technology, this goal-oriented rationality gains relative autonomy towards human beings. Once institutionalized, Weber points out, these subsystems have their own internal dynamics. As a result of this, the modern individual experiences these systems more and more as autonomous external forces on which he or she has no influence. Basically, this autonomization of goal-oriented rationality is the reason why Weber portrayed Western society as a suffocating "iron cage" (1988:265). In a similar context, Mannheim (1940) compares the anxieties of modern humans aroused by their rationalized environments, with those of premodern people:

> Just as nature was unintelligible to primitive man, and his deepest feelings of anxiety arose from the incalculability of the forces of nature, so for modern industrialized man the incalculability of the forces at work in the social system under which he lives . . . has become a source of equally pervading fears (Mannheim, 1940:59).

In short, the works of Weber and Mannheim point out that the process of rationalization manifests itself as a "blind", autonomous force over which people have limited control. When we look more closely at the development of modern rational technology, Ellul (1965) confirms this assumption. In *The Technological Society*, he states:

> A whole new kind of spontaneous action is taking place here, and we know neither its laws nor its ends. In this sense it is possible to speak of the 'reality' of techniques—with its own substance, its own particular mode of being, and a life independent of our power of decision. The evolution of techniques then becomes exclusively causal; it loses all finality (Ellul, 1965:93).

Weber, Mannheim and Ellul write about the process of rationalization that increasingly dominates Western society, thereby, expelling religious and magical–mythical ideas. Their writings, however, can also explain the technoanimistic impulses found in *Wired*. If technology, based on purely rational principles, withdraws more and more from the control of humans and is increasingly seen as an autonomous, opaque or even "irrational" reality, then the step towards technoanimistic ideas and sentiments will be small. The developments in the technological disciplines of artificial intelligence and artificial life after World War II may have been decisive in this step. The specific combination of autonomy and intelligence in our new technological environment creates a fertile ground for late modern technoanimism and explains the feelings of humility that can be found in *Wired*. Like premodern people, these technical specialists are confronted with an autonomously "behaving" environment, whose deeper laws they can no longer completely comprehend. There is, of course, an important difference. This incomprehension is not caused by a lack of scientific knowledge, as Tylor assumed was the case with premodern animism. On the contrary, late modern technoanimism can be interpreted as the ultimate result of a superior level of scientific and technical knowledge. Artificially intelligent machines are an example of this. When these advanced creations enter the lifeworld, however, it becomes increasingly difficult to fully understand them. As in premodern society, this opens up a large space for magical–mythical and, especially, animistic representations of our material environment.

From this perspective, technoanimism can be seen as an unforeseen and "irrational" side effect of the accelerating process of rationalization. Rationalization does not, by definition, equate with disenchantment but can also mean re-enchantment. Generally, the conclusion of this paper resonates with the work of the sociologist Ullrich Beck, who claims that "in the risk society the unknown and unintended consequences come to be a dominant force in history and society" (1992:22). This statement refers to potentially catastrophic side effects of rationalization, such as the greenhouse effect or nuclear disasters. Apparently, as I have argued in this paper, technological progress is also accompanied by the mystification of technology itself.

ALL LIKE ONE IN CYBERSPACE:
THE HOMOGENIZING LOGIC OF NET COMMUNITIES

Irina Aristarkhova
Department of Sociology
National University of Singapore

Introduction

Rheingold (2000), a pioneer in the systematic study of virtual communities, conceptualises them as social aggregations that emerge from the Internet when enough people carry on those public discussions long enough, with sufficient human feeling, to form webs of personal relationships in cyberspace. He was also one of the first to suggest that such virtual communities and the communications therein are efforts to compensate for the inadequacies experienced in real-life communities. His argument is that virtual communities are, in part, a response to the hunger for community that has followed the disintegration of traditional communities around the world. My paper seeks to analyze how Net communities reproduce and mimic, rather than problematize and compensate, for existing notions of real communities. I will show that insofar as real communities form the structural and discursive basis for the development of Net communications, the Net communities that derive therefrom are unlikely to become the borderless, heterogeneous and free communities that are dreamt of by cyber-utopians like Rheingold. The first part of the paper will examine the ways in which the structural, discursive and practical conditions that mediate the formation of Net communities tend to erect serious impediments to the growth of heterogeneous social formations. The second part of the paper examines how the conventional theorizations of community are founded on what I call "a logic of homogeneity", which discursively organizes the associations within these communities by a necessary and systematic exclusion of some "others". I will present a critique of these theories and formations of community through Jacques Derrida's notion of hospitality as a deconstructive and dissociative gesture that perpetually responds to the ethical demand of the heterogeneous, that is, of "others".

Homogenizing Communities

Historically, the concept of community has been theorized through notions of collective consensus based on homogeneity, forming the ground, thus, for unity and harmonious social interaction. Significant examples of scholars adopting this perspective are Durkheim, Tonies and Parsons.

Durkheim (1972) provides the classic example of such a consensus-based community. His concept of mechanical solidarity that is supposed to have mediated community formation in pre-industrial society is based on *similarity* in beliefs, activities and social forms. His concept of organic solidarity introduces social differentiations deriving from a complex division of labour, which in turn resulted from rapid industrialization, population growth and the rise of capitalism. This concept, which could have been foundational for the theoretical renovation of the heterogeneous presence of the "other" in community formation, is very quickly submitted to what I call the "homogenizing logic of community". Durkheim claims that such differences generated by the division of labour create a greater sense of one's interdependence with others in society, but he warns that there are those anomic individuals who are unable to adequately reconcile their differences with the rest of society. It could even be argued that the Durkheimian anomic individual is, in a sense, the "other" who is marginalized by way of irreconcilable differences. Another important theorist of community is Ferdinand Tonies. Tonies also espouses a dual model of community development. His notion of *Gemeinschaft* is characterized by an organic sense of community, fellowship, family and custom, as well as a bonding together by understanding, consensus, and language. *Gesellschaft* is characterized by a form of hyper-individualism in which relations among people become mechanical, transitory and contractually oriented. Tonies argues that the processes of urbanization and industrialization would result in the destruction of *Gemeinschaft* and, consequently in the destruction of traditional community, security and intimacy. While there are clear resonances with Durkheim's differential concepts of solidarity, Tonies seems to be ideologically and morally opposed to the *Gesellschaft* community, which fails socially because of its inability to adequately police the differences within.

Such theories that conceive of communities as being essentially based on unity are problematic because the very concept of unity implies "sameness"—whether assumed or sought after—and "sameness" itself is more of a theoretical construct than an empirical fact. As such, in all unifying gestures, a *principle of homogeneity* is implied, whereby things are submitted to an equation that cancels out their individual differences so that a larger unity based on some chosen feature(s) of "sameness" can be *forged*. The history of communities is, therefore, seldom one free of violence, for the heterogeneous elements that are not proper to the homogenizing logic of a certain community are necessarily and violently erased.

As Allucquere Rosanne Stone shows in her book, *The War of Desire and Technology at the Close of the Mechanical Age* (1996), issues of control and user surveillance had been crucial even in the earliest stages of the formation of Net communities. Her discussion of a social experiment in community formation is interesting. Greenstone and James from California started a small business called the CommuniTree Group, based on the concept of a conference tree, their main goal being the promotion of an idea for an electronic community. They used the so-called Forth programming language, which was so opaque in comparison with other existing languages that it was practically incomprehensible to those outside the community. Those involved employed this language to associate themselves with a chosen community and its habitus.

Stone writes that "with each version of the BBS system, the CommuniTree Group supplied a massive, detailed instruction manual—which was nothing less that a set of directions for constructing a new kind of virtual community" (1996:109). From the beginning, fantasy was a constitutive part of this "community" imagery: "They saw the terminal as a window into a social space . . . It is . . . clear that virtual communication required a propensity toward play or fantasy on the part of the participants, either as a precondition of the interaction or as a concomitant" (1996:110–11). Stone also compares virtual communication with the "lucid dreaming in an awake state—a participatory social practice in which the actions of the reader have consequences in the world of the dream or of the book" (1996:121). It is noteworthy that such notions of collective imagination and fantasy used to describe Net communities have also been employed by others to depict the "nation" and "community".[1]

---

[1] For example, Slavoj Zizek, especially in his *Looking Awry and They Know Not What They Do* (1991), and Benedict Anderson in his *Imagined Communities* (1983).

Therefore, just like other communities, Net communities also involve elaborate schemes to construct and regulate the collective imaginary of its constituents.

In the case of CommuniTree, as soon as the Net community started growing, the programme was jammed with obscene and scatological messages. This jam came as a result of a pre-installed code that exiled such messages into the hard disk and, given the exclusive and opaque qualities of the Forth language, the safe and prompt removal of these improprieties was made practically impossible. The life of the Tree came to an end. The main lesson that those men learned from it was a drive to incorporate into programmes "provisions for monitoring and disconnection of 'troublesome' participants", which would be written in an accessible code so that such policing mechanisms would be available at both server and user levels. Such measures "facilitated easy removal of messages that did not further the purposes of the system operators" (Stone, 1996:115). Thus, it is no surprise then that the second generation of online conference software for virtual communities was already accompanied with more surveillance and control. We are not just talking of routine "monitoring of all networks" as is done by the National Security Agency of the US government, but of "local surveillance" instituted by "individual system operators". One early example of such a community is Fujitsu's Habitat, which employed the so-called Oracles programme that enabled one to observe both the official records of participants and their online actions.

The effective achievement and maintenance of homogeneity demand a vigilant policing and removal of the various heterogeneous elements that threaten to contaminate it. The historical development of real communities as well as of Net communities that are sustained by them have been based on protection and surveillance of their limits through the use of policing techniques, including censorship and exile of deviant users. Terry Harpold points out that there is a tendency to equate "freedom to connect" with "freedom to surf", even though the *possible* movements of data within any Net domain do not always equate with its *actual* movements. It is a historical fact that the political regimes charged with the management of any nation's Net connectivity have policed the kind of information made available at any point in time. Such policing could be motivated by a variety of rationales, ranging from racial and religious sensitivities to existing moral, ethical and legal codes. Net communities were not, even in their heyday, spaces for free access, play and negotiation. They were,

from the very beginning, "governed" (another often-forgotten etymological meaning of the term "cyber"—*kubernare* as in "govern") spaces
with clear notions and demarcations of *propriety* (the "dos" and the
"don'ts") and *property* (rightful ownership). It is for the safeguarding
of its own definitions of propriety and property that Net communities
institutionalize policing mechanisms; these inevitably mark them out
as exclusive communities. In fact, Nikolas Rose, in his most recent
book, *Powers of Freedom* (1999), proposes that the notions and constructions of community in its contemporary form actually constitute
a sector of government, what he terms "government through community". Drawing extensively on Foucault's notion of governmen-
tality, Rose argues that it is a mistake to frame this mobilization of
the community as an elaborate system of social control, even though
such control necessarily accompanies it. He claims that

> in the institution of community, a sector is brought into existence
> whose vectors and forces can be mobilized, enrolled, deployed in novel
> programmes and techniques which encourage and harness active prac-
> tices of self-management and identity construction, of personal ethics
> and collective allegiances (Rose, 1999:176).

Following Rose's arguments, these practices of Net surveillance, Net
policing as well as the active mobilization of the Net for the purposes of articulating notions and experiences of "community", need
to and can be analyzed in terms of what I call, "a governmental-
ization of Net communities".

In addition to the active measures that police the propriety of
activities on the Net, there are also certain homogenizing conditions
and conventions that are structurally intrinsic to Net technologies of
communication. Siegfried Zielinski (1996:279–290) claims that the
primary proprietary conventions of Net communications are, what he
calls, *algorithmic*, and which are necessarily adverse to an actual heterogeneity of experiences. The Boolean "algorithmic" of ones and zeros,
which forms the operational basis of computers and, therefore, the
Net, is a "signifying practice of unambiguity" (Zielinski, 1996:283)
where definite computational procedures are worked out for effective
and generalized applicability to a specific set of problems. Zielinski
argues that while certain aspects of knowledge and experience can
be "communicated exceptionally well by the means of electronic networks" because they submit well to algorithmic conversion; that is,
they are "capable of being generalized, reproduced, serialized—

processed in symbolic machines", there are certain "other" kinds of
experience and knowledge that would always elude such codification.
He claims that these experiences are not very unlike what Bataille
termed "the heterological", which, in being attentive to "the other",
is very often characterised by *excess*. In fact, he says that

> excess . . . is bound up with a specific place and in the presence of the
> Other, the extreme muse, the experience of a duration tied to a specific
> locality, the accident, the surprising turn of events, passion, pain . . . For
> these unique events the networks are an impossible place, and this
> impossible place is already fleeing from them, before they have even
> had time to approach it properly (284).

While Zielinski's argument of heterogeneity being necessarily anti-
thetical to algorithmic conversion seems too essentialized, it does
make sense to acknowledge that the proprietary conventions of "the
algorithmic" do not entirely cohere with those of "the heterological".
Thus, in addition to the highly intentional schemes of Net policing,
it seems that the very operational foundations of computers and Net
communications may be inherently inimical to and, thereby, exclusive of heterogeneous experiences and knowledge. Such policing and
exclusivity constantly problematize the euphoric optimism that sur-
rounds the notion of Net communities among users and activists.
Zielinski advises:

> the claim made for the universality of telematic networks and the dig-
> ital code as its informative content include an exaggerated and mis-
> leading promise of use value, namely, the existence of the possibility
> of an all-embracing, one-for-all order, that in the course of the his-
> tory of human thought and nature has always been a hollow dream
> and often evoked by the culture industry for its own ends. One-for-
> all is not the great whole, but the complexly individual, the hetero-
> geneous (284).

It is noteworthy, however, that this "one-for-all order" Zeilinski speaks
of is more often operationalized on the Net not by its restrictive
algorithm, but by the homogenizing proprieties of the dominant languages that are used within.

According to 1999 statistics provided by *Global Internet Statistics*, the
most commonly and extensively used language in the Net is English,
followed by German, Chinese, French and Dutch. The historical
development of English as the lingua franca of the Internet, as well
as its seemingly overwhelming use on the Net, is related to the fact
that the United States of America, which technologically initiated

the Net revolution, has also understandably been the most active to culturally integrate and embrace Net communications. The average Internet node intensity—which means the ratio of active nodes to overall population—in the USA is nearly 1 to 6. Compare this with the average Internet node density worldwide, which is 1 to 40. In a shocking counter-position to these figures is that of the Democratic Republic of Congo, which goes up as high as 1 to 440,000. (Mike Jensen, 1998, cited in Harpold, 1999, no. 23). That the cultural hegemony of the English language in international Net communications has historically instituted a homogenizing influence in the development of Net communities is a well-documented fact that does need to be rehearsed here. It would be useful, however, to briefly cite two case examples of linguistic hegemony on the Net: one from Japan with reference to the transition from English to Japanese; and another from the Russian Federation, where the Russian language has had a homogenizing influence on the Net communications of its various ethnic minorities.

Kumiko Aoki, in her 1994 article, "Virtual Communities in Japan", begins with a rather problematic assertion that "communication and computer technologies has enabled networking of people regardless of their geographical and temporal differences", but provides us with a rare and excellent account of one non-English based Net community. For example, Japanese Unix NETwork (JUNET) was the first nationwide non-commercial computer network designed for e-mail/e-news exchange. It was started in October 1984 by two public universities (Tokyo Institute of Technology and Tokyo University) and one private university (Keio University) through public telephone lines (at 9600 bps), through the use of Unix to Unix copy protocol (UUCP). When JUNET began international communications, it had to be in English or Romanized Japanese, and it was not until much later that *kanji* support in the form of a windowed user interface to the messaging systems was included. Interestingly, the amount of public traffic as well as JUNET membership has increased dramatically since then. Of course, this data is old by today's standards of technological developments (Aoki wrote the article in 1994) but the point I would like to make on the issue of language differences and encoding difficulties stands for non-English speaking virtual communities. Even with the introduction of *kanji* support, there are technical peculiarities that impede the easy transition to and use of Japanese. One important impediment for Japanese Net communities in internationalizing their Net links is the problem of *encoding*. Aoki shows that a few encoding systems that emerged in Japan and were developed by Japanese and American companies are very often incompatible. For example, Japanese Industrial Standards (JIS) encoding is being used for external information interchange, but it is not very efficient for internal storage or processing on computer systems. Another encoding system, Shift-JIS encoding, was originally developed by ASC II Corporation in collaboration with Microsoft and mainly used as internal code for Japanese PCs and KanjiTalk (the Japanese operating system for Apple Macintosh) as well as the millions of inexpensive Japanese language *waapuro* (word processors) that have flooded the market. It uses a combination of a one-byte eight-bit code and a two-byte eight-bit *kanji* code, while JIS uses a two-byte seven-bit code, thus, the conversion between Shift-JIS and JIS requires a very complex algorithm (Aoki, 1994). This is only one of many examples of encoding difficulties that slow down and frustrate the development of effective Net communications in Japan.

Another significant element of heterogeneity, seldom analyzed, is that of the cultural differences in communicational strategies employed by different Net communities. Aoki stresses that Japanese culture places tremendous importance on the context of communication that results in text-dominated cyberspace, which is perceived by many Japanese as an inappropriate and even an asocial substitute to real meetings and real communities. Aoki writes that the Japanese tend to read between the lines more than Net-users in the West, with the help of such cues as facial expressions, tone of voice, posture, etc. Thus, what in the USA is perceived as the most celebratory gesture of Net communities might be seen as irrelevant in other cultures. Though Aoki's account borders somewhat on essentializing Japanese cultural differences, there is a genuine need to avoid the obliteration of such differences by some utopian image of borderless Net communities, where geographical location and cultural background do not matter.

The next example is from Russia, where I have been undertaking research on the development of Net communities with particular reference to its complicities with Russian nationalism. The homogenizaton of Net communication through the use of the Russian language (and English as an alternative) is a practice that is seldom reflected upon as problematic and/or limited. In a manner coherent with the governmental emphasis on Russification, a policy first introduced by Catherine the Great in the second half of the eighteenth century, the Soviet regime had made education in the Russian language compulsory for its many minorities since 1922. This institutionalized education in and familiarity with the language may seem like a good justification for the continued use of that language to bring about better Net communications and, thereby, more unified Net communities in Russia. The minority communities in Russia, however, have historically resisted Russification, and the Russian language was very often seen as an extension of Russian imperialism. While it may be argued that the minorities could, in fact, employ the dominant language to their advantage on the Net, there is also much to be said about the systematic marginalization of minority languages that is justified and institutionalized by such practices. Moreover, the Net practice of using English as an alternative to Russian shows that the existing Net communities strive more for the English-speaking "outside" than for exploring or linking up with differences "inside". It seems, thus, that the Net communities in Russia are more interested in achieving a sense of community—if at all—with those "outside" Russia. While one may applaud in this the loosening of the thus-far impermeable Russian border, one cannot but bemoan the institutionalized neglect of "others-within" perpetrated by such Net practices. The problems of encoding Cyrillic for international Net links still persists in many parts of Russia, and often requires special computer peripherals and software.

The notion of homogeneous Net communities has been sustained by the belief that Net communications transcend and dissolve existing cultural, geographical and technological differences between and within real communities. A growing body of research, however, is puncturing such illusions; most notably, research in cybergeography and the work of postcolonial cybertheorists.

Cybergeographical and Postcolonial Critique

Martin Dodge, a chief proponent of cyber-geography defines it as "the study of the spatial nature of computer communications networks, particularly the Internet, the WWW, and other electronic 'places' that exist behind our computer screens that popularly refer to as cyberspace." This field encompasses "a wide range of geographical phenomena from the study of physical infrastructure, traffic flows, the demographics of the new cyberspace communities to the perception and visualization of these new digital spaces" (Martin Dodge, http://www.cybergeography.com/about.html). In short, it is interested in analyzing the real-space concomitants and implications of cyberspace. Michael Batty, another cybergeographer, proposes a distinction between what he calls "cyberplace" and cyberspace. Cyberplace, according to him, is "the substitution, complementation and elaboration of physical infrastructure based on manual analogic technologies with digital" ones. Here, he includes "all the wires that comprise the network that are being embedded into man-made structures such as roads and buildings" as well as "the material objects that are used to support this infrastructure such as machines for production, consumption and movement" (Batty, 1997:346).

Terry Harpold, in his brilliant essay, "Dark Continents: A Critique of Internet Metageographies" (1999), critiques the notion of free proliferation of Net communities and CMC by pointing to the structural conditions of such "cyberplaces" that mediate and support Net connectivity. He argues that various maps that have been used to represent Internet traffic, and diffusion and distribution in the world, are discursively and historically implicated in obscuring the socio-economic and political differences between countries and the Net communities they sustain. For example, he points out that the different conditions of access—specifically, bandwidth; and speed of transmission and quality of access (for example, image resolution, audio transmissions, video feed, etc.)—are not indicated in statistical and geographical data of Internet connectivity. Harpold writes that there are huge differences in the operating bandwidths used by different countries and even within any one country (the most common bandwidth is in the range of 1544 kbps which does not provide you with full motion video, and some of the more advanced and professional ISPs offer up to 44736 kbps—this is 1999 data). Such differences in access bandwidths and speeds result in significantly less sophisticated kinds of communications issuing from and within these geographically marginalized Net communities. In addition to limiting the scope of communication, the temporal lapses and glitches in their communications tend to constitute them as "less advanced" and "slow" destinations with which to enact Net links.

The conditions of actual Net access are further complicated by a variety of social, political, cultural and geographical factors. Research has shown that a significant proportion of the *total available network bandwidth* in any country is reserved usually for MNCs with regional headquarters in the cities, and/or for university and government agencies. This means that network nodes that are geographically located outside the metropolitan centres have very little access to the full range of Net facilities. Most of them may be restricted to simple store-and-forward e-mail only. Also, in most developing countries, the lack of a comprehensive and well-maintained telecommunications infrastructure and power grid poses serious constraints to the development of digital networks.

For example, in Russia, the majority of all Internet Service Providers (ISPs) and the Net communities they support are based in and emanate from Moscow and St. Petersburg. Such geographical monopolization is symptomatic of Russian history, in which these capitals capitalize on being centres of political and economic infrastructure that jealously maintain their control over these privileges. The relevance of the geographical locations of Net communities has rarely been addressed, especially since too much attention has been placed on the borderless and placeless nature of cyberspace. The socio-political and economic implications of the physical location of Net providers and operations, however, need to be examined much more carefully before one celebrates the ecumenism of cyberspace. Russian urbanization has actively encouraged the centralization of activities and resources in either of these two major cities. This has created a situation where local and foreign investors/organizations investing in new technologies have tended to work from/with these more "centralized" Net groups, which have subsequently come to represent "Russian cyberspace". Even the privately-funded elementary courses in Internet usage for women in Moscow and St. Petersburg take for granted the cultural and linguistic homogeneity of those great Russian metropolises. Thus, women of other ethnic and religious backgrounds, so "visible" today in Russian capitals, are left out of those programmes. Thus, it seems that the exclusionary practices of the Russian real communities have not been seriously challenged, but merely reinforced in their Net communities and their practices.

McLuhan has written that the development of electronic communication technologies has essentially abrogated space and time so that we can live in a borderless "global village". While many acknowledge the McLuhanesque vision of a global village to be a distant dream, their reasons for believing so have been predominantly technological. Many believed (and still do) that it is merely a question of the limits of present technology that stand in the way of realizing truly

global Net communities. In recent years, however, a group of postcolonial theorists have begun to actively theorize cyberspace and Net
communities. Olu Oguibe, Tetsuo Kogawa, Guillermo Gomez Pena
and Maria Fernandez are some notable examples of what I call *postcolonial cybertheorists*. In addition to pointing out the fallacies in arguments for the globalization of free and heterogeneous Net communities,
many of these theorists actively advocate various "local" Net strategies for the appropriation and effective deployment of these communication technologies. For the purposes of laying down some of
the central arguments of this very exciting group of thinkers, I will
quickly present the ideas of Olu Oguibe.

Olu Oguibe, in his *Forsaken Geographies: Cyberspace and the New World
'Other'* (1996), presents a sweeping critique of what he calls "cyberism",
with its promises of the "brave new world" and a "digital nirvana".
He writes

> Electronic mail and the web-browser, with all their unarguably posi-
> tive potentials, nevertheless become veritable tools for the construction
> and fortification of an other world, outside the borders of which every-
> thing else is inevitably consigned to erasure and absence.

He considers existing cybercommunities to be not only unaware but
more importantly, irresponsible in relation to those who "do not and
cannot belong" to it. He states, thus, that

> Cyberspace as we have seen it, is not the new, free global democracy
> we presume and defend, but an aristocracy of location and disposi-
> tion, characterized, ironically, by acute insensitivity and territorialist
> proclivities.

In an interview, "On Digital Third-Worlds", from that same year,
Oguibe speaks of how the developments in information and communication technologies have followed the contours of bygone colo-
nialism and global capitalism. Oguibe does not dismiss cyberspace
and the Net communities hosted within simply as sites of neo-colo-
nialism and nothing else. He sees his task as a postcolonial cybertheo-
rist to be one of presenting

> the challenge to all those who possess and understand this new tech-
> nology; namely that we begin to explore with greater seriousness and
> humanism, means of extending the numerous, practical possibilities of
> this new technology to the greater majority of humanity.

According to him, these neglected spaces, what he calls "forsaken geographies", need to be embraced by a systematic extension of cyber-technology and Net connectivity to these areas; in short, the excluded needed to be included. While there are acknowledged dangers of economic neo-colonization in such a quantitatively driven expansion of Net connectivity by the importation of Net technologies, Oguibe argues that such risks must be taken in order to invalidate and redress the existing hierarchies of Net access and communications.

It has been argued thus far that the structural, practical and dis-cursive conditions of Net communities are centred on notions of association by homogeneity, exclusivity and closure. One common thread in all of the abovementioned criticisms is that the notion and ideal of community is itself desirable, and that the removal of those disruptive conditions and impediments to community would make free Net communities possible. The structural and cultural differences identified between socio-political entities, exemplified by their specific national borders, languages and identities, are seen as temporary impediments deriving from their postcolonial conditions and global capitalism. The technological limits to community formation are bemoaned as significant but surmountable problems on the road to dynamic global Net communities. Throughout these carefully considered criticisms, however, the notion of community itself remains "unthought". The question of whether the notion of community itself is constitu-tively incompatible with the formation of free and heterogeneous social formations in real life and on the Net has yet to be posed. The problem of closure and exclusivity is not unique to Net commu-nities; I would argue that *insofar as they are communities, they are exclusive.* The associative conditions that have been historically deemed fun-damental to community formation need to be re-examined. I would like to frame the various critiques mentioned above as having pre-sented a call for attention to those conditions that fissure and unset-tle Net communities from within; what I would like to call, following Derrida, the dissociative conditions for community. Each of the crit-icisms highlighted the failure of Net communities to somehow address the differences that arose from and/or were intrinsic to the com-munities as such—the difference and heterogeneity of the "others". Thus, in the next part of my paper, I will, using Derrida, deliber-ate on the notion of community by posing difference, heterogeneity and otherness as the very constitutive and dissociative conditions of community formations, both Net and real.

The Dissociative Condition of Community

Jacques Derrida has presented several scathing critiques of such unity-based notions of community in many of his works. He claims:

> if by community one implies, as is often the case, a harmonious group, consensus, and fundamental agreement beneath the phenomenon of discord or war, then I don't believe in it very much and I sense in it as much threat as promise (1995:355).

He says that "the privilege granted to unity, to totality, to organic ensembles, to community as a homogenized whole . . . is a danger for responsibility, for decision, for ethics, for politics" (1997:13) exactly because of their negative implications for "the relation to the other". Derrida, thus, presents the possibility of thinking of a community based not on unity but, instead, on dissociation.

Derrida's critique of community as well as those of a variety of other French theorists, have been largely based on their continuing critical engagements with the writings of Bataille on community. It is noteworthy that the earlier works of Jean Luc Nancy, *The Inoperative Community* (1991); as well as that of Maurice Blanchot, *The Unavowable Community* (1988; partly a reaction to and reading of Nancy's text), have structured much of the contemporary Continental debates on community, including those of Derrida (though the latter has not been particularly forthcoming in acknowledging this debt). In both the works of Nancy and Blanchot, there is a clear interest in articulating the dissociative presence of the other instead of actively denying it, though the individual arguments of Blanchot and Nancy as to how the other presents itself within the community differ significantly. Due to the lack of space, let me just briefly present the views of Nancy as exemplified in his book, *The Inoperative Community*.

In the early parts of the book, Nancy reflects:

> the emergence and our increasing consciousness of decolonized communities has not profoundly modified the givens of community nor has today's growth of unprecedented forms of "being-in-common" through channels of information as well as through what is called a multi-racial society triggered any genuine renewal of the question of community (p. 22).

It is the question of community that Nancy elaborates and deliberates upon in the rest of the book. According to Nancy, the notion of community, both in its philosophical and sociological guises, has traditionally been centred on a fusion of beings creating a unified organic whole, wherein a "dream of transparent social organization based on a specular recognition of the self in the other" is realized. Such a community he labels as "immanentist", insofar as it seeks to produce its own *essence* as a work; that is, a community is realized through the work of its members to actively create it based on notions of what is predefined as essential and proper to it. In opposition to such an immanentist community, Nancy sought one based on an attention to the alterity of others. This so-called "inoperative community" is workless and idle because it refuses to create itself as a work. It is a community of *partage*, which means both sharing as well as division, where the very sharing is sustained by the recognition of division between "me" and "you" (*toi est tout autre que moi*).

Though this argument on community and its relation to Derrida is itself worthy of some careful discussion, it is well beyond the scope of the present paper. Derrida's dissociatively structured community is the real focus of my paper today, and that demands beginning with Derrida's critique of Heidegger. The privilege that Heidegger places on the "gathering" (*Versammlung*), as opposed to the notion of dissociation, for the constitution of community is heavily criticized by Derrida exactly for its negative implications of "the other" and to difference(s). He says, "once you grant some privilege to gathering and not to dissociating, then you leave no room for the other, for the radical otherness of the other, for the radical singularity of the other." In fact, Derrida redefines the notions of "dissociation" and "separation" not as "obstacles to community", as they are commonly conceived, but the very condition of possibility for any community. "Dissociation, separation, is the condition of my relation to the other. I can address the Other only to the extent that there is a separation, a dissociation." Derrida also argues that such a relation does not and cannot entirely overwhelm or possess the other through knowledge, understanding or emotional investment. This is because the other remains itself throughout the relationship. This is what he calls, along with Levinas and Blanchot, "*rapport sans rapport*, the relationless relation", where "the other remains absolutely transcendent. I cannot reach the other. I cannot know the other from the inside or so on." This relationless relation based on a separation is not a bad thing, Derrida says, for

> this is not an obstacle but the condition of love, friendship and of war, too, a condition of the relation to the other. Dissociation is the condition of community, the condition of any unity as such (Derrida, 1997).

Dissociation, however, only provides the initial condition for any community since it establishes heterogeneity as a necessary ground upon which to build community. What is required, he proposes, is a whole new way of thinking about and constituting communities. This Derrida seeks to articulate through another concept, that of *hospitality*.

Hospitable Community

Derrida provides an interesting way of addressing the notion of community with dissociation as its condition in his recent, yet-unpublished article, "Questions of Responsibility: Hostility/ Hospitality". In it, he opposes a community based on unity that results from fusion and identification and which is, therefore, necessarily against some other. The community of unity is, for him, based on a "unity-against" a collective other. It invokes an etymological connection between *communio* as a gathering of people and a fortification (*munnis*); an arming of oneself in opposition to some other. As such, the erection of a community is inherently allied to the construction of a defence mechanism that is vigilant to and exclusive of some other as foreigner and outsider. The homogenizing logic of community development is constantly attentive to those heterogeneous elements within itself only to enable their effective elimination or assimilation. Community as based on unity, fusion, identification, defence, closure and exclusivity needs to be redefined through, what he calls, hospitality.

Derrida points out that, etymologically, the term "hospitality" is related to the notion of "hostility", since the root of the former, *hospes*, is allied to an earlier root of the latter, *hostis*, which interestingly meant both "stranger" and "enemy". Thus, hospitality, as in *hostilis*, stranger/enemy + *potes*, "(of having) power", came eventually to mean the power the host had over the stranger/enemy. John Caputo, in an interesting commentary on Derrida's notion of hospitality, notes that "the 'host' is someone who takes on or receives strangers, who gives to the stranger even while remaining in control" (Caputo, 1997:111). It is clear that the "host" is in a necessary position of power insofar as he or she[2] circumscribes the parameters within which the

---

[2] I develop a cyberfeminist critique of Levinas' and Derrida's notion of hospitality in a forthcoming article in a collective book, *Next Protocols*, and in my cyberart work, *Virtual Chora* (www.aristarkhova.org).

needs and comforts of the stranger/enemy are attended to. In addition to this circumscription, the host's "power over" the stranger, Derrida suggests, results from his or her ownership of the premises that is thus offered up. Given the fact that hospitality is dependent on ownership before it is offered hospitably to the other, Derrida argues, an essential tension is built into its structure. This is because it is difficult to give over to the other when you continue to own.[3] The aporia for the giver is the tension of wanting to give but also having to have what is given away, for it is having that makes possible the giving. Derrida says that this aporia, which could well paralyze any efforts at hosting the other, is exactly what needs to be worked through rather than denied. In fact, hospitality is only possible when one resists this paralysis by moving towards what Derrida calls a "hospitality beyond hospitality", wherein the very impossibility of a hospitality based on ownership as limit-condition is pushed to/at the limits. In having erected its possibilities on their very impossibility, claims Derrida, hospitality—like deconstruction—is a *to come* (*avenir*). The aporia of a hospitality *to come* is constituted by one's inability to know entirely or surely its specific qualities and as such, it is to be struggled with *performatively*.

Derrida's critique of communities is aimed at their tendency to construct a defensive unity, a "we", based on the negation and continuous marginalization of some others. Communities are, Derrida believes, essentially *inhospitable structures*; thus, lodging hospitality as a deconstructive *graft* within this structure of the community promises to keep it open to/for others. Hospitality allows communities "to make their very limits their openings"; thus, it ensures that there is always a possibility of hosting the other. This issue of how to host the other is today more pertinently raised with reference to Net communities, which have inherited not only some of the promises of earlier real communities but also their problems.

---

[3] A primary aporia of Derrida's notion of hospitality is of how the host is to simultaneously (and generously) negotiate his or her exclusive ownership of that which he or she offers up inclusively to the other as guest. He asserted the need to deal with this impossibility by constant contestation of its limits, enacted through acts of generosity that are performatively excessive to ownership.

Conclusion

In the age of globalization, cultural difference becomes both subject to persecution and a subject of fascination; difference is required as never before: to form a global community. The idea of "global" makes sense only when there are distances to cover, only when there is a diversity to encounter, only when there is a fascination with the "other". The global depends on local differences, and on heterogeneity. Does it, however, depend on it only to eliminate it later? The price for this homogeneity is not, I am afraid, the loss of intimacy or tradition within Russian (Net) communities as it has been projected by many; rather, it is an inherent violence in this drive to homogeneity, the murder of difference that creates by itself the possibility of any community, the elimination of hospitality on which any community is based, and a shutting of doors for others who do not want to belong at the expense of their difference.

Trying to dissolve too fast into some homogenized Net community, with its only naively imagined absence of cultural and sexual specificity and borderless spaces, we are closing many openings made possible by cyberspace. This closure connects online communities with traditional communities, which, for centuries, resisted their debts to difference and heterogeneity. We can conclude that so far, cyberspace has been used in a way that does not offer anything new; the only condition for entering it seems to be an elimination of difference and a forgetting of "otherness". Yet, this has been a condition for a real life community—policing of difference and governing it have been its main functions. Unpredictability of the other seems to be resolved in the production of the "other", in mimicry of the "other"—speaking for both, being for both. Occupying both spaces—of the host and the other/guest—we do not have the two, but one and the same who is splitting into many ones. Being both, we lie to ourselves that we celebrate diversity; speaking for others shuts them up. Hospitality can be carried out not only when we have something to offer (as owners) but also when we are not pretending that nothing belongs to us. Here, cultural and sexual specificity does not necessarily imply sameness and belonging to one singular culture or gender, it does not imply some kind of disembodied imagined construction like the notion of nation; rather, it implies a sensitivity to and awareness of its own cultural and sexual heterogeneity, of the multiplicity and politics of what is called "geographical embodied location". While recognizing the limits of the community, Derrida advised a strategic use of these limits as openings. It is such an opening that I have tried to identify here.

THE VIRTUAL COMMONS:
HALLUCINATION, HYPE OR HETEROTOPIA?

Michael D. Mehta
Department of Sociology
University of Saskatchewan

> Cyberspace. A consensual hallucination experienced daily by billions of legitimate operators, in every nation, by children being taught mathematical concepts . . . A graphic representation of data abstracted from the banks of every computer in the human system. Unthinkable complexity. Lines of lights ranged in the non-space of the mind, clusters and constellations of data. Like city lights, receding . . . (Gibson, 1984).

In 1884, Edwin Abbott wrote a delightful story about the adventures of a square-shaped creature in a two-dimensional world called "Flatland" (Abbott, 1992). Not realizing that more than two dimensions existed, the square's worldview is altered radically by a visitor from the third dimension. The confused square could no longer see the world in two dimensions; his frame of reference had shifted. Many of us have much in common with the square in this story, and are reeling from the shock of being thrust into cyberspace. No longer is our world the same as it was 10 years ago. The Internet, combined with virtual reality and a variety of enhanced computer network applications, including online banking and reservation systems, have altered our sense of place, time, and even self. What effects is the Internet having on how we view the world?

There are two competing visions of the Internet; namely, a neo-utopian, technological-determinist view and a dystopic, technocratic view (Dery, 1995). The neo-utopian vision is represented best by the work of Marshall McLuhan (1962) and is based on the pastoral "global village" metaphor. The information age, according to McLuhan, began with the telegraph in 1844. This snapped us out of the typographic trance that the printing press put us in, and led to an imploding effect where time and space shrank. The introduction of movable type, followed by the portable book, fostered a worldview that structured Western consciousness from the fifteenth century on. It crystallized in the Enlightenment and attained its apotheosis in industrial modernity. There is an insistence on linearity, compartmentalization, classification, and detached observation—all hallmarks of the scientific method. According to Lewis Mumford (1962), this was exemplified by the mechanical clock, which introduced or fostered a regularity of production, regular work hours and standardization of products. The Internet is expected to usher in a golden age of democracy similar to the ancient Greek agora or New England town hall. Electronic voting and the potential to empower grassroots movements are claimed as the biggest virtues of the Internet. Information age guru Mark Poster (1995) claims that electronic communication enhances significantly our postmodern potentialities by allowing us new relations between human and machine; greater decentralization; a new space—time complex; and the obliteration of racism, sexism, and homophobia. In a sense, this entails the development of a reconstituted identity through cyberspace.

The dystopic vision of the Internet is that instead of a global village, we have a "paradise re-tribalized". This is not what former US President George Bush called the "kinder and gentler society". Instead, many live in fear of downsizing, "foreign devils", obsolescence, and technological displacement. Our notion of community is changing, with economic, social, and racial tensions "Balkanizing" our society. There is even fragmentation of the online community. The thousands of newsgroups in Usenet are an illustration of this fragmentation. Consistent with this vision is the cybergothic nightmare told by William Gibson in his 1984 science fiction thriller *Neuromancer*. In Gibson's novel, swirling multimedia merge and mutate in consensual hallucination to fuel a greed for bits and bytes. Hackers connect their central nervous systems directly to computer networks to fight for encrypted information in cyberspace. Individuality and privacy erode in a search for power and profit. In this fictional world, there is a destabilization of traditional notions of ethnicity and nationhood. Some believe that Gibson's world is fast becoming a reality, thanks in large part to the Internet.

In this paper we will discuss the following questions: How is this wired world affecting our society? What are the impacts on individuals, organizations, and governments? Is it possible to develop virtual community standards in cyberspace, and on what level? Can the Internet really promote a more democratic, egalitarian world? What impact do the infrastructural needs and costs associated with building and maintaining the Internet have on content-based regulation like the Communications Decency Act?

Running through a Maze of Possibilities:
The Effects of Computer-mediated Communication

Psychologists and physiologists are beginning to understand better the effects of novel behavioural patterns on neurological structures in the brain. Rats forced to run the same maze hundreds, or even thousands, of times have brains that are structurally different than their non-maze running relatives. By turning repeatedly to the left or right in a pre-arranged maze, rats rewired their brains, thus, increasing their efficiency at this task, and perhaps even passing along knowledge to their offspring. Is it too far a stretch to suppose that a computer user's repeated use of a mouse and keyboard can have similar affects on the human brain? Do hypertext files, with a search technique involving many jumps and leaps through interconnected databases, lead to shorter attention span, fragmented knowledge, and information overload? How do new technologies facilitate the collection of information about our consumer behaviour, movement, and health status? Are the liberating effects of these technologies counterbalanced by the surveillance function they facilitate?

The Internet as Global Superpanopticon: Raging against the Machine

The rapid growth of the Internet and its shift towards a commercially-oriented marketplace where electronic transactions are common, presents a serious threat to privacy. Not only must consumers ensure that products or services ordered through the Internet with credit cards remain beyond the gaze of the unscrupulous, but they should be concerned about how much easily personal information can be collected. The debate over the future form of electronic currency is closely linked to this issue, as is the future of encryption software.

Consumers have become used to the idea that money as a medium of exchange need not be physical in the sense of currency like shells, beads, coins and bills. In Canada during the past few years, the one and two dollar bills have been replaced by coins. The Canadian government claims that more durable currency cuts the cost of replacing worn-out bills. To me this seems odd considering how many transactions are now digital. Instead of exchanging hard currency, funds are sent electronically through computer networks and stored on value-added cards. The popularity of credit cards, ATM machines, debit cards and electronic fund transfers have predisposed consumers to a new form of electronic currency—digital cash for Internet transactions.

Presently, two competing forms of electronic currency are available: Digicash and NetBill. The Digicash system is similar to how paper currency is exchanged (Chaum, 1992). A bank dispenses electronic tokens of specific denominations that may be exchanged between two network users (for example, consumer and retailer). Like paper currency, Digicash allows for the anonymous transaction of tokens issued by central authorities. By contrast, the NetBill system is similar to how money is exchanged using cheques (Sirbu and Tygar, 1995). Parties using this form of electronic currency exchange promissory notes that require verification and approval before transactions are completed. Concern about privacy and the tracing of transactions involving NetBill exchanges make some suspicious of how the Internet will evolve. In some ways, privacy has been traded for the privilege of participating in electronic commerce. French philosopher Michel Foucault provides a useful way to examine these issues in greater depth.

In 1975, Foucault published a seminal book on the history of the modern prison system. His central argument is that the purpose for the new prison system established after the French Revolution was to get away from punishment based on the arbitrary rule of the monarch and the use of torture (Foucault, 1979). As such, this represents a radical transformation in the deployment of power wielded by the state. The recourse to torture as a system of state punishment became less possible and desirable in an increasingly "democratic" and "enlightened" context. The new bourgeois regime undertook a major reform of the state penal system based on the humane and equal treatment of prisoners. As part of this reform, the French National Assembly launched a competition for the design of a new prison that would be cost-effective to run from the state's point of view, and which would help create model prisoners.

Jeremy Bentham entered the competition and suggested the panopticon, an observation tower located at the centre of the prison (Bentham, 1995). Using an open plan, iron bars are placed on the sides of each cell facing the panopticon, thus, making the occupant totally visible to a gazing guard. An outside window in each cell provided natural light and additional visibility. This system was designed to achieve a "political economy" of the running costs of an institution. A single guard could simultaneously observe all the prisoners.

Another original and important feature of the panopticon is that it is a one-way observation system where prisoners are unable to see if a guard is actually observing them. This meant, in theory, that there could be no guard in the panopticon (the ultimate political economy!), yet prisoners would have to behave as if there were an observing guard. Prisoners, even without an actual gazing guard, felt the power effects of the panopticon. This meant that individuals in each cell would have to learn to practise self-control and behave as "good" prisoners who followed prison regulations at all times. Despite the absence of institutionalized physical violence against prisoners, this constant gaze had normalizing effects—not only on conduct— but on self-perception, personality, and way of seeing the world. How far does the metaphor of the panopticon relate to the Internet (Mehta and Darier, 1998)?

The panopticon is an example of institutional centralization: archi-tecturally, it is a tower in a prison, which is itself the institution of the state's monopoly on detainment. The real novelty of the panop-ticon is the disciplinary use of constant visibility as an instrument of power applied to the entire prison population and to each individ-ual prisoner. Until then, the use of dungeons and dark cells only confirmed the absolutism of the monarch over his subjects. With the Enlightenment, constant visibility is added to the increased central-ization of disciplinary institutions.

Bentham's dream of total visibility and unencumbered gaze is being realized beyond his wildest expectation by electronic innova-tion. A constant gaze (or monitoring) of the entire population is now technologically possible, from credit rating, financial transaction analy-sis, health records, police files, cameras in public spaces, and mar-keting surveys that gauge consumer preference. More importantly, increasingly sophisticated new data processing technology enables the effective sorting of large amounts of information. The electronic panopticon is the latest instrument of the political economy of power (Lyon and Zureik, 1996). There is, however, a major change in the scale and range of the gaze. No longer are prisoners and factory workers the only individuals under observation. The electronic panop-ticon has us all under scrutiny. Nevertheless, the actual effectiveness of this gaze does not rest solely on technology but on the constructed willingness of a population to participate in it, and even to demand it.

The panopticon becomes the privileged source of observation of the behaviour of individuals and how they respond to various rules and commands. Therefore, the panopticon plays two central functions:

it facilitates the collection of data on individual and group behaviour, and allows for actual experimentation of new techniques of social engineering. In many psychology undergraduate texts, students read about something called the "Hawthorne effect" and about the "scientific management" approach proposed by Frederick Winslow Taylor. In the early 1930's a series of studies to improve the efficiency of workers in an assembly line considered the effects of different levels of lighting on productivity. Researchers were surprised to discover that any change in level of illumination, up or down, resulted in increased production. Apparently workers were responding to being observed, and scrutiny of their work habits encouraged greater productivity.

In the context of a modern prison, there is a direct link between the gazing function of the panopticon as a data collection system and as a normalizing instrument. Beyond the prison system, there is a similar instrumental trend in society. The Internet has become part of this new panopticon, and is being organized to maximize visibility. A key question to ask is: if the Internet functions as a panopticon, who is in the guard tower?

For some, this question is linked to the issue of who owns the Internet. On one level, ownership is equated with the physical infrastructure, including telephone lines and switches, satellites, microwave relays, etc. For example, CompuServe's dominance in the international market is due, in part, to its telephone networks that reach from Alaska to American Samoa. The implications of assigning control of the Internet to those who own its hardware have far-reaching consequences. The restructuring of time and space (both physical and social) depends heavily on how the issue of ownership is dealt with.

Who owns the Internet is a question often asked by people new to the network. The answer commonly given is that it is owned by no one and everyone at the same time. The Internet operates like a co-operative with governments, universities, service providers and other businesses providing small pieces of the infrastructure. The backbone of the Internet is "owned" by the US National Science Foundation and is run under contract to Merit—a joint venture between IBM and MCI. The backbone is the long-haul communication lines that provide connections to the various networks around the world. In North America, the lines that connect together servers are owned by local telephone and cable companies. This co-operative relationship works because self-interest compels organizations to maximize connectivity and efficiency. An international body known as the Internet Society establishes general guidelines for networking, and a non-profit organization known as Internic is responsible for domain name registration and associated grievance procedures. In sum, the Internet is run in a non-hierarchical, diffuse manner.

Another related issue has to do with access and those who are excluded from participating in this communication revolution. Although the Internet has the potential to overcome many of the traditional systemic barriers to access, an individual still needs a computer and modem, a telephone line, access to an Internet service provider, and leisure time to learn the intricacies of navigating a complex labyrinth of computer networks. Since such barriers still exist, it makes sense, intuitively, that most users of the Internet are technically-oriented and relatively well-educated.

Not only do economic barriers prevent the poor from participating in the electronic world, but it also limits their ability to participate in what is being packaged as electronic democracy. Government agencies and politicians are becoming more accessible through e-mail, and many have web sites on the World Wide Web. As in the physical world, however, not being enumerated means not having a voice. Those without access to the Internet quickly become invisible. In a sense, the global superpanopticon gazes only at those "worth" gazing at, and there has been considerable resistance to such monitoring.

At present, the Internet and activities related to shaping its future rests in the hands of the technically savvy, those who can write computer software to cancel or otherwise modify messages sent by others. This situation creates an interesting dynamic among a variety of forces where new power configurations among communicating individuals exist. Not only do governments, corporations, systems administrators, and law enforcement agencies attempt to control the flow of information on the electronic highway, individuals and special interest groups also play a role.

The Panopticon Within: Sexual and Non-sexual Interaction under Scrutiny

Computer users have found that high-quality monitors, Internet links to chat lines, Cu-SeeMe video reflector sites, pornographic newsgroups, and virtual reality simulations have added a new dimension to sex. The amount of computer pornography available on the

Internet and in adult bulletin boards is startling to many. The sophistication and quality of this pornography is surprising. In some ways, computer-mediated sexual interaction is the ultimate form of "safe sex", assuming one is careful to protect computer equipment from viruses. Nowadays, many fear contracting sexually transmitted diseases like AIDS, and with the short life span of relationships including marriage, a fear of intimacy may make computer-mediated interaction more appealing, and less threatening.

Eventually, full body suits will immerse virtual reality buffs in three-dimensional computer-generated environments. The benefits to airline pilots (and their future passengers) who can learn to fly in simulators, and to surgeons who can operate on virtual patients while learning new skills, are obvious. The potential to propel sex into this virtual world has captured the imagination of many, and movies like *Lawnmower Man* show both the benefits and dangers of human sexuality merging with silicon chips. Howard Rheingold (1991) speculates that virtual reality will soon involve the use of prosthetic devices that he calls "teledildonics". With teledildonics, the feel of male and female genitals are simulated using data sensing input/output devices designed to emulate their real-world counterparts.

The promise of virtual reality to create a world to retreat to is not without risk. Research by NASA and the US military demonstrated that 30 percent of people placed in a virtual reality simulator sufferer "flashbacks" and disorientation when returned to the non-virtual world (Strauss, 1995). A sensory conflict between what one sees and what one thinks one sees creates this problem. Perhaps the body's sensory systems need time to adapt to this new, substance-less world. Our interpersonal and social interactions may also suffer from the same technologically imposed structure.

Sexual and non-sexual interaction over the Internet between individuals using Internet Relay Chat (IRC) is another example of how a virtual self has been constructed. Since users participating in online fora can narrate their identities unfettered by physical and social constraints, there is an opportunity to experience a different type of social world where gender, age, race, and so on, can be altered. In this way the Internet is challenging the very notion of self.

Mark Poster told the story of how a reconstitution of gender had devastating affects on individuals connected to an online community (Poster, 1994). A group of women who met online to discuss personal issues were victimized by a reconstitution. After spending several months getting to know one another in this virtual world, one of them admitted to the group that he was not a woman but a man. In this case, honesty was the worst thing possible. The group disintegrated after several hostile exchanges. The "lie" broke the cohesiveness of this group, and social exchanges within the community were halted. The Internet might be the building site of a virtual self, but virtual communities seem to be less stable and predictable than their real-world counterparts.

Humans are literally becoming the flesh component of an electronic system where carbon-based life forms are connected to computers. In this context, there appears to be two possible strategies of resistance. The first is a whole-scale rejection of technology—a return to the quiet, less complicated days of yesterday if you will. Certain communities like the Hutterites of Manitoba and the Mormons of Utah have extolled the virtues of a simpler life for decades, and do not have an official presence in cyberspace. The second option is to embrace the race to virtuality, thus, becoming the "dedicated flesh" in the system. For example, hackers become anarchists to undermine the authoritarian structures that corporations and other institutions impose on those areas of the Internet under control. Yet, they do not often question the nature of privilege inherent in the Internet's structure. They use technological solutions to deal with the symptoms of social problems. By being technically savvy, computer hackers use technology to protest the direction of society.

This is precisely the chronic nightmare of network managers. Not only must system operators protect data from hackers who breach security, they must be vigilant against having equipment infected by computer viruses. In their simplest form, computer viruses are small programs that work by attaching a copy of themselves to an executable file. When an infected file is run, the virus replicates and does what it was designed to do. A relatively benign virus, known as "Yankee Doodle" first appeared in 1989, and played the song "Yankee Doodle" on a computer's internal speaker at a predetermined schedule. More damaging viruses like "Eddie" and "Diana P." spread slowly, sometimes imperceptibly, through a company's computer network, hitting the hard drives of computers, and deleting or damaging files and software en route. To stop viruses from spreading further, a company may have to shut down an entire network. For companies, viruses can mean the loss of data, lost time required for eradicating the virus, lost revenue, and possibly, lost customers.

Users of the Internet are at a greater risk from computer viruses. Pirated software is probably the greatest source of danger since FTP sites allow users to upload software to archives and to download available software. The Internet is littered with potholes and speed traps that have powerful effects on our behaviour. These obstacles slow down the race to virtuality by undermining the social, political and economic organization of this new information and communication infrastructure.

Community Standards in Cyberspace:
Using a Rubber Yardstick to Measure a Moving Target

As comet Hale-Bopp made its way through the northern skies in March and April of 1997, the world was shocked to hear about the mass suicide of a group of cultists, known as "Heaven's Gate", in San Diego. Apparently members of the cult believed that a UFO was following the comet, and that by terminating their existence here on earth, they could "hitch a ride" with the alien craft to a better world. With the Internet, the cult managed to spread their message to thousands around the world.

Through their web site, www.heavensgate.com, cult members made available information about their beliefs and distributed an elaborate, hypertext-based suicide note (Quitter, 1997). In this case, we see a marginalized group of people reaching out to the world through the Internet to build and help maintain their community of followers. Many believe that members of this suicide cult were misguided, and perhaps some feel sad about what happened to them. Nevertheless, the Internet helped get their message out in a controlled fashion. Instead of relying on traditional media like television, radio and newspapers, fringe organizations can jump the queue and use the Internet to communicate to large audiences. This quick, relatively inexpensive, customizable form of communication is ideally suited for facilitating the development of virtual communities, but there are drawbacks and limitations, and only certain kinds of communities thrive in cyberspace.

A community is a group of like-minded people tied together by rules and laws, customs and taboos, beliefs, and economic and social arrangements. Until recently, most communities existed within a defined geographical location that often mirrored national, provincial, territorial and local levels of social organization. For example, a country like Canada is composed of several interlocked, yet distinct

communities, but these communities are part of a larger body—
Canada. In cyberspace, the concept of community means something
different. No longer do geography or economic and social arrangements influence the formation and maintenance of communities in
the wired world. Some questions worth considering include: How
are such groups formed and what characteristics do members of virtual communities have in common? How permanent are these groups,
and is it possible for cyberspace to replace face-to-face interaction?
What effects do virtual communities have on temporally and geo-
graphically-bound communities like the nation-state?

Reaching Out to Touch Someone: How Do I Sign Up?

The Internet is an unusual place to meet people, but even the most
introverted can make contact with strangers without ever venturing
outside. Through an Internet service provider, you can exchange
messages with another person through e-mail, participate in a newsgroup, chat with IRC, or use voice-based and video-based technology. As the technology improves, and data compression algorithms
and equipment allow for more information to be squeezed through
the strained bandwidth, we can expect to see more interactive applications available through the Internet. At the present time, text-based
interaction with e-mail, Usenet and IRC offer the simplest and quick-
est forms of social interaction. The more bandwidth-intense applications for sound and video are slow, unstable and cumbersome.

When we meet someone in the "real" world, we rely on stereo-
types, body language, modes of speaking, accents, styles of clothing
and hair, and even body odour to judge a person. There are con-
stellations of beliefs that we hold for placing someone into a pre-
conceived stratum of society—social class, level of education, ethnicity
and race and, ultimately, their social desirability. In the text-based
part of the Internet, most of these external markers are absent, and
virtual communities are formed along different lines.

In theory, the Internet should be the most democratic, classless form
of social interaction. Individuals can communicate unfettered by the
prejudices arising from face-to-face interaction. In reality, the Internet
is elitist, exclusionary, and an instrument for electronic colonization.

The dominance of English as the primary language of the Internet
has become a sensitive issue for many around the world who see the
growth of this communication and information network as a cultural

and linguistic form of imperialism. There is a fear that the Internet, and the role it plays in re-mapping the "global village," will further erode vulnerable cultures and national identities by transporting not just English-based information, but "Western" culture including its values, mores, and even its slang (Pollack, 1995).

Some argue that this situation is purely a technological feature and nothing more. Computers represent information as a series of bits (for example, zero or one, on or off). This information is then transferred using a code known as ASCII (the American Standard Code for Information Interchange), which represents each character of a natural language by a sequence of zeros and ones. Binary coding allows for a maximum of 256 characters (for example, $2^8 = 256$). As a result, ASCII cannot handle many characters other than those in the English language.

A coding system known as Unicode helps overcome this problem. Instead of coding characters with a series of eight units, Unicode uses 16 so that 65,536 possible characters can be coded (for example, $2^{16} = 65,536$). This coding system allows for all the characters of the world's languages to have their own unique sequence and, therefore, helps alleviate some of these concerns. The dominance of English—or rather American—as the standard Internet language, however, may be too entrenched already. The global drive of the Internet also resulted in a flurry of activity to develop online language translation software. Some Internet servers like CompuServe use automatic translation to allow English, French, German and Spanish speakers to participate in online discussion groups. The accuracy of such software, however, leaves much to be desired.

In addition to English dominating the Internet, individuals with better typing skills, accurate spelling and faster computer and modem connections have a considerable advantage. This text-based world, and the virtual communities fostered by it, reward the better educated and more affluent. Like the "real" world, such attributes reflect advantages that follow class, race, gender and socio-economic differences. In a sense, the Internet is allowing the rich nations of the world to band together in the creation of a virtual world where the poor and disenfranchised cannot enter. Like having a muscle-bound security guard standing in front of a posh restaurant, or a high-security fence and guardhouse surrounding a gated community, the Internet protects its denizens from the unwelcome contact and intrusion of the technologically disempowered.

Perhaps virtual communities fill a need not satisfied in the "real" world, but this technology does not exist in a cultural vacuum, and neither is it value-free and neutral. In his book, *Technopoly*, Neil Postman (1992) wrote about the transformation of societies resulting from technology. Postman outlines a typology for three forms of cultural impacts created by technology. The first type of impact is on tool-using cultures, where the tool (a type of technology) affects the culture into which it is introduced. As an example, Postman tells the story of Dutch sociologist Egbert de Vries' research on the introduction of matches to an African tribe. In this tribe, a fire was lit following an act of sexual intercourse. One of the participants in the sexual act would have to visit a neighbour's tent to bring back a burning stick to light a fire, thus, making adultery difficult to conceal. When matches were introduced to the tribe, no longer was it necessary for sexual partners to expose themselves to public scrutiny—they could light their own fire. This relatively simple technology, a match, had the potential to impact on tribal rituals, sexual attitudes, social cohesiveness and, perhaps, the rate of adultery. On another note, this analysis feeds a form of technological determinism. Perhaps the introduction of matches to the tribe only had minor and temporary effects. In this light, technology allows the dominant relations in a society to remain the same. In modern society, technologies of the silicon age may have similar impacts. It is difficult to see how the introduction of the personal computer and the Internet has restructured the financial, social and institutional foundations of Western society. Arguably, such technologies strengthen pre-existing, dominant social relationships and make change more difficult to achieve.

The second type of impact created by technology is on more advanced, science-based cultures. Postman refers to this as technocracy, and outlines the historical developments of the scientific method and the ascendancy of rationality. My research on nuclear power plant safety and how decisions based on probabilistic risk assessment, toxicological and epidemiological analyses, and seismic margin study is an illustration of this (Mehta, forthcoming). Decisions made by technocrats, using skills purchased from technicians, represents a transformation in the source of social power, and allow certain technologies to dominate many facets of our existence.

The third effect of technology on culture covered by Postman is known as technopoly. Technopoly results when technology becomes culture, and vice versa. Like television, the Internet has helped firmly entrench computer technology into our culture. Not only do many of us spend our working days on the computer, but our leisure time is spent playing computer games, searching the Internet for services and information, budgeting home finances, storing and viewing photographs and recipe collections in electronic form, and for some, viewing pornography. The computer has become a prime source of information and entertainment.

The computer has taken on a new prominence in our lives, and many homes display proudly their newest computer in the family room, next to the television set. Here, we see how technology has become synonymous with culture. We are surrounded with equipment that constantly reminds us that work and leisure are one and the same thing, that Internet access means not having to drive to the local café or shopping mall, and that friendships and other types of relationships can be sought in the safe haven of cyberspace. Is it any wonder that virtual communities exist, considering the dominance of computer technology in our lives?

There are several problems associated with constructing a lifestyle based on the centrality of computer technology. On a physical level, the sedentary nature of working with computers probably exacerbates the decline in health noted in several Western countries. There is also considerable scientific debate on the health effects associated with exposure to the electric and magnetic fields generated by computers and monitors. On a social level, there is concern that computer-mediated interaction is replacing face-to-face human interaction. Perhaps our relationship with machines is creating a cyborg culture where we aspire to process information logically and efficiently. Social relationships are messy and profoundly biological in nature. The cyborgification of human nature may change our sense of community and self in unexpected ways. On an economic level, computer technology is creating a new kind of worker. Many believe that the introduction of computers into the workplace has created a new class of worker—the digital literati. On a small scale, computer technology has created several new millionaires in Silicon Valley and other parts of the world. The vast majority of workers who use computers, however, are electronically tethered and perform menial tasks. Such workers are easily replaced and subject to the smallest changes in the marketplace. There are several other impacts associated with this lifestyle that I recommend the reader think about.

The Stability of Virtual Communities

Today's computers are things to marvel at. Weighing less than ten pounds, a laptop computer with a Pentium microprocessor can do more calculations in a second than computers 20 years ago could perform in several hours. The ubiquity of the home computer has transformed how many of us work and play. Unless a computer is connected to a network, like the Internet, however, the computer remains little more than a glorified calculator. Certainly, it is bigger, faster, and more graphical but when isolated, it soon becomes obsolete and boring for many of us. The Internet has helped bridge many of the technical problems associated with compatibility, and now the slowest 286 computer can communicate with the fastest Pentium through what is known as the TCP/IP protocol. This technical feat of engineering means that almost anyone with a computer built in the past ten years can participate in cyberspace, and be part of a virtual community.

Virtual communities are an important part of the information society because they demonstrate that the electronic transfer of information around the world is more than an activity for governmental and corporate elites. Such communities also show how the project of modernity has failed. As Mark Poster noted, electronic communication technologies enhance significantly our postmodern possibilities by creating new loci of speech, reconstituting self-identities, and rendering borders ineffectual. How do these transformations affect virtual communities and their embeddedness within the information economy?

In *Under Technology's Thumb*, William Leiss (1990) claimed that concepts like the information revolution, information society and information economy represent a new form of technocratic thinking. For Leiss, these concepts show that public policy is being used to "soften up" the public so that they more readily accept new technologies. Information society metaphors are being used to inject new values and social behaviours that reinforce the inevitability of these changes and, therefore, bolster the new markets being developed. Are virtual communities a way to push us along this path, or are they an undesirable by-product?

Virtual communities operate within the information society, but are in most cases, are strongly resistant to being thrust into the information economy. For example, pornographic newsgroups heat up with "flame wars" when commercial posters of pornography become too active. In this study, I have noticed that the community of Usenet denizens who regularly post to a particular newsgroup became quite irate when a commercial poster "spammed" a newsgroup. Spamming is equivalent to distributing flyers in a neighbourhood or mass faxing an advertisement. In pornographic newsgroups, spamming also refers to commercial services that post too many "soft core" image files. Most of the opposition to spamming in Usenet followed a mass posting of "Playboy" and "Penthouse" style images. Very few people objected to the explicit images posted by commercial services. The virtual community, in this case, is more accepting of these commercial images and is, therefore, tolerating some parts of the information economy while rejecting others.

The stability of a virtual community in Usenet is dependent on how members of the community respond to spamming, and how dedicated spammers are to their cause. The newsgroup community of alt.sex.pedophilia was almost destroyed when an individual using the name "Mad Hacker" posted thousands of threats and off-topic messages to the group during the spring and summer of 1996. Instead of posting images and exchanging ideas, beliefs and opinions, members of this group were dedicated to hunting down and stopping Mad Hacker. What prevents someone from doing the same thing in any newsgroup? For example, could a person of Armenian descent spam a newsgroup devoted to Turkish culture because of the Armenian genocide? Could an American spam a Canadian newsgroup because they disagreed with Canada's trade agreements with Cuba? Virtual communities, if they are to survive, must be able to withstand these attacks.

*The Effects of Virtual Communities on the "Real" World:
A Withering Away of the State?*

When the first "manned" rocket boldly leapt through the earth's atmosphere in 1961, we became aware that an important step towards the colonization of distant planets had been taken. In a way, a seed of hope was planted; maybe we could escape the earth if pollution or nuclear war made life here unlivable. For me, it is no coincidence that a spate of movies and science fiction novels about colonizing space (for example, *Star Trek*) emerged around the same time that scientists like Rachel Carson and Barry Commoner began writing about serious environmental problems. The practicality of evacuating billions of people, coupled with an awareness that there is nowhere to go at this moment, makes this option unthinkable. We better find another option (like reducing the amount of pollution we create), or retreat into a different kind of world, maybe a cyber world. This latter option is not feasible, however, since we still need to sustain a body to operate computers.

By the 1970s, many people living in the Western world were addicted to their television sets. Several studies over the years show that the average Canadian watches 28 hours of television per week, while the number of viewing hours for children is even higher. We have retreated into a broadcast world where advertisements for products and services enter our homes on a daily basis. Instead of interacting with one another, many of us sit in front of our television sets, absorb product information, and begin to hold worldviews that resonate with the programming we are exposed to. In many cases, these worldviews depict our society as a violent and dangerous place where strangers should not be trusted. As atomized consumers sitting in front of the "box", we have little or no motivation to participate in the political life of our communities and nations, and our "real" world community is devoted to work and shopping. Cyberspace is changing this through the formation of virtual communities, but not without considerable resistance from governments and corporations.

The Internet is a "Wild West", and governments and corporations find it a threatening, chaotic, and unpredictable place. The formation of virtual communities may represent acceptance of the information age, but the benefits of governing or doing business online are minimal at the present time. The companies that seem to be thriving online are information services and the pornography industry. Even though more people are working from home by computer—a form of telecommuting—big business and government are attempting to gain control of the Internet through regulatory restructuring and tough laws against contentious content, especially pornography.

These actions have led some to speculate that the Internet, as we know it, is dying and will soon be replaced by a newer, "better" Internet II. It is hard to ignore the complaints of those who claim that the Internet is too big, difficult to finds things on, and filled with trivial and sometimes inaccurate information. Governments and corporations are desperately trying to convince us that the Internet is dangerous, unruly, and filled with "crackpots" who should not be trusted. In other words, things are out of control, but if you let us take over the Internet we will make it a better place. Handing the Internet to corporations and governments will probably mean the death of virtual communities. Instead of fostering an online world where anyone can communicate with anyone else, it is likely that a "controlled" version of the Internet will become more like watching television: one-way, packaged, and filtered. Virtual communities are nowhere near as much a threat to the "real" world, as the "real" corporate world is to such communities.

Cyberdemocracy: Does Your Vote Count?

At the end of the twentieth century, advocates of liberal democracy are faced with a curious dilemma: the collapse of socialist governments around the world means that its ideological ascendancy has never been more complete, yet many are becoming increasingly disillusioned with the political process. As this alienation increases, technology is called upon to cure our most pressing political problems. Many believe that the Internet will create the conditions for the direct participation of citizens in decision-making and, thus, save democracy. It is claimed that the Internet can deepen understanding of policy issues, broaden participation, increase the accountability of officeholders, and register votes and public opinion.

Enlightenment philosopher Jean-Jacques Rousseau believed that democracy could be created through a public meeting of citizens, and that access to information was a necessary pre-condition. In a democratic society, it is presumed that public understanding of issues is necessary for "good" government. Government must be responsive to the will of citizens. Many have noted that even the most totalitarian regimes must generate some level of public support to rule effectively. To accomplish this goal, government needs to stimulate public debate and make available information regarding the various options under consideration. How can the Internet help deepen public understanding of policy issues?

Unlike television, radio, newspaper, and other forms of broadcasting, the Internet allows for the interactive exchange of information. With e-mail, for example, asynchronous exchanges of information are possible. E-mail does not depend on the simultaneous availabil-

ity and attention of sender and receiver. Therefore, e-mail increases
the ability of individuals to be active participants in a dialogue
extended over time and space, rather than as passive recipients of
"canned" programming.

There is an assumption that access to information and the exchange
of ideas is necessary and sufficient to broaden public participation.
One often hears of libraries and shopping malls providing free access
to the Internet. It is assumed that even the homeless can participate
in public debates or contact politicians through e-mail. I seriously
question this position and want the reader to be aware that access
to equipment is not the same as access to a resource. For example,
most home computers sold today come with a modem, yet the majority of people who own computers do not have access to the Internet.
The equipment is, of course, the minimum requirement for access,
but there is more involved. By offering free Internet access in public places like libraries, and in semi-public places like shopping malls,
two essential ingredients are missing: knowledge about how to use
the equipment and access to the interactive side of the Internet.

One can argue that this knowledge gap is surmountable, and that
with time and assistance, the technologically illiterate will learn how
to surf the Internet. This is exactly my point. Learning how to surf
the World Wide Web is akin to learning how to use a fancy television
remote control. I can teach almost anyone to use a search engine
and customize a search in a few hours, but I would only be teaching
someone how to browse. Browsing through web sites is not by itself
participating in a virtual community, nor is it a political act either.
By offering access to the Internet without empowering people to create their own web sites, use chat and video-conferencing technology,
such access becomes a passive sport. How can we broaden public
participation by increasing access to the Internet if all we are doing
is teaching people how to browse? Maybe what we are really after
is the creation of new markets, or the consolidation of existing ones.

If you watch enough television or look carefully at magazine advertisements, you have probably noticed that many companies now give
their web site addresses. Presumably consumers can look up the web
site of their favourite brand of laundry detergent or toothpaste, and
get product information. What we have here is an advertisement in
one medium cross-referencing a different type of advertisement in
another—an advertisement in an advertisement, if you will. The
casual browser can access this information through the Internet and,

thus, reinforce the commercial development of this network. There comes a point in this development, however, when access and public participation intersect. This is when the accessibility issue becomes problematic.

A commercially-oriented service makes money by knowing how to market itself. In short, the Internet is a tool for accessing different markets on a local and international level. Since we already know that most users of the Internet are from advantaged groups to begin with, commercial services wishing to make money through the Internet must target this audience. Based on demographic information about users, companies can strategically market products and services. At the same time, industry is called upon to help build the network, and to wire remote communities. The goal for governments is to create the necessary market conditions to stimulate industry to invest in building and maintaining infrastructure. This, however, is a fine balancing act. Why would industry invest large amounts of capital in wiring remote communities when demographics suggest that the biggest markets have already been tapped? For example, in Canada, Internet access in major cities like Toronto, Montreal, Vancouver, Calgary and Halifax already provides industry with a large market. The cost of wiring small towns like Corner Brook and Kenora provide diminishing marginal returns. Government must force industry's hand by offering all kinds of concessions, none of which are politically popular nowadays. We need to be sold on the notion that concessions are important to the well-being of our country, be it national unity, protection of cultural industries, or electronic democracy. How is this done?

There has been an erosion of trust and confidence in government and industry over the past few decades. Instead of more government, many are demanding a leaner, more efficient, less bureaucratic form of government. For example, in the Province of Ontario, the Progressive Conservative government of Premier Mike Harris cut social service programmes, privatized former crown corporations, amalgamated municipalities, and downloaded the costs of social programmes like welfare and garbage collection to municipalities. Even though many of these choices have led to considerable social dislocation and anguish, this government is still popular in the polls.

Residents of Canada who wish to contact a member of parliament or the prime minister can take advantage of free postage for sending letters. This system was put in place originally so that barriers for contacting politicians would be lessened for the poor. By the late 1990s, all political parties in Canada, and many politicians and senators in the United States of America, had web sites to facilitate a different kind of contact: electronic contact. Not only do these web sites usually provide e-mail addresses but also information about a politician's background, political orientation and beliefs, policy positions, and platforms for upcoming elections. It is assumed that this way of disseminating information and enhancing contact improves the accountability of office-holders.

Whenever technology is developed, there is a need to evaluate its impacts on society, the natural environment, and other technologies. One of the promising features of the Internet is that it can be used to collect public opinion data and votes. It is assumed that direct democracy leads to more responsive and accountable government and, presumably, to greater citizen satisfaction. Let us look at some of the technical and social barriers to implementing this form of democracy, and then consider the possible impacts electronic voting may have on different types of issues.

Surveying public opinion and registering votes through the Internet is not a simple task. On the technical side, there needs to be a way to ensure that a person can vote only once on any particular issue or election. It has been suggested that personal identification numbers (PINs), like those used when accessing an automated teller machine, can solve much of this problem by matching a secret number to voting status. For example, once your vote has been included, the system automatically de-lists you from voting again. The problem I have with this system is that it is not too difficult for a hacker to create a software package to run millions of possible combinations of PINs and, thus, vote several times once a valid PIN has been randomly uncovered. To overcome this problem, PINs need to be long and complicated with probably 12 or more digits and letters. If voters have to recall long strings of characters, errors become more likely, and participation will probably decrease. It is possible to have a personal computer store your PIN, and send this number automatically when voting, but another problem emerges. If a family of five shares a common computer, for example, it is possible that one member of the family can vote on behalf of all five by simply clicking a mouse. To ensure that the person voting is the person sending the PIN, more elaborate mechanisms are needed. This can include voice confirmation prior to voting, or may involve a different scenario altogether.

The technical problems associated with collecting votes from home through the Internet probably mean that the first generation of federal level elections using such technology will rely on kiosk systems in public places. Instead of registering a vote in the comfort of your home, you may have to go to a polling station to vote on a networked computer. Although such measures are likely to improve the speed and efficiency of the electoral process, much of the convenience is lost. It is unlikely that the public will respond favourably to this kind of voting, and the collection of public opinion data will be more difficult.

There are other technical issues associated with electronic voting, but we will not go into them any further. I am also somewhat concerned with the security and privacy issues arising from this technology. Although one has to trust that government will not link a vote to your identity, when it comes to public opinion polling, this is unlikely. In Ontario, only the public sector is required by law to maintain the anonymity and confidentially of your personal information (Cavoukian, 1995). The private sector is not required to maintain privacy, and can and does exchange and sell personal information. Electronic opinion polling makes it easier to collect and compile information and, therefore, help marketers be more strategic. What about public opinion polling on issues such as abortion, euthanasia, free trade, Quebec sovereignty, etc.? This is where social limitations become evident.

When I visited the State of California in 1989, residents were voting for a new governor. I was surprised to hear that California residents not only vote for local politicians, but also vote on a variety of issues known as propositions. There is a limited number of propositions allowed on the ballot, and residents vote on such things as level of taxation, child care reform, and affirmative action policies. The issue that most surprised me was a vote on whether or not police officers should be allowed to use radar units to catch speeders on the state's roadways. Apparently, some people in California believe that such technology is an infringement on their right to speed, and mustered enough support to ensure that this became an issue. It is not too difficult to guess the outcome of this proposition: California's police officers are not allowed to use radar on city streets. If an issue like this can get on a ballot, what prevents all kinds of other issues from being voted on through electronic opinion polling?

In Canada there are several issues where greater public consultation is both desirable and necessary. For example, Canadians have not yet had the opportunity to vote on such issues as the legality of abortion, capital punishment, use of reproductive technology, the unilateral secession of Quebec, etc. In our political system, it is assumed that the local Member of Parliament represents the interests of her constituents, and votes accordingly. This is rarely the case, and there have been several notable examples of politicians being punished for not following their party's position. Additionally, when Canadians go to the polls to elect a new leader, rarely are these kinds of issues given centre stage. Instead, we vote on such things as free trade, deficit fighting practices, and employment creation programmes. In my opinion, there is a need to open up the debate on many of these neglected social issues, but I am unsure about whether or not an electronic form of polling will work. In short, electronic democracy is an intriguing but imperfect device for reviving democracy. Perhaps we need to devote more thought and energy to improving our existing system, without looking to technology as a panacea for social problems. The reconstruction of the Internet as a broadcast medium makes democratic enhancement even less likely. Is there really any kind of technology that enhances democracy?

Wiring the Virtual Commons: Content versus Infrastructure

In 1968, Garrett Hardin noted that a "tragedy of the commons" occurs when a common resource pool is overused (Hardin, 1968). For example, a patch of publicly-owned farmland can be used by local farmers to graze cattle. It is in the interest of each individual farmer to graze more cattle on this land since it maximizes his profits. This self-maximizing behaviour, however, can eventually degrade the land to a point where it becomes unusable for all farmers, and a tragedy of the commons results. The same thing may happen to the Internet due to excessive congestion, since it seems to belong to everyone, yet is protected by no one (Gupta, Stahl, and Whinston, 1995). This tragedy is made worse because concern over contentious content is hindering the development of the needed infrastructure for wiring homes and businesses to the Internet. In this case, the tragedy is both social and technological, and its impact on the formation of virtual communities is potentially devastating.

Like the issue of accessibility, the content versus infrastructure debate depends on the incentives provided by government for business to enter cyberspace. Normally, incentives include start-up funding for local Internet service providers, tax concessions and preferential capital development loans, training programmes through industry/academic joint ventures, and reform of existing regulation. Now that much of the necessary infrastructure is in place in urban parts of Canada and the USA, two other questions need to be addressed: How can these incentives be used to stimulate the development of new markets while strong content-based regulation for controlling the flow of pornography, hate literature, etc. are being implemented? How can we ensure that rural communities and people living in urban "ghettos" have access to the digital economy?

In a general sense, regulation is about controlling through rules, laws; and principles the actions of people, corporations, and governments. The balancing act in capitalist countries is to control the risks arising from dangerous activities with the economic and social benefits of following a particular course of action. From another perspective, how can we balance the rights of the individual against the needs of the collective? When talking about the Internet, this balancing act hinges upon regulating content and building infrastructure, and the debate over Internet service provider liability is key.

When the US Communications Decency Act was debated in the House of Congress in early 1996, Internet service providers expressed concern that strong content-based regulation would kill their fledgling companies (Rowan, 1996). Large service providers like America Online and CompuServe expressed serious concern that they were being singled out due to their size and dominance in the market, and stated that strong content regulation would place a heavy burden on them to screen the activities of thousands of customers. In this case, a large company is at a disadvantage since it is more likely to be noticed if a failure to perform a censoring role is made, and since it has the burden of screening user activities. The large Internet service providers rightly viewed the CDA as anti-competitive, yet such regulations were sold as part of a larger Telecommunications Act that was mostly deregulatory. This inconsistency between the larger bill and its CDA component is worth considering in detail.

The history of regulating the telecommunications industry in the USA explains why there are many discrepancies between the CDA and the larger reform bill. In 1934, the US Congress passed the Communications Act for regulating the sole provider of long distance service, AT&T (Kall, 1996). At this time, broadcasting was limited to AM radio, which was heavily regulated to avoid signal interference due to the small amount of bandwidth available. For almost 50 years, the Communications Act remained unchanged even though considerable changes had occurred in the technology. In 1982, AT&T was broken into smaller, independently-owned regional companies, and the long-distance telephone market was opened to competition. Another major change in 1984 established the Federal Communications Commission (FCC) as an authority over cable operators. Concerned that cable and telephone companies would converge to form larger services within a given region (a monopoly), the FCC regulated them separately and required that they not combine services. The Telecommunications Act of 1996 changed this, and cable and telephone companies were allowed to compete for each other's markets.

The Telecommunications Act is a late, but welcome piece of legislation that finally shows that the US government understands that traditional differences between radio, television and telephone are evaporating due to technological innovation. Communication satellites and cellular telephone networks are two illustrations of this. That is, sending an image file, sound byte, or text-based message is electronically the same thing. The representation of data is the same no matter what is sent, and the sophistication of today's modern telephones, home computers and television sets mean that appliances used to receive data are flexible and non-discriminatory. This is where the content debate comes into play. Computer networks and computers are inherently insensitive to content: a picture of a mountain range scanned from *National Geographic* is elementally the same as one from *Hustler*. Additionally, telephones can now receive video signals, some television sets have built-in telephones, and home computers are used to receive both television signals and telephone calls. The convergence of these technologies is pushing regulators to change outdated regulatory structures based on older conceptions of how technologies differed.

Mitchell Kapor, co-founder of the Electronic Frontier Foundation and founder of Lotus Development Corporation, sees the convergence of these technologies as a necessary part of creating "high-capacity broadband networks by cable and telephone companies" (Kapor, 1993). For Kapor, the success of the Internet is tied to how well integrated these services are, and how consensus among business, government, and regulators is achieved. At this point, there are three areas of consensus among these constituents, and each area shows clearly how the infrastructural needs of the Internet are indissolubly wedded to the content passing through it.

First, there is agreement that the Internet will be developed and maintained by the private sector, not government. In Canada, the federal government has strongly supported this notion, and has put in place funding opportunities for the private sector to take necessary risks to develop new markets (Information Highway Advisory Council Secretariat, 1996). The rapid commercialization of the Internet is an indication that business is interested, yet there is still a role for government. Government should remain involved in supporting research, help promote standards for inter-operability and interconnectivity, and protect the interest of citizens in certain areas including privacy, security and accessibility. In a sense, not much has changed; telephone and cable companies still play a dominant role in bringing information to the public. With the Internet, they have to bear most of the cost of developing the physical network and maintaining high-capacity servers for the growing number of people entering cyberspace. Government should be responsible for ensuring that sovereignty and national identity are protected while promoting cultural industries.

Second, there is an awareness that the Internet will have to be built on the remains of the existing telephone and cable companies. Instead of replacing coaxial and copper wire connections, the Internet will operate through a hybrid network. Fibre optic cables will connect with copper and coaxial wires to distribute messages. Since in most urban areas fibre optic cables act as primary conduit for cable and telephone companies, the opportunity to wire more homes to the network is relatively high. The actual wires that run to individual homes and businesses, however, are likely to be coaxial and copper, and the cost of replacing this last segment of the connection with fibre optics is not justified. In rural and remote areas, this hybrid network creates more of a problem. In many rural parts of Canada and the USA, older telephone switches and copper wires connect homes. Some areas still use multiparty telephone lines that make connecting to the Internet impossible. People living with "party" lines cannot even use fax machines. Many of these areas do not have cable either, and rely on antennas and satellite receiver dishes. For these communities, the cost of running fibre optics into homes or setting up a reliable satellite relay system is high.

Third, there is awareness that the future of the Internet is likely to be video-driven. Cable and telephone companies are investing heavily in figuring out how to deliver movies on demand. For the moment, consumers are forced to rely on the programming of television networks for their movie viewing, rent movies, or use "pay-per-view" services. With higher capacity networks and improved compression technology, it is hoped that consumers will be able to order movies in real-time through their cable or telephone company, or perhaps some combination of the two. For example, you may be able in the near future to telephone a service provider and request a particular movie at a specified time. Much like ordering a pizza for delivery, this service will allow you to customize when and how you watch the movie ordered. With conventional pay television, viewers are forced to watch movies at pre-arranged times. With this service, greater flexibility is offered. Cable companies, in particular, are keen on developing video-on-demand because of the threat posed by direct broadcast satellite services (DBS). Here, we see a different kind of content issue at work. To compete in a deregulated marketplace, cable and telephone companies must provide more service to customers in the form of video-on-demand. Personally, I see these changes as an important step to improving both customer service and the greater integration of telecommunications networks into the Internet.

These changes in our world coincide with what Don Tapscott, in his book *The Digital Economy* (1996), refers to as the "new world disorder". In this disordered world, there is convergence of computers, communication networks and content through interactive multimedia. With a decline in the cost of processing and storing data, and the growing use of distributed communication networks, our world is undergoing profound changes. Some like MIT's Nicholas Negroponte (1995) find these changes "exhilarating" because of their impacts on the erosion of nation-states, whereas others, including myself, believe that a digital economy may be more elitist, exclusionary, and socially and environmentally damaging than the one it replaces.

Conclusion

The Internet is intricately tied to the forces of globalization, and fits a post-industrial worldview in which profitable and progressive industries are assumed to provide satisfying, high-paying jobs. In this post-industrial information economy, a transformation of society is expected. Such a transformation is expected to push Western society further along in its evolution to a service economy, where "white-collar" and professional workers dominate, and where increased reliance on computers and information technology enhances our postmodern potential by improving the quality of life (for example, having more leisure time).

The Internet, by definition, is the opposite of centralization; as a result, a conflict between this technology and the state appears inevitable. The shift from a highly centralized information and communication infrastructure to a decentralized set of interconnected networks has generated concern about issues of jurisdiction, privacy and censorship. There are also concerns about the effects of this new technology on self-identity and social interaction through the formation of virtual communities. The Internet has helped create a new kind of global community where new community standards are being developed.

An illustration of these effects is the formation, often by market forces, of virtual communities that respect no geographical boundaries. This new "public sphere" represents an exclusive enclave of privileged, technologically-oriented and enabled individuals and groups that prosper from the globalizing effects of the Internet. Although the benefits of the Internet are real for many, the social dislocation stimulated by this technology generates a global economy and culture geared towards the internationalization of labour, the erosion of some nation-states and expansion of others, and places a severe strain on governance and public accountability. Here, we see the influence of globalization on economics and public policy and the broader implications for citizens, governments, and markets. These effects include, but are not limited to, changes in the global economy, evolution of nation-states, and a re-definition of social contracts and associated deficits in democratic practices.

THE REAL IN THE VIRTUAL:
SPEECH, SELF AND SEX IN THE REALM
OF PURE TEXT

STELLA KOH

Department of Sociology
National University of Singapore

Preamble—The Ecstasy of Communication

"Connected!" is the catchphrase of our times; cyberspace has been hailed a milestone in technological history. "(T)echnology is no longer a means of mastering the human environment, but . . . it becomes the human environment" (Lajoie, 1995:164). The exponential increase in the number of people who partake of computer-mediated communication (CMC) is a sign of the times. The sheer number of individuals who interact via modems disproves the ominous predictions that have been made about the alienating effects of computer technology. Being hooked up to cyberspace opens up social and informational vistas. The dormant potential of the Internet that can be harnessed for our social and intellectual growth, as well as for entertainment, is mind-boggling. The birth of new technologies brings forth bursts of creative energy, and sometimes, these new experiences and ways of seeing expand our horizons.

"Cyberspace" is a term coined by the Canadian writer William Gibson in the seminal cyberpunk novel, *Neuromancer* (1984). Gibson terms it a "consensual hallucination" (ibid.) where people communicate in imaginary, non-physical spaces. As a result of the rapid technological advances made in CMC, the concept of communication in cyberspace no longer remains a work of fiction, but has its place in our everyday lives. Some of these new communication technologies that are widely used in our day-to-day activities include e-mail, electronic bulletin boards, Multi-User Domains (MUDS), the World Wide Web, ICQ and Internet Relay Chat (IRC). Each of these technologies has stupendous consequences for human interaction. This paper explores how one such CMC technology, IRC, has changed the experience of communication. The arrival of a new technology brings considerable change into our personal and social lives (McLuhan, 1964). This realization—that technology has more than just utilitarian functions—is an important one. Technology is increasingly mediating our social relations and self-identities. The ubiquity and prevalence of virtual encounters in everyday life have implications for social life and society that cannot be dismissed casually. IRC is a new frontier in the realm of human communication. It is one of the most social places in cyberspace. It is a "great good place" (Oldenburg, 1997) of sorts, where the "lonely crowds" (Riesman, 1961) go to satisfy their need for sociality and/or intellectual companionship—but with a modern twist, because unlike the "great good places" of the past, IRC does not have a physical location. It is an imagined space whose existence is sustained by the imaginations of the IRC masses. One's ticket to IRC—a computer, a modem and a telephone line.

The data presented here comes from two sources: online ethnographic fieldwork[1] and from interviews conducted with 54 respondents. Over a period of several months, I kept a log of the interactions that took place on IRC for textual analysis. I also drew on logs that were given to me by some of the respondents. The first of several concerns in this paper is displayed in the title of the paper, that is, an exploration of how elements of the "real"[2] world seep in the virtual realm. The classification of our experiences into the binary divisions of "real" and "virtual" is to privilege one entity and to downplay the significance of the other.[3] On IRC, however, such binary divisions are rendered less distinct when the "real" and "virtual" realms

---

[1] In this study, non-systematic purposive sampling methods were used. The 54 respondents were found through personal contacts, snowballing and approaching strangers online. Representative sampling was impossible to carry out for two reasons. First, the high entry-and-exit rate of users on IRC caused the sample population to fluctuate frequently. Second, to avoid detection, some users used a command to make themselves "invisible"; therefore, the list of online users on display was always incomplete. All observed interactions took place on the Galaxynet server. Galaxynet is one of the servers on IRC. It is the server used by the majority of Singapore users.

[2] In Goffman's (1974:21) frame analysis discourse, the "real" or real life, would constitute a "primary framework". Subsequently, all interactions "framed entirely in terms of a primary framework are said to be real or actual, to be really or actually occurring" (ibid.:47). Virtual reality (VR) is usually cast as the opposite of the "real".

[3] In the Derridean tradition, entities are cast against their opposites, so that one entity, the "positive" term, subjugates the other, the "negative". The "negative" is then conceptualized as inadequate or derivative, and subsequently, seen to be "lacking". Also, see Chayko (1993).

morph into one, and when the "human" and the "machine" merge in one's adventures in cyberspace. It is in the light of such developments that an examination of the blurring of such boundaries is warranted. I shall address this issue by examining the transformative character of IRC on the experiences of communication, identity and sexuality. Social encounters on IRC are a running commentary of their real-life counterparts. What then does the vitality of the IRC scene say about the "real" world?

We Are the Moving Matrix

IRC is both a form of public life and a form of private social life. People meet in virtual chat rooms, known as "channels", where conversations and discussions are held in the presence of other IRC users. Paradoxically, while IRC users are connected to others, they usually do so in isolation at their computers. Despite the distinction made between written and spoken forms of communication by language and linguistics scholars, the mode of communication on IRC marries both the written and the spoken form. The result is a hybrid form of synchronous, interactive chat; that is, chat taking place in real time. IRC chat resembles face-to-face spoken language, except that the conversations are typed out. IRC text has a postmodern character. The line between the author and the reader is rendered indistinct, as IRC users are both the producers and the consumers of the text. They are producers in that they co-author the conversation that appears on other people's screens. What they contribute to the conversation or discussion in channels forms part of the text that moves up and off the screen, and they are consumers in that they read what appears on their screen. As both producer and consumer, an IRC user is simultaneously limited and emancipated by the medium. The collective amount of text created is massive since there are thousands of users. Juxtaposed with the quiet hustle and bustle of real life, where strangers pass one another by, is a subterranean world of sorts where strangers chat eagerly with each other via modems.

IRC chat essentially comprises typed utterances that are modelled on the form of spoken conversation. As typing is slower than speaking, brief and succinct responses are usually given to reduce lapses in conversation. Chatting with a slow typist can be frustrating and one is likely to lose interest in the conversation and to just move on to the next chatting partner. There is a tendency for IRC users to reduce words or phrases to the shortest possible forms, but that will still allow them to be recognizable. Speedy responses are valued more than impeccable grammar and spelling. As such, typographical errors, spelling mistakes and incorrect grammar are all part of IRC chat. The use of acronyms and abbreviations is also common. Chats take place either in channels or through private messaging. Channels can be topic-based forums, or they can simply be a "great good place" for people to "hang out". Each channel has a name, which may or may not reflect the conversational interests of the people in it. Channels are denoted by the symbol "#". For example, #music and #philosophy are channels that focus on music-related chat and philosophical discussions, respectively. Conversation styles can range from light-hearted banter to scholarly discussions to cheesy flirtation sessions. The overall atmosphere on IRC is relaxed and informal.

Communication, as we know it in real life, consists of two components—the verbal component and the non-verbal. Both components are crucial to communication, and consequently, to the formation of relationships. Non-verbal communication includes body language, facial expressions, gestures, etc., which can change the meaning of messages in both subtle and dramatic ways (Stone, 1962). Communication on IRC, however, lacks the non-verbal component since IRC communication is entirely textual. IRC users are aware of the importance of non-verbal behaviour and have displayed ingenuity and creativity in coming up with a range of paralanguage techniques (Walther, 1992) to enrich online communication. There are three ways by which nuances in messages are conveyed: the use of "emoticons", the use of "actions", and the use of textual emphasis and word variations.

"An emoticon is an emotional icon, or a pictorial expression of the emotions of the moment" (Fudpucker, 1992:557). Emoticons are a combination of keyboard symbols to form facial expressions and are to be read sideways. They are used to denote emotions or moods like anger, happiness, humour, sadness, indignation, shock, fear, etc. Here are some other commonly used emoticons:

:(denotes sadness or unhappiness
:~ a crying face
;) a face with a wink, a cheeky smile or a lewd smile
:P a face with the tongue sticking out, which denotes indignation or cheekiness

:X a face with lips sealed
:O a face showing shock or surprise
8) a face with a pair of spectacles on

Conversations are usually liberally peppered with emoticons to give a more nuanced and intimate meaning to messages. For example, let us compare using "hello" and "hello :)" as a greeting. The former sounds neutral and impersonal, while the latter conveys warmth and friendliness. The addition of a "smiley" emoticon to a greeting can work wonders in increasing one's congeniality ratings on IRC. "Actions" are used to express an action or an event, either by sandwiching the action/event between two asterisks, or by invoking the action command. For example, instead of saying "I am sneezing" or "I am frowning", actions like "*sneeze*" and "*frown*" are used, respectively. Alternatively, the action command can be invoked. For example, if my username on IRC is "Muse", and if I want to give someone a hug, I would type "/me hugs you". The action would then appear on the other users' screens as:

*Muse hugs you.

The emphasis of certain words, through the use of keyboard symbols, is used to lend tone and to mimic speech as used in face-to-face conversations. Textual emphases like punctuation and the highlighting of words are adopted to create the effects of tones and exclamations in speech. Capital letters are used to denote shouting:

<Muse> DON'T YOU DARE DO THAT!!!!

Underscores and asterisks are used to emphasize words:

<Muse> that was *not* a nice thing to do at all
<Muse> I had _such_ a bad day today

To draw out the sound of a word, reduplicated letters are used:

<Muse> this is waaaaaaaaaaaaay cooooooooooool !! wooooooohooooooooo !!!!

Pauses in speech are indicated by the use of "...":

<Muse> well ... i don't know ... let me think on that ...

In (traditional) CMC studies, it is proposed that the lack of social cues (known as the "cluelessness model") in communication should lead to a lack of spontaneity in communication styles (Spears & Lea, 1992). We do not, however, see this situation on IRC. The use of emoticons, actions and textual emphasis can inject spontaneity, liveliness and a sense of intimacy in IRC chat. Even though interactions on IRC are computer-mediated, users are frequently forthcoming in their self-disclosures, and the relationships between them can get personal. This could be because people "need to have some distance from . . . intimate observation by others in order to feel sociable" (Sennett, 1976:15). As one respondent commented,

> I can talk to people more easily online because I feel more comfortable talking online than in real life. Online chatting is much more relaxing, since there's no need to worry about how sloppy you look. So you tend to talk more and open up more to people. When you spend so much time talking and telling each other private things, it's easy to grow close.

IRC is a play-space for the disembodied self. The IRC atmosphere is predominantly recreational, playful and experimental. IRC operates on a different plane of reality from real life. The reality of IRC accommodates fantasy and role-playing behaviour. Wittgenstein (1953) posits that language plays a pivotal role in the functioning of cultures. The discursive language rules that guide communication influence the prevailing notions of rationality that exist in that culture. In IRC culture, the tone of conversations is predominantly informal and playful and is untouched by the utilitarian character of daily living in real life; "playing may serve as relaxation from work, as a sort of tonic inasmuch as it affords repose to the soul" (Huizinga, 1949:161). Play is an end in itself and serves no other purpose than personal enjoyment and relaxation. It does not involve "necessity or utility, duty or truth" (ibid., 158). IRC users frequently enjoy "playing pretend". Two IRC users explain:

> I behave like a kid. I can be as fun and playful as I want and no one will tell me to grow up and act my age. It gets crazy but people play along. You bounce bounce bounce, snuggle up to people. (laughs) Sometimes, I just want to act a little silly.

On IRC, play is not a solitary activity. Others collude to sustain play, leading to a willing suspension of believe, en masse. Collusion is vital in sustaining the play atmosphere on IRC. How else would one explain how the following play scene carried on uninterrupted:

```
*gnasher jumps around the channel on a pogo stick!
*boingboing*
*luna trips gnasher with her foot!
<juno> hahahahahaaaa go get 'im luna!
<gnasher> heeeeeeeey, nooooooo faaaaaaaair! you
spoilsports!
<eh-oh> I wanna play too leh
<gnasher> sorry buddy, only got room for one *boing!*
<gnasher> but I'll let ride piggyback ;)
<luna> come play eh-oh =)
*gnasher gives luna a lascivious leer
<gnasher> luna:wanna ride on my stick ? hehehehehehee
*luna gives gnasher a vicious kick. Idiot :P
<gnasher> ouchhh *rubs sore booty*
```

Although IRC has an open and liberal culture, it is evident that social control mechanisms do exist online. A general code of behaviour, guided by "Netiquette", is expected of IRC users. "Netiquette" outlines acceptable cyberspace conduct. Some things to avoid are "dumping" huge amounts of text into the channel, using expletives and harassing others. Typing entirely in upper case is also disallowed as it is construed as shouting. Failure to adhere to those unwritten rules is likely to warrant a user's temporary removal, or even a ban, from a channel. Another method of punishment is the withdrawal of attention. This acts as a potent social control mechanism because people log on to IRC in search of company, attention and conversation. The use of social control mechanisms constitutes a (re)establishment of the social/moral boundaries of the (online) society (Durkheim, 1938). The collective conscience is alive. In the words of another respondent:

> It can't be a free for all, so there're rules and standards. People who don't follow the protocol get shunned or kicked out. That's just the way it is.

Even as people seek out new experiences online, they inadvertently replicate the social relations that exist in real life.

New IRC users usually need a period of time to acclimatize themselves to online culture. Gaining knowledge of the general IRC culture, however, is no promise that one can survive online chatting unscathed. This is because some channels have their own culture and their own set of rules and regulations. What is acceptable in one channel could very well be unacceptable in another. For example,

while certain channels prohibit the use of vulgar language, it is the
norm in other channels to use vulgarities:

> <Lola> can u pls dun use vulgaritie?
> <warped> get the fuck out if you don't like it,
> this is how we speak here

> <cutemike> hahaha!!! shuddup you shithead
> <Dunce> this is yr last warning. another expletive
> from u and you'll be banned ok, i am not joking

Anonymity is a double-edged sword. It can be liberating, but it can
also lead to the display of anti-social behaviour, like flaming. Flaming
is expressive behaviour that frequently includes swearing, insulting,
name-calling (Siegel, Dubrovsky, Kiesler and McGuire, 1986), and
the use of profanities and ad hominem-type arguments. Flaming is
a phenomenon that people find fascinating. This is perhaps due to
the fact that many very rarely see insults and offensive remarks being
unleashed with such unadulterated ferocity in real life. Flaming does
not necessarily involve logic or well-crafted arguments. This is how
flaming works:

> <wonky> shit your own head EhiNz
> <fresto> mnm . . . tsk tsk . . .
> <MnM> FUCK YOU FRESTO
> <wonky> or better still shit MnM's
> <EhiNz> wat the mother fucker are u all kao bei
> abt???
> <MnM> U WANNA PICK A FIGHT YOU LITTLE SHIT
> <EhiNz> wonky:same to u too go fuck ni nah bu eh
> cb can???
> <wonky> fuck yourself
> <fresto> #nus used to be a nice place
> <fresto> till you twits messed it up
> <fresto> mnm . . . sheesh . . . take the hint and go away
> <MnM> FRESTO FUCK YOU
> <MnM> FRESTO FUCK YOU[4]

In a nutshell, flaming proceeds thus: if I say "You're stupid", you
may retort with "Well you're stupid and your mum smells funny".
The purpose of flaming is to out-talk, outsmart and verbally pulverize

---

[4] In this paper, I have left all typographical, grammatical and spelling errors contained in the data uncorrected.

your opponent, logic notwithstanding. The combination of anonymity and the resulting lack of sanctions bring out the worse in people. One is able to heap verbal abuse on another user gratuitously, and then log off scot-free.

Online (Id)entities—The Electronic Id Unleashed

Interactions on IRC are sustained by the creative and imaginative use of language. The absence of physical cues and the paucity of social cues create a fertile ground for the imagination, giving free reign to the individual's interpretive facilities in creating idealized images (Stone, 1995). It is for this reason that Turkle (1996) calls IRC a Rorschach inkblot test. Very often, there is no congruence between the signified (person) and the signifier/s (persona/s). The signified is absent and in its absence, one's fantasies are projected onto the signifier. Identities on IRC have a distinctively postmodern character—they are multiple, fluid and mutable. On IRC, a person can re-invent himself/herself if he/she has the skills to play the role convincingly. As such, the authenticity of identities is rarely verifiable because in most cases, the real life identity of the person behind the nickname cannot be traced. For example, it is fairly common to see male users having a bit of fun by adopting a female persona, and getting away with it. Interactions proceed based on the information one has about the persona, not the person; the being-in-pixels is not the being-in-body. Interactions like these may seem strange, but the IRC world is inhabited by personas. IRC users frequently do air-brushing work on their proclaimed self/selves, while their chatting partners paint idealized pictures of them. Individuals try to influence the way others perceive them by manipulating their self-presentations (Goffman, 1959). This process of gaining intersubjective recognition by others is crucial in the development of identity, because no one can construct identity independently of others. On IRC, people get a chance to play roles and try out new identities in the presence of other people. Emboldened by the anonymity that the medium provides, they play out their ideal selves—selves they have always wanted to be but could not or dared not to be (Turkle, 1995).

According to the symbolic interactionist perspective, the self is presented, developed and constituted through social interaction (Stone,

1962). Traditionally, identity claims stem from two sources: appearance (non-verbal) and discourse (verbal) (ibid.). Goffman (1959) observes that identity claims may be established in two ways:

> The expressiveness of the individual (and therefore his capacity to give impressions) appears to involve two radically different sign activities: the expression that he gives, and the expression that he gives off. The first involves verbal symbols or their substitutes, which he uses admittedly and solely to convey the information that he and the others are known to attach to these symbols. This is communication in the traditional and narrow sense. The second involves a wide range of action that others can treat as symptomatic of the actor, the expectation being that the action was performed for reasons other than the information conveyed in this way (ibid., 2).

Goffman's work on the presentation of self (or selves) in everyday life and his dramaturgical perspective of social life as drama is especially pertinent to the study of social life on IRC; because IRC is a virtual stage where people, masked by anonymity, play with their identities. On IRC, one has greater control over one's self-(re)presentation, since most of the aspects of the "give off" component cease to be relevant. With the absence of the physical body, the need to monitor one's posture, choice of clothes and accessories, grooming, accent, tone, gestures, etc. disappears. All that is left to monitor is one's typed utterances, that is, the text. Hence, identity claims are easier to make online. Now, not only are identity claims easier to work on, even one's mental and emotional states are made more accessible. Studies report that CMC leads to greater (private) self-awareness, and that one becomes more aware of the covert aspects of one's self/selves (Matheson and Zanna, 1988). It appears that CMC allows individuals to devote less cognitive resources to monitoring their physical bodies, so that the focus on their internal states may be magnified. An IRC user was quoted as saying:

> IRC is textual so I have to articulate my feelings, which I might not do in real life. Articulation of feelings sort of leads to self-discovery because it forces you to be introspective.

Freud (1945) argues that the taming and suppression of the id is necessary before an individual is allowed entry into a culture/society. There are two aspects to an individual's self-identity: the civilized aspect (the socialized "self") and the uncivilized aspect (the suppressed id). The idea of a dual-faceted self is resonated in several sociological and psychological theories. Mead's (1962) conception of the self runs along the same lines as Freud's. According to Mead, the self consists of two components: "me" and "I". "Me" is the socialized component of the self, while "I" is the innovative and creative component of the self. Mead suggests that it is the "I' part of the self that makes it unpredictable and unique. Goffman, too, argued that there is an unsocialized component of the self that propels an individual to deviate, on occasion, from social rules and rituals (cited in Lemert and Branaman, 1997:xlvii). These three theories are in conflict with the idea of a unitary, stable and essential self.

Erikson's (1963) theory of identity development maintains that revealing and committing oneself in what is perceived as "unreality" is the first step in the exploration of identity. Using the virtual realm as a testing ground to play out and experiment with new experiences can lead to self-discovery:

> I've learnt about how minds tick through throwing people into unlikely situations and seeing their reactions. Myself, I've also been caught offbalance and from there, I learnt more about myself—my flaws, strengths, quirks. I don't think real life can offer that many new situations for me to try out.

Sometimes, virtual "selves" surface from identity play. Although these "selves" only surface online, they have consistent personalities and are regarded by IRC users as part of their identity:

> The 'me' when I'm online and the 'me' in real life are different, but they're both part of me.

Identity play flourishes on IRC because there is less restriction on behaviour in the virtual realm:

> IRC creates a different set-up. It allows more (social) space since real life constraints are out of the way. You meet new people, try new experiences and experiment with your identity.

In real life, we are often constrained by social norms. To step outside these social norms, and/or to fail in self-representation attempts is to risk being in an embarrassing situation. Indeed, embarrassment is a powerful motivator of (non)behaviour. Online, people are free to try out different roles/identities in new and different social situations. This can lead them to realize what they are (or what they are not), and what their potentialities and limitations are. Indeed, in play, we learn.

Kenneth Gergen could have been writing about IRC when he posited that "(a)ll selves lie latent, and under the right conditions (they) spring to life" (1991:159). For some IRC participants,

> The creative part of me comes out online. In real life, I'm just an executive in mental straitjackets.
>
> Online, people know me by my two personalities. Doinky's the fun one, the playful one. When I'm Doinky, I behave like a kid. For 'Ice', it's closer to my (real life) personality.

Playing with identity (re)constructions could make us realize that the "self" is full of potentialities and that we have a repertoire of selves we can draw on. IRC reveals the field of possibilities, in which the real world "self" is but one configuration in the vast grid of possibilities. On IRC, one gets to practice assessing one's multiple selves. IRC makes a good testing ground because anonymity provides us with a feeling of security that buffers against our anxiety of being embarrassed in social interactions. Even though IRC users are free to try out and discard as many identities as they wish, the fact is that sometimes, IRC users do construct and maintain certain identities for themselves via the processes of role creation and (selective) self-disclosure (Baym, 1995). Some online personas are so stable and consistent that, after a while, other IRC users are able to recognize them by their distinctive personality and conversational style:

> Sometimes, for the fun of it, I enter my regular channel using a new name. But some of the chatters spot me after a while. They say I have a certain way of speaking.

Cruising, Cybersex and the Dream Machine

The most common form of cybersex involves two people describing to each other, in a dramaturgical manner, what they are "doing" to each other and to themselves. Cybersex is also known as "hotchat", "cyber", or "talking sexy/dirty". The other type of cybersex identified here involves role playing by the participants. In this variation, both users decide on a setting or storyline before going on to role play. Some of the more popular settings include rape scenes, having sex with a colleague, seducing a stranger in a public place and scenarios involving sadomasochistic practices. Descriptions are often graphic, vivid and detailed. Typically, users type with one hand whilst masturbating themselves with the other hand. In many cases, participation in these two types of cybersex can elicit such heightened feelings of arousal that the users reach physical orgasm. More often than not, there is no pretence of emotional involvement in cybersex; it is the virtual equivalent of a one-night stand. Once both persons are satisfied, they inform each other and log off. Cybersex can take place either in a channel (or "on the main"), which is public domain, or in one-to-one chat, where two persons engage in private messaging. Cybersex very rarely takes place on the main, and even when that happens, it is usually done as an attention-getting tactic. Most users prefer to have cybersex in the private domain of one-to-one messaging. Besides cybersex, people also cruise for real sex, phone sex and dates on IRC channels. Its (legendary) appeal is tremendous since it is convenient, accessible and safe. It is also a relatively cheap way of cruising for sex-related activities and dates. Cruising, be it for heterosexual or homosexual partners, usually takes place in the more popular channels like #sex, #cybersex, #phonesex, #teens, #Singapore, #singapore20+ and #singapore30+, where there is a sizeable crowd.[5] When you enter a channel, it is quite unlikely that anyone will initiate a conversation with you on the main. Instead, you are likely to receive private messages from other people in the channel, asking you for your gender and age. In the more popular channels, it is not uncommon to see a barrage of advertisements calling for sex-related activities on the main:

> RichMan is looking for temporary girlfriend. . . . msg me now if u are interested. . . . minimum 6500 sg cash. . . . sincere . . . thanks!!!!

> <jackyWoo> any girls need sex?
> <jackyWoo> i need to fxxx a girl

> <[Guyver]> any ger wan to have f o n e s e x with a guy ? msg me

> <aSugarDad> golden candie$ for beng boys in return for hot sticky ice-cream

> <camwonde> hi any girls wanna see me mastubate msg me plsssss

---

[5] A channel is considered to have a sizeable crowd when the number of users in the channel totals up to about 100.

<BeCkHaM07> Hi . . . Everybody . . . I am feeling pretty horny here.I must first Intro myself as an Undoubtedly and i mean really Clean guy. Coz i have never had any intimate scenes with anybody . . . so i am dying to.As for wat i actually want . . . i just wanna show you how i masturbate . . . right in front of you . . . u dun have to strip dun even have to do anything . . . just see mi cum . . . if u want u can join mi . . . do for mi watever but
your decision is my choice i will respect u

<cute_hunk> any veri wet & horny babes around noW??? pls msg mi thanks

<KaPpA^BoI> me very rich man any gal get accumpany for a nite . . . . . . dun mistake for sex juz touching n kissing n sleeping together hugging can. the fees goes like this . . . stuff like hp n money n cash cards r given 10 gals r needed . . . . . . be quick!!!

<^Ethan^> any girls interested in making some easy money??? pls msg me. . . .

Cruising is akin to fishing, where one hopes to get a catch. Sometimes, however, one can cruise for hours and yet leave empty-handed:

It's like fishing. Sometimes you get a catch, sometimes you don't. Mostly, you just wait and hope. You wait a whole lot.

Due to the difficulty of landing a desired chatting partner, those cruisers who do manage to find a suitable one will persevere in trying to get him/her to engage in any sex-related activity. Even when the other party insists he/she does not want cybersex, phonesex or hotchat, some users can be doggedly persistent:

<deMarco> im 26/m n very experienced
<Eden> im not interested in cybersex. just here to see what happens
<deMarco> why don't i give 'practicals'?
<Eden> my curiosity doesnt stretch that far,no thanks
<deMarco> okok, we have clean chat. care to describe yrself?
<Eden> hobbies?
<deMarco> wat do u look like.weight/height/physical.
tell me what u're wearing now. wearing underwear?
<deMarco> u virgin? do you masturbate?
<deMarco> got bf? do petting?
<Eden> well, it was very nice talking to you, goodbye
<deMarco> wait, wanna have phonesex??? don't go . . . pls . . .
<Eden> well, im obviously wasting yr time so let's just say bye and u go look for someone else?
<deMarco> u're the only female I can find . . . I need u . . . to help me wank . . . pls. . . . im feeling very horny now . . . I need it . . .
<Eden> sorry, cant help, goodbye.

(10 minutes later)

> \<deMarco\> hello?? feel horny now???
> \<deMarco\> hellooooooooo??

The anonymity afforded by the medium allows people to unleash their desires online, as evidenced by the language used:

> \<straight8\> hey baby, bored ? wanna cyber ?
> \<straight8\> my rod's hard and steaming, all ready for you. i can give you a good fuck ;)
> \<straight8\> come onnnnnn, let's have some fun i'll have you moaning in no time

Vulgarities and sexually explicit words are used freely and frequently. Durkin and Bryant (1995) offer an interesting explanation for the gratuitous use of such language by IRC users. Such language, they argue, may be viewed as intellectual graffiti. It allows "an outlet for the person's carnal thoughts or (for) a manifestation of sexuality" (ibid., 193). The use of such language is a deliberate expression of disdain for the "square" world (Cohen, 1965) that forbids them from using language of this sort.

Paradoxically, cybersex involves anonymity, secrecy and distance, even as participants engage in one of the most intimate human experiences. Anonymity adds to, rather than detracts from, the cybersex experience, since it allows the participants to project their fantasies onto the other. Cybersex works "not through a celebration of actualities, but through an orchestration of potentials, an organization of appearances" (King, 1996:95):

> Cybersexing is the release of your imagination and creativity. You adopt the persona of a superstud and imagine your partner is Cindy Crawford. Imagine it's the real thing and then wank.
> It's the visualization. That's why people ask for physical descriptions. Everyone lies and say they're beautiful, so that everyone's happy. It adds to the jerking off and makes it fun. Better than porn 'cuz it's interactive.

Imagination is the key to having fantastic cybersex. "The participants mobilize erotic tension by taking advantage of (the lack of information)—filling in missing information with idealized information" (Stone, 1995:95). The cybersex experience involves a "romantic idealization of sexual encounters worthy of the most airbrushed Hollywood art" (Reid, 1996:341).

Cyborg theory is a radical and refreshing way to look at the relationship between sexuality and the development of technology. In hooking up to cyberspace to experiment with one's sexuality, one inadvertently blurs the man–machine distinction (Stone, 1995). In a sense, the computer acts as a prosthesis of sorts. The act of having cybersex blurs the boundaries between "human" and "machine", since the access to one's sexual side requires the aid of the computer, the modem and the telephone line. The experience of cybersex threatens the difference between the imaginary and the real "by becoming at once imagination and reality" (King, 1996:97), as human, machine and wires are amalgamated into one; they are all part of the whole organism that is engaged in cybersex. The human being begins to take on some semblance of a cyborg.

In Singapore, the control over sex-related materials has always been tight. The phenomenal growth of the Internet, however, has suddenly opened up avenues for access to sex-related material, pornography and cruising (Ho, Baber and Khondker, 2002). This sudden wealth of information and access can turn people heady with excitement. This, compounded by the fact that the bulk of IRC users are teenagers or young adults[6] coming to terms with their sexuality, has resulted in the explosion of an unprecedented wave of sexual experimentation and interest in sex-related activities.[7] IRC has been utilized by some not only to find cybersex partners, but also to seek out partners for real-life sexual intercourse, phone sex and dates. They use IRC as a platform for seeking out sexual encounters that would be difficult or impossible to come by in real life.

Epilogue—Paradoxes and Dialectics

IRC is a technology that is profoundly dialectical. It liberates yet constrains. It connects yet isolates. Its users are simultaneously pro-

---

[6] Out of a total of 54 respondents in this study, only one was above the age of 30 years. The remaining 53 respondents ranged in age from 16 to 28 years. This demographic trend is reflected in several studies that have been done on users of text-based VR mediums. See Reid (1996) and Rheingold (1993).

[7] The webmaster of a Singaporean commercial sex web site (www.sammyboy.com) revealed that his site registers 4,000 hits a day from Singaporean users. The web site features forums for sex-related discussions and also provides monthly reports on where and how to find the best sex workers in Singapore and in the region.

ducers and consumers. The paradoxical nature of IRC, as a medium of interaction, makes it an excellent tool for the examination of some of our taken-for-granted assumptions and ideas. It is clear that communication models, notions of self and even notions of what it means to be human become problematic in cyberspace. As a result, the binary divisions between those categories and concepts dissolve, leading to a multiplication of the number of "realities" we encounter. The seepage of the real into the virtual realm is perhaps seen most clearly in the phenomenon of cybersex, where sex has become hyperreal; simulations have displaced the real (Baudrillard, 1994). The human–machine distinction dissolves in the act of cybersex, where the human "morphs" into a cyborg. How does one define the cybersex experience when the medium is taken to be unreal, and yet the elicited reactions are real? More importantly, can such binary divisions still hold? Chayko (1993) argues that "it is time to frame experiences not in terms of either/or distinctions but to classify them along a continuum of reality with which we attempt to gauge . . . the 'degree' of reality" because the either/or way of comprehending our social world today is no longer compatible with our experiences. Critics of VR technologies may argue that IRC is just a game, and that it is a total waste of time. Despite those criticisms, it remains evident that online encounters have the potential to enrich our experience(s). The diversity of people on IRC exposes one to new experiences and new opinions that are refreshing to people who have stagnated into a routine lifestyle. Our cyberspace experiences can jolt us into being more reflexive. The way technologies are defined depends on the way people construct the meanings. Let the users of IRC decide for themselves the "reality" of their experience. We should not, as a knee-jerk response, privilege the "real" unthinkingly. We need to learn to live between the two worlds. More importantly, we need to learn to utilize the opportunities for connection with others that the virtual world offers, so that our lives can be enriched. IRC is neither "real" nor "virtual"; rather, it is a social space that belongs in our everyday life. We should not be too concerned with theoretical quibbles over what is real and what is not real. Instead, we should recognize that it is what human beings can do and are now doing in these new social spaces that should be the crux of the issue.

REFERENCES

Books and Articles

Abbate, Janet (1999) *Inventing the Internet*. Cambridge, MA: MIT Press.
Abbott, E. (1992) [1884] *Flatland: A Romance of Many Dimensions*. New York: Dover Publications.
Accenture (2001) "Rhetoric versus Reality—Closing the Gap", March 30, 2001. www. accenture.com/xd/xd.asp?it=enWeb&xd=industries/government/gove_method.xml
Adam, Barbara, Ulrich Beck and Joost van Loon, eds. (2000) *The Risk Society and Beyond*. London: Sage.
Adler, M. (1986) *Drawing Down the Moon*. Boston: Beacon.
Alexander, Cynthia, ed. (1998) *Digital Democracy*. New York: Oxford University Press.
Anderson, Benedict (1983) *Imagined Communities*. London: Verso and New Left Books.
Ante, S.E. (1999) "Preparing for Y2K: Been There, Done That", *Wired* January.
Aoki, Kumiko (1994) "Virtual Communities in Japan: Their Cultures and Infra-structure", *Asia-Pacific Exchange (Electronic) Journal* 2(1). University of Hawaii, Kapiolani Community College. http://naio.kcc.hawaii.edu/kcc/apex-j/v2-1.html
Appelbaum, R. and J. Henderson, eds. (1992) *States and Development in the Asian Pacific Rim*. Newbury Park, CA: Sage.
Archibugi, Daniele, Jeremy Howells, and Jonathan Michie, eds. (1999) *Innovation Policy in a Global Economy*. Cambridge: Cambridge University Press.
Baber, Z. (1996) *The Science of Empire: Scientific Knowledge, Civilisation, and Colonial Rule in India*. Albany: SUNY Press.
Ban, A. Pakir, and K.C. Tong, eds. (1992) *Imagining Singapore*. Singapore: Times Academic Press.
Bataille, Georges (1992) *Theory of Religion*. Translated by Robert Hurley. New York: Zone.
Batty, Michael (1997) "Virtual Geography", *Futures* 29(4/5): 337–352.
Baudrillard, Jean (1994) *Simulacra and Simulation*. Translated by Sheila Faria Glaser. Ann Arbor: University of Michigan Press.
Baym, Nancy K. (1995) "The Emergence of Community in Computer-Mediated Communication", in Steven Jones, ed., *Cybersociety: Computer-Mediated Communication*. California, London, India: Sage Publications, pp. 138–163.
Beck, Ulrich (1992) *Risk Society: Towards a New Modernity*. London: Sage Publications.
Beck, Ulrich, Anthony Giddens and Scott Lash (1994) *Reflexive Modernization*. Cambridge: Polity Press.
Bell, Daniel (1976) *The Post-Industrial Society*. New York: Basic Books.
Bentham, J. (1995) *The Panopticon Writings*. Edited by M. Bozovic. London: Verso.
Berkun, S. (1995) "Agent of Change", *Wired* April.
Berman, M. (1988) *All That Is Solid Melts into Thin Air: The Experience of Modernity*. London: Penguin.
Bijker, Wiebe E., Thomas P. Hughes and Trevor Pinch, eds. (1989) *The Social Construction of Technological Systems*. Cambridge, MA: MIT Press.
Boogars, G.E. (1956) "The Tanjong Pagar Dock Company, 1894–1905", *Memoirs of the Raffles Museum* series 3. Singapore: GPO.
Bourdieu, P. (1998) *Practical Reason: On the Theory of Action*. Cambridge: Polity.
Borgman, Albert (1999) *Holding on to Reality: The Nature of Information at the Turn of the Millennium*. Chicago: University of Chicago Press.
Borsook, P. (1994) "Listening to Silicon", *Wired* March.
———. (1995) "The Goddess in Every Woman's Machine", *Wired* July.

———. (2000) *Cyberselfish: A Critical Romp through the Terribly Libertarian Culture of High Tech*. New York: Public Affairs.

Burn, Janice M. and Maris G. Martinsons, eds. (1997) *Information Technology and the Challenge for Hong Kong*. Hong Kong: Hong Kong University Press.

Burton, P.F. (1995) "Regulation and Control of the Internet: Is it Feasible? Is it Necessary?" *Journal of Information Science* 21: 413–428.

Calhoun, C., ed. (1992) *Habermas and the Public Sphere*. Cambridge: MIT Press.

Calhoun, C. (1998) "Community Without Propinquity Revisited: Communication Technology and the Transformation of the Urban Public Sphere", *Sociological Inquiry* 68(3): 373–397.

Cameron, J. (1965) *Our Tropical Possession in Malayan India*. KL: Oxford University Press.

Caputo, John, ed. (1997) *Deconstruction in a Nutshell*. New York: Fordham University Press.

Castells, Manuel (1989) *The Informational City*. Oxford: Blackwell.

——— (1992) "Four Asian Tigers with a Dragon's Head: A Comparative Analysis of the State, Economy, and Society in the Asian Pacific Rim", in R. Appelbaum and J. Henderson, eds., *States and Development in the Asian Pacific Rim*. Newbury Park, CA: Sage, pp. 33–70.

——— (1996) *The Rise of Network Society*. Oxford: Blackwell.

——— (1997) *The Power of Identity*. Oxford: Blackwell.

——— (1998) *End of Millennium*. Oxford: Blackwell.

——— (2000a) "Rise of the Network Society", *The Information Age: Economy, Society and Culture* volume 1. Cambridge: Blackwell.

——— (2000b) "End of Millennium", *The Information Age: Economy, Society and Culture* Volume 3. Cambridge: Blackwell.

Castells, M. and P. Hall (1994) *Technopoles of the World: The Making of 21st Century Industrial Complexes*. London: Routledge.

Cavoukian, A. (1995) *Who Knows? Safeguarding Your Privacy in a Networked World*. Toronto: Random House.

Chan, Heng Chee (1971) *Singapore: The Politics of Survival*. Singapore: Oxford University Press.

Chan, Heng Chee (1975) "Politics in an Administrative State: Where Has the Politics Gone?", in Seah Chee Meow, ed., *Trends in Singapore*. Singapore: Singapore University Press.

Chaum, D. (1992) "Achieving Electronic Privacy", *Scientific American* 267(2): 76–81.

Chayko, Mary (1993) "What is the Real in the Age of Virtual Reality? 'Reframing' Frame Analysis for a Technological World", *Symbolic Interaction* 16(2): 171–181.

Chissick, Michael and Alistair Kelman (1999) *Electronic Commerce: Law and Practice*. London: Sweet & Maxwell.

Chng, M.K., A. Tyabji, L. Low and B.N. Tay (1986) *Effective Mechanisms for the Enchantment of Technology and Skills in Singapore*. Singapore: ISEAS.

Choo, C.W. (1997) "IT 2000: Singapore's Vision of an Intelligent Island", in P. Droege, ed., *Intelligent Environments: Spatial Aspects of the Information Revolution*. New York: Elsevier, pp. 49–65.

Chua, Beng Huat (1991) "Not Depoliticized by Ideologically Successful: The Public Housing Programme in Singapore", *International Journal of Urban and Regional Research* 15(1): 24–41.

——— (1995) *Communitarian Ideology and Democracy in Singapore*. London: Routledge.

——— (1997) *Political Legitimacy and Housing: Stakeholding in Singapore*. London: Routledge.

Cobb, J.J. (1999) "A Spiritual Experience of Cyberspace", *Technology in Society: An International Journal* 21(4): 393–407.

Cobb, Kreisenberg, J. (1995) "A Globe, Clothing Itself with a Brain", *Wired* June.

Cohen, A.K. (1965) "The Sociology of the Deviant Act: Anomie Theory and Beyond", *American Sociology Review* 30: 5–15.

Comte, A. (1997) *Het Positieve denken*. Meppel: Boom Pers.

Creset, Sed (1999) *E-commerce Asia: Cyberstrategies for Asia's Multi-Jurisdictional Environment.* Hong Kong: Asia Law & Practice.

Davis, E. (1998) *Techgnosis: Myth, Magic and Mysticism in the Age of Information.* London: Serpent's Tail.

—— (1996) *Technoculture and the Religious Imagination. A Digitally Remastered Remix of an Improvised World-Jam,* delivered at Metaforum III. http://www.techgnosis.com/technoculture.html.

—— (1995) "Technopagans: May the Astral Plane Be Reborn in Cyberspace", *Wired* July.

Department of Statistics (2000) *Yearbook of Statistics Singapore.* London: Routledge.

Derrida, Jacques (1992) *The Other Heading: Reflections on Today's Europe.* Translated by Pascale-Anne Brault and Michael Naas. Bloomington: Indiana University Press.

—— (1995) *Points . . . Interviews, 1974–94.* Edited by Elisabeth Weber; translated by Peggy Kamuf. Stanford: Stanford University Press.

—— (1997) "The Villanova Roundtable: A Conversation with Jacques Derriea", in John Caputo, ed., *Deconstruction in a Nutshell.* New York: Fordham University Press.

—— (1999) *Adieu to Emmanuel Levinas.* Translated by Pascale-Anee Brault. Stanford: Stanford University Press.

Dery, M. (1995) "Mcluhan through the Rearview Mirror", *Educom Review* November/December: 22–28.

—— (1996) *Escape Velocity: Cyber Culture at the End of the Century.* New York: Grove Press.

Devan-Nair, C.V. (1973) *Toward Tomorrow: Essays on Development and Social Transformation in Singapore.* Singapore: Singapore National Trade Union Congress.

Dibbel, J. (1995) "Viruses Are Good for You", *Wired* February.

Dodge, Martin at http://www.cybergeography.org/about.html

Dreyfus, Hubert L. (2001) *On the Internet.* London: Routledge.

Droege, P., ed. (1997) *Intelligent Environments: Spatial Aspects of the Information Revolution.* New York: Elsevier.

Du Gay, P. (1996) *Consumption and Identity at Work.* London: Sage.

Durkheim, Emile (1938) *The Rules of Sociological Method.* Translated by S.A. Solovay and J.H. Mueller. Chicago: University of Chicago Press.

—— (1972) *Selected Writings.* Edited by Anthony Giddens. Cambridge: Cambridge University Press.

Durkin, K.F. and C.D. Bryant (1995) "Log on to Sex", *Deviant Behaviour: An Interdisciplinary Journal* 16: 179–200.

Ellul, J. (1965) *The Technological Society.* New York: Alfred A. Knopf.

Erikson, Eric (1963) *Childhood and Society.* New York: Norton.

Etzkowitz, H. (1996) "Conflicts of Interest and Commitment in Academic Science in the United States", *Minerva* 34: 259–277.

—— (1997) "The Entrepreneurial University and the Emergence of Democratic Corporatism", in H. Etzkowitz and L. Leydesdorff, eds., *Universities and the Global Knowledge Economy: A Triple Helix of University-Industry-Government Relations.* London: Pinter, pp. 141–152.

Everard, Jerry (1999) *Virtual States: The Internet and the Boundaries of the Nation-State.* New York: Routledge.

Felker, Greg and K.S. Jomo, eds. (1999) *Technology, Competition and the State. Malaysia's Industrial Technology Policy.* New York: Routledge.

Fisham, Etha, ed. (1991) *Pubic Policy and the Public Good.* New York: Greenwood Press.

Fitzsimmons, James A. and Mona J. Fitzsimmons, eds. (2000) *New Service Development: Creating Memorable Experiences.* Thousand Oaks: Sage Publications.

Foucault, M. (1979) [1975] *Discipline and Punish: The Birth of the Modern Prison.* New York: Vintage.

Frauenfelder, M. (1998) "Do-It-Yourself-Darwin", *Wired* October.

Freeman, C. (1997) "The 'National System of Innovation' in Historical Perspective", in D. Archibugi and Michie, eds., *Technology, Globalisation and Economic Performance.* London: Cambridge University Press, pp. 24–49.

—— (1995) "The 'National System of Innovation' in Historical Perspective", *Cambridge Journal of Economics* 19: 5–24.

Freud, Sigmund (1984) "The Unconscious", in *On Metapsychology: The Theory of Psychoanalysis.* Pelican Freud Library, 11. Harmondsworth: Penguin.

Fudpucker, Orville (1992) "PC Magnet", *PC Magazine* 74: 557.

Gandy, Oscar (1993) *The Panoptic Sort.* Boulder: Westview.

George, Cherian (1999) *Singapore, the Air-Conditioned Nation: Essays on the Politics of Comfort and Control.* Singapore: Landmark Books.

Gergen, Kenneth (1991) *The Saturate Self: Dilemmas of Identity in Contemporary Life.* New York: Basic Books.

Gibson, Willam (1984) *Neuromancer.* London: Grafton.

Gibson-Hill, C.A. (1956) "Singapore Old Strait and New Harbour", *Memoirs of Raffles Museum* series 3. Singapore: GPO.

Goffman, Erving (1974) *Frame Analysis: An Essay on the Organization of Experience.* Cambridge, MS: Harvard University Press.

—— (1959) *The Presentation of Self in Everyday Life.* New York: Anchor Books/Doubleday.

Goh, C.B. (1995) "The Role of State and Society in the Development of Science and Technology in Singapore". Ph.D. dissertation. Australia: University of New South Wales.

Goh, K.S. (1972) *The Economics of Modernisation and Other Essays.* Singapore: Asia Pacific Press.

Goldsmith, J. (1995) "The Last Human Chess Master", *Wired* February.

Gomez, James (2000) *Self-Censorship: Singapore's Shame.* Singapore: Think Centre.

—— (2000) *SHAME.* Singapore: Think Centre.

——, ed. (2001) *Publish and Perish: The Censorship of Opposition Party Publications in Singapore.* Singapore: National Solidarity Party.

—— (2001) "Singapore: New Technologies, Old Values", in Sheila E. Coronel, ed., *Access to Information in Southeast Asia.* Manila: Philippine Centre of Investigative Journalism.

Gramsci, A. (1971) "State and Civil Society", in Quentin Hoare and G.N. Smith, eds., *Selections from the Prison Notebooks.* New York: International Publishers, pp. 135–205.

Gross, Paul and Norman Levitt (1994) *Higher Superstition: The Academic Left and its Quarrels with Science.* Baltimore: John Hopkins University Press.

Gruber, M. (1997) "In Search of the Electronic Brain", *Wired* May.

Gupta, A., D.O. Stahl and A.B. Whinston (1995) "The Internet: A Future Tragedy of the Commons?" Paper presented at Conference on Interoperability and the Economics of Information Infrastructure, Rosslyn, VA, 6–7 July 1995. An electronic version can be found at http://cism.bus.utexas.edu/alok/wash_pap.html.

Habermas, Jurgen (1970a) "On Systematically Distorted Communication", *Inquiry* 13(3): 205–218.

—— (1970b) "Towards a Theory of Communicative Competence", *Inquiry* 13(4): 360–375.

—— (1989) *The Structural Transformation of the Public Sphere.* Cambridge, MA: MIT Press.

Hacker, K.L. and J. van Dijk, eds. (2000) *Digital Democracy.* London: Sage.

Hacking, Ian (1990) *The Taming of Chance.* Cambridge: Cambridge University Press.

Hague, Barry N. and B. Loader, eds. (1999) *Digital Democracy.* London: Routledge.

Hamilton, M.B. (1995) *The Sociology of Religion: Theoretical and Comparative Perspectives.* New York: Routledge.

Hanegraaff, W. (1996) *New Age Religion and Western Culture: Esoterism in the Mirror of Secular Thought.* Leiden: E.J. Brill.

Hanson, Ward (2000) *Principles of Internet Marketing.* Cincinnati, Ohio: South-Western College Pub.

Hardin, G. (1968) "The Tragedy of the Commons", *Science* 162: 1243–1248.

Harpold, Terry (1999) "Dark Continents: A Critique of Internet Metageographies", *Postmodern Culture* 9(2).

Headrick, D.R. (1981) *The Tools of Imperialism: Technology and European Imperialism in the 19th Century*. New York: Oxford University Press.

——— (1988) *The Tentacles of Progress: Technology in the Age of Imperialism 1850–1940*. New York: Oxford University Press.

Henry, Clement M. and Robert Springborg (2001) *Globalization and the Politics of Development in the Middle East*. New York: Cambridge University Press.

Hill, Michael (1997) *The Policy Process in the Modern State*. London: Prentice Hall.

Hill, M. and K.F. Lian (1995) *The Politics of Nation-building and Citizenship in Singapore*. London: Routledge.

Ho, Kong Chong, Zaheer Baber and Habibul H. Khondker (2002) "Sites of Resistance: Alternative Websites and State-Society Relations", *British Journal of Sociology* 53(1): 149–156.

Holmes, D., ed. (1998) *Virtual Politics: Identity and Community in Cyberspace*. London: Sage.

Huff, Toby E. (2001) "Globalization and the Internet: Comparing the Middle Eastern and Malaysian Experiences", *The Middle East Journal* 55(3) (Summer): 439–458.

Huizinga, Johan (1949) *Homos Ludens: A Study of the Play-Element in Culture*. London: Routledge & Kegan.

Infocomm Development Authority (2001) *Catalyst for Change*. Singapore. IDA 2000: Bringing Singapore to the world.

Information Highway Advisory Council Secretariat (1996) "Building the Information Society: Moving Canada into the 21st Century." Ottawa: Minister of Supply and Services Canada. An online version of this document can be found at http://info. ic.gc.ca/info-highway/ih.html

Jayaseelan, Risen (2001) "Lessons in e-Government", *The Edge*. Net@lue2.0: 2f.

John, K.J. (2001) "The Malaysian GEM Story: Leapfrogging to a K-Society". 7 May: 16. www.nitc.org.my/resources/papers.html

Johnson, C. (1995) *Japan: Who Governs? The Rise of the Developmental State*. New York: W.W. Norton.

Johnson, G. (2000) "Only Connect", *Wired* January.

Jones, Steve (2000) "The Bias of the Web", in Andrew Herman and Thomas Swiss, eds., *Cultural Theory and the World Wide Web*. New York: Routledge.

Jordan, Tim (1999) *Cyberpower: The Culture and Politics of Cyberspace and the Internet*. London: Routledge.

Joy, B. (2000) "Why the Future Doesn't Need Us", *Wired* April.

Kaku, Michio (1997) *Visions: How Science Will Revolutionize the 21st Century*. New York: Anchor Books.

Kall, M. (1996) "The Telecommunications Act: The Good, Bad and Unknown", *MacWeek*, 12 February 10(6).

Kapor, M. (1993) "Where is the Digital Highway Really Heading? The Case for a Jeffersonian Information Policy". This paper can be found online at http://www. db.nl/Archief/wired/kapor.on.nii.html

Katz, J. (1995) "The Medium is the Medium", *Wired* July.

Kelly, K. (1994) *Out of Control: The New Biology of Machines, Social Systems and the Economic World*. Oxford: Perseus Books.

——— (1995) "Singular Visionary", *Wired* June.

——— (1999) "Nerd Theology", *Technology in Society: An International Journal* 21(4): 349–354.

Kelly, K. and S. Reiss. (1998) "One Huge Computer", *Wired* August.

Kennedy, P.M. (1971) "Imperial Cable Communications and Strategy 1879–1914", *English Historical Review* 86: 728–752.

King, Richard C. (1996) "The Siren Scream of Telesex: Speech, Seduction and Simulation", *Journal of Popular Culture* 30(3): 91–101.

Kirsner, S. (1998) "Moody Furballs and the Developers Who Love Them", *Wired* September.

Kosiur, David R. (1997) *Understanding Electronic Commerce*. Redmond, Washington: Microsoft Press.

Lajoie, Mark (1996) "Psychoanalysis and Cyberspace", in Rob Shields, ed., *Cultures of the Internet: Virtual Spaces, Real Histories, Living Bodies*. London, Thousand Oaks, New Delhi: Sage.

Latour, Bruno (1998) "Thought Experiments in Social Science: From the Social Contract to Virtual Society". "1st Virtual Society?" Annual Public Lecture. Brunel University, London, 1 April.

Lau, A. (1992) "The National Past and the Writing of the History of Singapore", in K.C. Ban, A. Pakir and K.C. Tong, eds., *Imagining Singapore*. Singapore: National Arts Council.

Leiss, W. (1990) *Under Technology's Thumb*. Kingston: McGill-Queen's University Press.

Lemert, Charles and Amy Branaman (1997) *The Goffman Reader*. Oxford & Massachusetts: Blackwell Publishers.

Leonard, A. (1996) "Bots are Hot!", *Wired* April.

—— (2000) "As the MEMS Revolution Takes Off, Small is Getting Bigger Every Day", *Wired* January.

Levinson, P. (1995) "Web of Weeds", *Wired* November.

Lim, Alwyn (1999) "Mapping the Body Electric: Discursive Formation of the Intelligent Island". Honours Thesis. Department of Sociology, National University of Singapore.

Lim, K. (2000) "Moments of Magic". Performed and recorded by E. Lim, W. Fann and T. Chua. In *Sing Singapore 2000* CD-ROM. Singapore: National Arts Council.

Lim, L.Y.C. (1978) "Multinational Firms and Manufacturing for Export in Less Developed Countries". Ph.D. thesis. Michigan Ann Arbor.

Luckmann, T. (1967) *The Invisible Religion: The Problem of Religion in Modern Society*. London: Macmillian.

—— (1996) "The Privatization of Religion and Morality", in P. Heelas, S. Lash and P. Morris, eds., *Detraditionalization: Critical Reflections on Authority and Identity*. Oxford: Blackwell Publishers, pp. 72–86.

Ludvall, B.A. (1988) *National Innovation Systems*. London: Pinter.

—— (1999) "Technology Policy in the Learning Economy", in D. Archibugi, J. Howells and J. Michie, eds., *Innovation Policy in a Global Economy*. London: Cambridge University Press, pp. 19–34.

Luhrmann, T.M. (1989) *Persuasions of the Witch's Craft: Ritual Magic in Contemporary England*. Cambridge: Harvard University Press.

Lyon, David (1988) *The Information Society: Issues and Illusions*. Cambridge: Polity Press.

—— (1994) *The Electronic Eye*. Cambridge: Polity Press.

—— (2001) *Surveillance Society*. Philadelphia: Open University Press.

Lyon, David and E. Zureik, eds. (1996) *Computers, Surveillance and Privacy*. Minnesota: University of Minnesota Press.

Mahathir, Mohammad (1998) *Mahathir Mohammad on the Multimedia Super Corridor*. Subang Jaya, Malaysia: Pelanduk Publications.

Makepeace, W.A., R.J. Braddell and G.S. Brooke, eds. (1991) *One Hundred Years of Singapore*. Two volumes. Singapore: Oxford University Press.

Malaysia (1991) *Sixth Malaysian Plan, 1991–1995*.

—— (2001) *Eighth Malaysian Plan, 2001–2005*.

Mannheim, K. (1936) *Ideology and Utopia: An Introduction to the Sociology of Knowledge*. London: Routledge and Kegan Paul.

—— (1946) *Man and Society in an Age of Reconstruction: Studies in Modern Social Structures*. London: Routledge, Kegan and Paul.

Marres, Noortje and Richard Rogers (1999) "Depluralising the Web, Repluralising Public Debate: The Case of the GM Food Debate on the Web", in Richard

Rogers, ed., *Preferred Placement: Knowledge Politics on the Web*. Maastricht: Jan van Eyck Editions, pp. 113–136.

Marshall, J. (1994) "Zippies!", *Wired* May.

Matheson, K. and M.P. Zanna (1988) "The Impact of Computer-Mediated Communication on Self-Awareness", *Computers in Human Behaviour* 4: 221–233.

McLuhan, Marshall (1962) *The Gutenberg Galaxy: The Making of Typographic Man*. Toronto: University of Toronto Press.

—— (1964) *Understanding Media: The Extensions of Man*. London: Routledge & Kegan Paul.

Mead, George H. (1962) *Mind, Self and Society*. Chicago: Chicago University Press.

Mehta, M.D. (forthcoming) *Risky Business: Nuclear Power and Public Protest in Canada*. Kingston: McGill-Queen's University Press.

Mehta, M.D. and E. Darier (1998) "Virtual Control and Disciplining on the Internet: Electronic Governmentalitiy and the Global Superpanopticon", *The Information Society* 14: 107–116.

Merton, R.K. (1970) *Science, Technology and Society in 17th Century England*. New York: H. Fertig.

Mills, C. Wright (1971) *The Sociological Imagination*. Harmondsworth: Penguin.

Ministry of Culture (1969) *Singapore Yearbook 1969*. Singapore: Ministry of Culture, Information Division.

Ministry of Trade and Industry (1991) *The Strategic Economic Plan: Towards a Developed Nation*. Singapore: SNP Publishers.

Ministry of Science and Technology (1975) *Science and Technology for 2 Million*. Singapore.

Mirza, H. (1986) *Multinationals and the Growth of the Singapore Economy*. London: Croom Helm.

Moravec, H. (1988) *Mind Children: The Future of Robot and Human Intelligence*. Cambridge: Harvard University Press.

Mumford, L. (1962) *The Transformations of Man*. New York: Collier Books.

Murray, G. and A. Perera (1995) *Singapore: The Global City-state*. Kent, UK: China Library.

Nancy, Jean Luc (1991) *The Inoperative Community*. Translated by Peter Connor. Minneapolis: University of Minnesota Press.

National Computer Board (1992) *A Vision of an Intelligent Island*. Singapore.

National IT Working Committee (1985) *National IT Plan*. Singapore.

National Science and Technology Board (1997) *National Science and Technology Plan: Securing our Future*. Singapore.

Negroponte, N. (1995) *Being Digital*. New York: Vintage.

Nelson, Richard R., ed. (1993) *National Innovation Systems. A Comparative Analysis*. New York: Oxford.

Nelson, Richard and Nathan Rosenberg (1993) "Technical Innovation and National Systems", in *National Innovation Systems: A Comparative Analysis* 3–21.

NITC/MIMOS (1999a) "The K-Economy and Its Implications". December 17, 1999. Dr. Tengku Azzman. Mimos Berhad, Technology Park, Malaysia.

—— (1999b) "K-Economy Policy Paper 1". Mimos Berhard, Technology Park, Malaysia.

—— (1999c) "K-Economy Advanced Paper." Mimos Berhard, Technology Park, Malaysia.

—— (2000) *Access, Empowerment and Governance in the Information Age: Building Knowledge Societies Series*. Vol. 1. Mimos Berhard, Technology Park, Malaysia.

Noble, F. (1999) *The Religion of Technology: The Divinity of Man and the Spirit of Invention*. New York: Penguin Books.

Oguibe, Olu (1996) "Forsaken Geographies: Cyberspace and the New World 'Other'". Paper presented at the Fifth International Cyberspace Conference, Madrid. Available at http://www.telefonica.es/fat/eoguibe.html#paper

Oldenburg, Ray (1997) *The Great Good Place: Cafes, Coffee Shops, Community Centers, Beauty Parlours, General Stores, Bars, Hangouts and How They Get You through the Day.* New York: Marlowe & Co.

Omar, Dr. Abdul Rahman, nd-1 "Competitiveness in the Knowledge Driven Economy. A Briefing on the Proposal for a Policy Framework". www.might.org.my
——, nd-2 "Technology Management Best Practice in Malaysia—Imperatives for the K-economy". Akademi Sains Malaysia.

Pauline, M., M. de Landa and M. Dery (1993) "Out of Control: A Trialogue on Machine Consciousness with Mark Pauline, Manuel de Landa and Mark Dery", *Wired* September/October.

Pearson, H.F. (1956) *A History of Singapore.* London: University of London.

Pesce, M. (1999) "Reductionism versus Holism: Multiple Models of the Spiritual Quest", *Technology and Society: An International Journal* 21(4): 457–470.

Plat, C. (1995) "Superhumanism", *Wired* October.

Pollack, A. (1995) "Cyberspace's War of Words", *The Globe and Mail* August 10, A15.

Poulsen, K. (1998) "The Y2K Solution: Run for Your Life!!", *Wired* August.

Poster, M. (1994) Lecture at York University. Toronto, 16 Oct. 1994.
—— (1995) *The Second Media Age.* Cambridge, MA: Polity Press.

Postman, N. (1992) *Technopoly: The Surrender of Culture to Technology.* New York: Vintage.

Priest, Susana (2001) *A Grain of Truth: The Media, the Public and Biotechnology.* Lanham, MD: Rowan & Littlefield.

Quittner, J. (1997) "Life and Death on the Web". This article can be found online at http://cgi.pathfinder.com/netly/opinion/0,1042,778,00.html

Reid, Elizabeth (1996) "Text-based Virtual Realities: Identity and the Cyborg Body", in Peter Ludlow, ed., *High Noon on the Electronic Frontier.* Cambridge, MS, MIT Press.

Reisman, David (1961) *The Lonely Crowd.* New Haven: Yale University Press.

Rheingold, Howard (1991) *Virtual Reality.* New York: Summit Books.
—— (1993) *The Virtual Community: Homesteading on the Electronic Frontier.* Reading, MA: Addison-Wesley Publishing Co.

Robertson, Roland (1992) *Globalization: Social Theory and Modern Culture.* London: Sage.

Rodan, Garry (1989) *The Political Economy of Singapore's Industrialization.* New York: St. Martin's Press.
——, ed. (1993a) *Singapore Changes Guard.* New York: St. Martin's Press.
—— (1993b) "Preserving the One-Party State in Contemporary Singapore", in Kevin Hewison, Richard Robinson and Garry Rodan, eds., *Southeast Asia in the 1990's.* St. Leonards: Allen and Unwin.
—— (1997) "The Internet and Political Control in Singapore", *Political Science Quarterly* 113(1): 1–30.

Rogers, Richard and Andrés Zelman (2001) "Surfing for Knowledge in the Information Society", in Greg Elmer, ed., *Critical Perspectives on the Internet.* Lanham, MD: Rowan and Littlefield.

Romm, Celia T. and Fay Sudweeks, eds. (1998) *Doing Business Electronically: A Global Perspective of Electronic Commerce.* London: Springer.

Rose, Nicolas (1999) *Powers of Freedom: Reframing Political Thought.* Cambridge University Press.

Rowan, G. (1996) "Internet Firms Try to Ward Off Regulators", *The Globe and Mail* 8 January, B1.

Salaff, Janet (1988) *State and Family in Singapore: Restructuring a Developing Society.* Ithaca: Cornell University Press.

Schiller, Dan (1999) *Digital Capitalism.* Cambridge: MIT Press.

Sennett, Richard (1976) *The Fall of the Public Man: On the Social Psychology of Capitalism.* New York: Vintage Books.

Siegal, J., V. Dubrovsky, S. Kiesler and T. McGuire (1986) "Group Processes in Computer-Mediated Communication", *Organizational Behavior and Human Decision Process* 37: 157–187.

Sirbu, M. and J.D. Tygar (1995) "NetBill: An Internet Commerce System Optimized for Networked Deliverer Services", San Francisco: IEEE ConCom, 6 March.

Smith, Merritt Roe and Leo Marx, eds. (1994) *Does Technology Drive History?* Cambridge, MA: MIT Press.

Spears, Russell and Martin Lea (1992) "Social Influences and the Influence of the 'Social' in Computer-Mediated Communication", in Martin Lea, ed., *Contexts of Computer-Mediated Communication*. New York: Harvester Wheatsheaf.

Stark, R. and W.S. Bainbridge (1985) *The Future of Religion: Secularization, Revival and Cult Formation*. Berkeley: University of California Press.

Strauss, S. (1995) "Cyber Sickness: A Malady of the '90s", Vancouver, BC: *Weekend Sun*, 26 August, B2.

Stone, Allucquere Rosanne (1995) *The War of Desire and Technology at the Close of the Mechanical Age*. Cambridge and London: MIT Press.

Stone, Gregory (1962) "Appearance and the Self", in Arnold M. Rose, ed., *Human Behavior and Social Processes*. London: Routledge & Kegan Paul.

Straits Times (1999) "My Son Won't Be Another LKY, Says SM", 13 December.

Tamney, Joseph B. (1996) *The Struggle over Singapore's Soul*. New York: Walter de Gruyter.

Tan, Felix B., Scott P. Corbett and Yuk-Yong Wong (1999) *Information Technology Diffusion in the Asia Pacific: Perspectives on Policy, Electronic Commerce and Education*. Hershey, PA: Idea Group.

Tapscott, D. (1996) *The Digital Economy: Promise and Peril in the Age of Networked Intelligence*. New York: McGraw-Hill.

Taylor, E.B. (1977) *Primitive Culture Vol. 1. Researches into the Development of Mythology, Philosophy, Religion, Language, Art and Custom*. New York: Simon & Schuster.

Thieme, R. (1996) "Getting Lost", *Wired* September.

Thong, James, Patrick Chau and Kar Yan Tam, eds. (2001) *Decision-making and E-commerce Systems*. Amsterdam, The Netherlands: North Holland.

Tremewan, Christopher (1994) *The Political Economy of Social Control in Singapore*. New York: St. Martin's Press.

Tsagarousianou, R., D. Tambini and C. Bryan, eds. (1998) *Cyberdemocracy*. London: Routledge.

Turban, Efraim, Jae Lee, David King and Michael Hung (2000) *Electronic Commerce: A Managerial Perspective*. Upper Saddle River, NJ: Prentice Hall.

Turkle, Sherry (1999) "Commodity and Community in Personal Computing", in Donald Schön, Bish Sanyal and William J. Mitchell, eds., *High Technology and Low-Income Communities*. Cambridge, MA: MIT Press.

—— (1996) "Parallel Lives: Working on Identity in Virtual Space", in Debra Grodin and Thomas R. Lindlof, eds., *Constructing the Self in a Mediated World*. London: Thousand Oaks, New Delhi: Sage.

—— (1995) *Life on the Screen: Identity in the Age of the Internet*. New York: Simon & Schuster.

Turnbull, C.M. (1989) *A History of Singapore: 1819–1988*. Singapore: Oxford University Press.

Ullman, E. (1999) "The Myth of Order", *Wired* April.

United Nations (1963) "A Proposed Industrialization Programme for the State of Singapore". Singapore: U.N. commissioner for Technical Assistance, Department of Economic and Social Affairs.

Verrips, J. (1993) "Het ding 'wilde' niet wat ik wilde": enige notities over moderne vormen van animisme in westerse samenlevingen", *Etnofoor* VI(2): 59–79.

Vinge, V. (2000) "The Digital Gaia", *Wired* January.

Walther, J.B. (1992) "Interpersonal Effects in Computer-Mediated Interaction: A Relational Perspective", *Communication Research* 19(1): 52–90.

Weber, M. (1988) *Gesammelte Aufsätze zur Religionssoziologie* 1. Verlag: Tübingen.

—— (1996) *Wissenschaft als Beruf*. Berlin: Duncker & Humblot.

Webster, A. (1991) *Science, Technology and Society: New Directions*. London: Macmillan.

Wertheim, M. (2000) *The Pearly Gates of Cyberspace: A History of Space from Dante to the Internet*. London: Virago.

Westland, J. Christopher and Theodore H.K. Clark (1999) *Global Electronic Commerce: Theory and Case Studies*. Cambridge, Mass.: MIT Press.

Whalen, J. (1995) "Super Searcher", *Wired* May.

Wilde, R. de (2000) *De voorspellers: Een kritiek op de toeomstindustrie*. Amsterdam: De Balie.

Wilhelm, Anthony (2000) *Democracy in the Digital Age*. London: Routledge.

Williams, D. (1996) "The Human Macro-organism as Fungus", *Wired* April.

Wilson, H.E. (1978) *Social Engineering in Singapore*. Singapore: Singapore University Press.

Winner, Langdon (1985) "Do Artifacts Have Politics?", in D. MacKenzie and J. Wajcman, eds., *The Social Shaping of Technology: How the Refrigerator Got its Hum*. Philadelphia: Open University Press.

—— (1993) "Social Constructivism: Opening the Black Box and Finding it Empty", *Science as Culture* 16(1): 427–452.

—— (1997) "Technology Today: Utopia or Dystopia?", *Social Research* 64(3): 989–1017.

Wittgenstein, Ludwig (1953) *Philosophical Investigations*. Oxford: Basil Blackwell.

Wong, F. and Y.H. Gwee (1980) *Official Reports on Education: Straits Settlements and the Federated Malay States 1870–1939*. Singapore: Pan Pacific Books.

World Bank (2001) *World Development Report 2000/2001*. New York: Oxford University Press.

Worseley, Peter (1968) *The Trumpet Shall Sound: A Study of Cargo Cults in Melanesia*. New York: Shocken Books.

Wright, A. and H.A. Cartwright, eds. (1998) *Twentieth Century Impressions of British Malaya: Its History, People, Commerce, Industries and Resources*. Singapore: Graham Brash.

Yeskel, F. (1996) "Invisible Worlds", *Wired* January.

York, M. (1995) *The Emerging Networks: A Sociology of the New Age and Neopagan Movements*. Rowmann and Littlefield.

Yoshihara, K. (1988) *The Rise of Ersatz Capitalism in Southeast Asia*. New York: Oxford University Press.

Zielinski, Siegfried (1996) "Thinking the Border and the Boundary", in Timothy Druckrey, *Electronic Culture: Technology and Visual Representation*. New York: Aperture Foundation Inc, pp. 279–290.

Zizek, Slavoj (1991) *Looking Awry: An Introduction to Jacues Lacan through Popular Culture*. MIT Press.

Web Sites

http://acnielsen.com/news/asiapacific/hk/19990610.htm
http://asia.internet.com/1999/3/0103–hk.htm
http://ec.fed.gov/
http://STIMAP.matrixlinks.ca/STLinks/STPolicyindex1.html
http://tdc-link.tdc.org.hk/edicentre/index.htm
http://www.bbbonline.org/businesses/code/index.htm
http://www.commerce.net/
http://www.commerce-net.com.sg/

http://www.cordis.lu/esprit/src/ecomcom.htm
http://www.cspp.org/gecreadinessguide/index2.html
http://www.digihall21.org
http://www.digital21.gov.hk/eng/
http://www.ec.gov.sg/
http://www.ecommerce.gov
http://www.freeway.org.hk/hkdsrc/
http://www.hkpc.com.hk
http://www.hongkongpost.com/
http://www.ida.gov.sg/Website/IDAhome.nsf/Home?OpenForm
http://www.ige.unicamp.br/~mpolli/stp.htm
http://www.info.gov.hk/itbb/it_ia
http://www.internetpublicpolicy.com/
http://www.ipi.org/ipihome.nsf
http://www.itpolicy.gsa.gov/
http://www.netrust.com.sg/
http://www.nua.ie/surveys
http://www.oecd.org/dsti/sti/it/ec/act/oslo_workshop.htm
http://www.oecd.org/publications/Pol_brief/9701_Pol.htm
http://www.scmp.com
http://www.tdc.com.hk
http://www.thestandard.com
http://www.thinkcentre.org
http://www.thinkcentreasia.org
http://www.utexas.edu/depts/ic2/austin99/
http://www.info.gov.hk/cpu/english/ecomm.htm

INDEX